Care in the Community: Illusion or Reality?

Edited by

Julian Leff

Institute of Psychiatry, London, UK

JOHN WILEY & SONS

Chichester · New York · Weinheim · Brisbane · Singapore · Toronto

Other Wiley Editorial Offices

John Wiley & Sons, Inc., 605 Third Avenue,
New York, NY 10158-0012, USA

VCH Verlagsgesellschaft
Pappelallee 3, 0–69469 Weinheim, Germany

Jacaranda Wiley Ltd, 33 Park Road, Milton,
Queensland 4064, Australia

John Wiley & Sons (Asia) Pte Ltd, 2 Clementi Loop #02-01,
Jin Xing Distripark, Singapore 129809

John Wiley & Sons (Canada) Ltd, 22 Worcester Road,
Rexdale, Ontario M9W 1L1, Canada

Library of Congress Cataloging-in-Publication Data

Care in the community : illusion or reality / edited by Julian Leff.
    p.   cm.
  Includes bibliographical references and index.
  ISBN 0–471–96981–8 (cloth).—ISBN 0–471–96982–6 (pbk).
  1. Mentally ill—Rehabilitation—Great Britain. 2. Community mental health services—Great Britain. 3. Deinstitutionalization—Great Britain. I. Leff, Julian P.
RC439.5C365   1997
362.2'0941—dc20   96–34256
                                                            CIP

British Library Cataloguing in Publication Data

A catalogue record for this book is available from the British Library

ISBN 0–471–96981–8 (cased)
ISBN 0–471–96982–6 (paper)

Typeset in 10/12pt Plantin from the editor's disks by Vision Typesetting, Manchester
Printed and bound in Great Britain by Biddles Ltd, Guildford

This book is printed on acid-free paper responsibly manufactured from sustainable forestation, for which at least two trees are planted for each one used for paper production.

CONTENTS

ABOUT THE EDITOR

Professor Julian Leff received his medical education at University Hospital Medical School, and trained in psychiatry at the Maudsley Hospital, London. He is research psychiatrist for the Medical Research Council (since 1968), and currently member of External Scientific Staff, Social Psychiatry Section, MRC Social, Genetic and Developmental Psychiatry Research Centre, Institute of Psychiatry (since 1995). He was awarded the Starkey Prize of the Royal Society of Health for outstanding contributions to mental health, in 1976. He established the Team for the Assessment of Psychiatric Services in 1985, and has been Honorary Director since then. Professor Julian Leff has published eight books, some of which have been translated into other languages, and over 200 papers in scientific journals and books.

CONTRIBUTORS

Michelle Asbury — *Personal Social Services Research Unit, University of Kent, Canterbury, Kent CT2 7NF*

Leona L. Bachrach — *19108 Annapolis Way, Gaithersburg MD 20879*

Maryland Psychiatric Research Center, PO Box 21247, Catonsville MD 21228

Barry Baines — *Alba Associates, 70 Orchard Court, Ash Close, Herne, Kent CT6 7NT*

Jennifer Beecham — *Personal Social Services Research Unit, University of Kent, Canterbury, Kent CT2 7NF*

Centre for the Economics of Mental Health, Institute of Psychiatry, 7 Windsor Walk, Denmark Hill, London SE5 8BB

John Carrier — *London School of Economics, Houghton Street, London WC2*

Andrew Fenyo — *Personal Social Services Research Unit, University of Kent, Canterbury, Kent CT2 7NF*

Angela Hallam — *Personal Social Services Research Unit, University of Kent, Canterbury, Kent CT2 7NF*

Centre for the Economics of Mental Health, Institute of Psychiatry, 7 Windsor Walk, Denmark Hill, London SE5 8BB

Rowena Kendal — *Department of Community Psychiatry, Institute of Psychiatry, De Crespigny Park, London SE5 8AF*

Ian Kendall — *School of Social and Historical Studies, University of Portsmouth, Burnaby Road, Portsmouth PO1 3AS*

Martin Knapp   *Personal Social Services Research Unit, London School of Economics, Houghton Street, London WC2*

Centre for the Economics of Mental Health, Institute of Psychiatry, 7 Windsor Walk, Denmark Hill, London SE5 8BB

Julian Leff   *TAPS Research Unit, 69 Fleet Road, Hampstead, London NW3 2QU*

Section of Social Psychiatry, Institute of Psychiatry, De Crespigny Park, London SE5 8AF

Robert Sammut   *Ashford Mental Health Centre, 1 Elwick Road, Ashford, Kent TN23 1PD*

Vivien Senn   *TAPS Research Unit, 69 Fleet Road, Hampstead, London NW3 2QU*

Noam Trieman   *TAPS Research Unit, 69 Fleet Road, Hampstead, London NW3 2QU*

Lucy Willetts   *West Berkshire Priority Care Service, 3 Craven Road, Reading RG1 5LS*

Walter Wills   *Dementia Relief Trust, 37–43 Sackville Street, London W1X 2DL*

Geoffrey Wolff   *Department of Community Psychiatry, Institute of Psychiatry, De Crespigny Park, London SE5 8AF*

ACKNOWLEDGEMENTS

The Team for the Assessment of Psychiatric Services is funded by the Department of Health, North East Thames Regional Health Authority and the Gatsby Charitable Foundation, currently administered through the Academic Department of Psychiatry, Royal Free Hospital School of Medicine, and directed by Professor Julian Leff.

Since the inception of TAPS, many research workers have contributed to the collection of a vast archive of data, some on a voluntary basis. The full list is:

Dr Jeremy Anderson
  (former Assistant Director)
Ms Michelle Asbury
Ms Jeni Beecham
Dr Chris Burford
Ms Kay Chahal
Ms Charlotte Cooklin
Dr Neil Coxhead
Dr Colin Crawford
Dr David Dayson
Mr Mark Dunn
Ms Frieda Durham
Miss Sara Finlayson
Ms Angela Fitzpatrick
Mrs Brenda Gardner
Mr Christopher Gooch
Miss Gillian Haddock
Ms Angela Hallam
Ms Joanna Hughes
Mr David Jones
Mrs Rowena Kendal
Professor Martin Knapp
Ms Rachel Lee Jones
Professor Julian Leff
  (Honorary Director)
Dr Flavia Leslie
Ms Ann Lewis
Mr Michael Luckie

Mrs Olga Margolius
Dr Oscar Martinez
Dr Simon Michaelson
Miss Kajori Mukherjee
Miss Kathryn O'Donnell
Dr Catherine O'Driscoll
Mr Dominic O'Ryan
Mr James Oerton
Miss Christine Peaker
Dr Louise Petterson
Mr Roman Raczka
Dr Sawsan Reda
Dr Robert Sammut
Mr Derek Scott
Ms Vivien Senn
Mrs Linda Sharon
Mr Clive Smith
Dr Juhani Solantaus
Dr Allan Thompson
Dr Graham Thornicroft
  (former Assistant Director)
Dr Dylan Tomlinson
Dr Noam Trieman
  (Assistant Director)
Mrs Maggie Wallace
Mrs April White
Ms Lucy Willetts
Mr Walter Wills

INTRODUCTION

Julian Leff
TAPS Research Unit

The hundred years before 1950 was the great century of the asylum. During that time, psychiatric hospitals continued to increase in number and size. Friern hospital, for example, was built on a green field site north of London and opened in 1851 by the Prince Regent. Its original capacity was 1000 beds, but it expanded progressively and also became increasingly crowded, so that at its peak in 1952 it contained 2400 patients. This pattern was typical of psychiatric hospitals in the UK, where the number of beds peaked in 1954 at 148 000.

The downturn in beds has often been ascribed to the introduction in 1954 of the first antipsychotic drug, chlorpromazine. However, a number of progressive hospitals, like Friern and Claybury in the UK and Massachusetts State hospital in the US, began to discharge patients and empty beds a few years before 1954. This is evidence that a change in the attitudes of staff began the decline in psychiatric bed occupancy, although it was certainly hastened by the advent of antipsychotic medication.

The number of hospitalised psychiatric patients went on decreasing in the UK from the 1950s onwards, with the result that by the 1980s most large psychiatric hospitals had been reduced to about one third of their peak size. The possibility of closing some of them completely began to be considered. In July 1983, North East Thames Regional Health Authority (NETRHA), which was responsible for six large psychiatric hospitals, announced its decision to close two of them, Friern and Claybury, over a ten year period.

This was seen as an opportunity to mount a prospective evaluation of the policy of replacing psychiatric hospitals with community services. The opportunity was to be seized because, although this policy had been promoted by successive governments over 20 years regardless of their political colour, it had never been adequately evaluated. A Mental Health Services Evaluation Committee was set up within the structure of NETRHA, which discussed the best way of going about an evaluation. It is to the credit of NETRHA as an organisation that it saw the value of supporting an evaluation of its own policy decision, and funding was agreed for one year in the first instance to establish a small research team.

The Team for the Assessment of Psychiatric Services (TAPS) was born in May 1985, and began modestly with one full-time research worker (interestingly, a sociologist, Dr Dylan Tomlinson) and an honorary director, myself. In considering the possible topics for research, it became evident that it was an almost limitless task, and that priorities had to be established. At least three different groups of patients were being served by the hospitals; the long-stay non-demented, people with dementia, and those staying for brief periods on the admission wards. Each group had different service needs which would require different research strategies.

The staff would have to change their attitudes and their practices if patients were to make a successful transition to the community. They would certainly have training needs for their new roles, and the extent to which these were met could be studied. The patients' relatives should be involved in the research since one of the aims of the policy was to move patients closer to their former homes. Since the long-stay patients were moving out of hospital into ordinary houses, the attitudes of the public towards their new neighbours and towards the policy would be an important focus of research.

The cost of care is high on the agenda for the National Health Service at present. Furthermore, there has been a vocal body of opinion that one of the main political motives for the hospital closure policy is to save money by providing community care on the cheap. Consequently, the Mental Health Evaluation Committee was very keen to include an economic component in the TAPS Project. The Personal Social Services Research Unit at the University of Kent was selected to provide a health economics input, and has worked closely with TAPS from early on.

The appointment of a sociologist as the first member of TAPS is an indication of the interest in policy issues. In particular, research could be focused on the process of decision making at all levels from care plans for the individual patient up to the regional planning committee.

It would also be informative to study the way in which decisions were implemented, or not, as the case may be.

The scale and breadth of possible research was daunting. Nevertheless, in the 11 years in which TAPS has been operating, all the above topics have been studied. The results of this diverse body of work, conducted by researchers from many different disciplines, are brought together in this book to give as comprehensive a picture as possible of the successes and failures of psychiatric community care.

Part I

The Rise and Fall
of the
Psychiatric Hospital

Chapter 1

EVOLUTION OF POLICY

John Carrier* and Ian Kendall[†]
*London School of Economics; [†]University of Portsmouth

NOT A LEAP IN THE DARK?

"Throughout history the plight of markedly mentally disturbed and/or deluded people has been an unhappy one, not just because of their underlying condition but also because of the reactions of those around them" (Taylor and Taylor, 1989, p.12).

"In the eighteenth century, madmen were locked up in madhouses; in the nineteenth century, lunatics were sent to asylums; and in the twentieth century, the mentally ill receive treatment in hospitals. That is the essence of the change which has taken place in the care and treatment of the insane in the past 200 years—a change which is more than a matter of terminology; for a 'madhouse attendant' is not the same as a mental nurse, nor is a 'mad-doctor' the professional equivalent of a psychiatrist" (Jones, 1955, p.ix)

Introduction

A further forty years have passed since Kathleen Jones made her judgement on the history of the mental health services in the UK, quoted above. These forty years have seen further changes in terminology with the emergence of a wide-ranging professional and political consensus in support of policies for community care. With the closing down of large nineteenth century mental hospitals the community-based mental health worker has replaced the hospital-based mental nurse. The resulting decommissioning of old buildings and the provision of a new service requires propitious political and economic circumstances. The political climate needs to be an enabling one, with general unanimity about the values of integration, community, other-directedness and altruism; and relationships between central and local government which are mutual, respectful and symbiotic. The ideal economic context would be one in which growth would be steady and sustained; and competition for public

Care in the Community: Illusion or Reality?
Edited by Julian Leff. © 1997 John Wiley & Sons Ltd.

resources would not be seen as a burden on the economy (Carrier, 1990). For the UK none of these ideal conditions have existed for the last two decades; perhaps an indication that the circumstances described by Taylor and Taylor (see above) might still apply.

It was as part of the operationalisation of the policy of "community care" in this less than propitious environment that North East Thames Regional Health Authority (NETHRA) took the decision to close Friern Barnet and Claybury Hospitals in 1983 (see Tomlinson, 1991, p. 76). It can be seen as a decision of some significance, indicating an acceptance that these classic nineteenth century asylums might have no useful role left to play in the future. This book is the result of more than ten year's research resulting from that closure decision and much of its content is based upon the work of TAPS researchers over that period. This chapter traces the history of the nineteenth century asylums and examines their changing role in the context of mental health policy in the twentieth century, including the decision-making process relating to the closure of two such asylums, Friern and Claybury.

BEFORE THE ASYLUM

Institutional care has a long history in the mental health services, and certainly pre-dated the social and economic changes associated with industrialisation and urbanisation in nineteenth century Britain. But this institutional care was of a rather arbitrary and haphazard nature. At least until the seventeenth century, Bethlem remained the only specialised institution and before the development of the county asylums, Bethlem was the only public institution for the mentally ill (see Scull, 1979, pp. 18–19 and Jones, 1955, p. 11) with perhaps "four or five thousand people suffering from psychotic disorders or mental deficiency in workhouses before 1789" (Jones, 1955, pp. 17–18). The implication is that towards the end of the eighteenth century matters may have changed little from medieval times when:

> "the insane were affected by . . . (a) . . . general, unsystematic approach to the deviant . . . some were left to their own devices . . . (others) . . . relied on their families . . . in only a small minority of cases was any effort made to relieve the family of this burden by gathering lunatics together in institutions" (Scull, 1979, pp. 18–19).

The first statutory recognition that "some of those suffering from mental disorder" required treatment came in 1744 (see Jones, 1972, p. 28) being part of a series of "lunacy reforms" associated with a group of charismatic individuals who "roused the conscience of mid-Victorian society" (Jones) and in so doing contributed to "a transformation of the cultural meaning of madness" (Scull, 1979, p. 64). In particular the 1845 Lunatics Act required the building of county asylums.

THE ASYLUM AND THE MENTAL HOSPITAL

The Rise of the Asylum

The County Asylum Act was passed in 1808, but it gave only permissive powers to Justices of the Peace to raise county rates for the building of asylums and by 1827 only nine county asylums were in operation (Jones, 1972, pp. 88–89). In the light of Table 1.1 the following observation identified a key trend, but was perhaps somewhat "premature" in its dates.

"By the mid-nineteenth century . . . virtually no aspect of . . . (the) . . . traditional response remained intact. The insane were clearly and sharply distinguished from other 'problem populations'. They found themselves incarcerated in a specialised, bureaucratically organised, state-supported asylum system which isolated them both physically and symbolically from the larger society" (Scull, 1979, p. 14).

It would be more accurate to say that for much of the nineteenth century many "persons of unsound mind" were under the care of the Poor Law authorities and by the end of the 1860s the ratio of workhouse to county asylum residents amongst "the insane" was still 1 : 2.29 (see, Hodgkinson, 1967, p. 575 and p. 590). The reasons for non-utilisation of the "specialised asylum system" included some that would be familiar to twentieth century reformers. There were separate authorities (for the asylum and the workhouse) with separate budgets and no particular reason to co-operate; the interests of the ratepayers being well-served by confining "pauper lunatics" in the cheaper environs of the

Table 1.1 The number and size of mental hospitals (county asylums) 1827–1890

Date	Number of county asylums/mental hospitals	Number of patients in county asylums/mental hospitals	Average number of patients per asylum/hospital
1827	9	1046	116
1850	24	7140	297
1860	41	15 845	386
1870	50	27 109	542
1880	61	40 088	657
1890	66	52 937	802
1900	77	74 004	961
1910	91	97 580	1072
1920	94	93 648 (104 298)	996 (1109)
1930	98	119 659	1221
1950		147 546	
1961		137 094	

Note: Figures in parenthesis for 1920 are those for total number of beds available as distinct from the total number of beds occupied. Many beds had then recently been freed from use as emergency beds for war cases, and the normal flow of civilian cases had not yet been resumed.
Sources: Goodwin, 1989, p. 43; Scull, 1979, p. 198; Jones, 1972, p. 357

workhouse regardless of their needs for "specialist care" (see, Scull, 1979, pp. 213–219). This position was changed by the 1874 legislation for Grant-in-Aid of pauper lunatics. The sum involved was four shillings per head, and it gave an incentive, previously lacking, for the Boards of Guardians (who administered the Poor Law), to transfer their paupers out of the workhouses and into the asylums (see, Jones, 1972, pp. 160–161).

It is really in the last quarter of the nineteenth century that the segregation of mentally ill people becomes more marked—there were now two and half times as many county asylums and over five times as many asylum residents as there had been in 1850 (see Table 1.1). The key role of the asylum was confirmed in statute by the Lunacy Act, 1890 by which the new local authorities (county councils and country borough councils created by the Local Government Act 1888) were required to build and maintain asylums, alone or under a joint agreement with a neighbouring authority (see Jones, 1960, Chapter 2).

The Private Madhouse and the Single Lunatic

Parallel to the development of the county asylums was a growing concern for the numbers of mentally ill people confined in private institutions (the "private madhouse") or in ordinary private households (the "single lunatic"). This concern related not only to the quality of care received by such people but also to the danger that they might be wrongfully detained for some, perhaps ulterior, reasons. The Madhouse Act, 1828, covered not only private madhouses, but also all subscription hospitals with the exception of Bethlem, and involved the establishment of inspection by a statutory authority and a more detailed form of certification of patients designed to obviate the possibility of illegal detention. The Lunatics Act, 1842, established, for a period of three years, the Lunacy Commissioners who were empowered to carry out inspections of all asylums and madhouses. This was followed by the Lunatics Act, 1845, which established a full-time inspectorate with duties of inspecting, licensing and reporting; as part of its provisions "a more detailed form of certification was devised . . . (which) . . . increased the legal safeguards against wrongful detention in each case" (Jones, 1972, p. 147).

Subsequently there appeared to be a divergence of professional and public views of mental illness. The Lancet Commission suggested that

> "patients labouring under mental derangement should be removable to a public or private asylum as to a hospital for ordinary diseases, without certificate . . . the power of signing certificates of lunacy should be withdrawn from magistrates" (quoted in Jones, 1972, p. 167).

The "public view" was perhaps reflected by the popularity of novels like Charles Reade's *Hard Cash* (1863) and Wilkie Collins's *Woman in White* (1869) in the plots of which wrongful detention in "private madhouses" played a key role (see Jones, 1972, pp. 161–64 and Taylor and Taylor, 1989, p. 12). If this was indeed the "public view", then it lent support to a "legalistic" approach and the need to safeguard individuals against wrongful detention in asylums. This approach was represented in statute by the Lunacy Act, 1890, which, as well as confirming the key role of the asylum in mental health services, also introduced:

"every safeguard which could possibly be devised against illegal confinement" (Jones, 1960, p. 40).

The situation at the end of nineteenth century, by contrast with the beginning, has been characterised as,

"a highly significant redefinition of the moral boundaries of the community. Insanity was transformed from a vague, culturally defined phenomenon afflicting an unknown, but probably small, proportion of the population into a condition which could only be authoritatively diagnosed, certified, and dealt with by a group of legally recognised experts; and which was now seen as one of the major forms of deviance in English society . . . with the achievement of lunacy reform the asylum was endorsed as the sole officially approved response to the problems posed by mental illness. And, in the process, the boundaries of who was to be classified as mad, and thus was to be liable to incarceration, were themselves transformed" (Scull, 1979, pp. 49–50)

Nineteenth century developments included both a rise of legal interest in the status of internees, and a key role for the medical profession in defining and redefining mental illness. They also included a commitment to building asylums—variously interpreted as "safe places", "forms of incarceration", or perhaps just "better places" than the workhouse or the "private madhouse" (Carrier and Kendall, 1996, Ch. 13). These developments and their differing interpretations serve as a useful precursor to understanding subsequent developments and contemporary concerns about caring for the ex-asylum patients. It is perhaps the responses to the subsequent redefinitions of mental illness that have proved most problematic.

Towards a "Medical Model"

While it has been noted that the asylum patients had been "diagnosed as a uniquely and essentially, medical problem" (Scull, 1979, p. 14), the treatment of mental illness and the care of mentally ill people had also been seen as something quite separate from physical illness and the care of physically ill people. But this division can be seen as breaking down in the first half of the twentieth century as evidenced by a number of statements and recommendations.

Firstly, for example, it began to be more widely argued that there was

"no clear line of demarcation between mental and physical illness . . . a mental illness may have physical concomitants, probably it always has, though they may be difficult of detection. A physical illness, on the other hand, may have and probably always has had mental concomitants, and there are many cases in which it is a question of whether the physical or the mental symptoms predominate" (From Report of the Royal Commission on Lunacy and Mental Disorder, 1926; quoted in Jones, 1960, p. 109).

Secondly, it was recommended that general hospitals should develop sections for the early diagnosis and treatment of mental illness (see, for example, 1918 Report from the Board of Control) and twelve years later the "asylums" became "mental hospitals" based on the concept of voluntary admissions introduced as part of the Mental Treatment Act, 1930.

Thirdly, there was an exploration of, and development of, physical treatments for mental illness in the inter-war years (e.g. ECT, neurosurgery, insulin coma treatment) (see, for example, Unsworth, 1987)

Away from Institutional Confinement

The Royal Commission of 1924–26 commented that the keynote of the past had been "detention" and the keynote of the future should be "prevention and treatment". The Commission also recommended that public funds be made available for community care. Three years later the Wood Committee recommended that greater use should be made of all forms of community care. In line with these comments and recommendations, there were a number of changes in "hospital regimes" and the role of the hospitals including the development of open wards and parole, occupational therapy, "therapeutic communities', day hospitals (by 1959 there were 45 day hospitals), night hospitals and outpatient treatment (see for example, Jones, 1960, p. 128, pp. 166–69, pp. 173–75 and Roberts, 1967, p. 26–29). There are two interesting observations to make about this move away from "institutional confinement" and towards "community care". Firstly, it is discernible alongside a continuation of the trend towards increases in both the number of mental hospitals and the number of mental hospital patients (see, Table 1.1). Secondly, this move is clearly discernible before the new drug treatments that have been associated with the development of policies for community care.

Towards the Delegalization of Mental Illness

In 1918 the Report of the Board of Control recommended that there should be treatment for a limited period without certification and in 1923 the Maudsley Hospital was opened to voluntary patients. The Mental Treatment Act, 1930 made provision for voluntary treatment and by 1932 seven per cent of all admissions were voluntary; by 1938 the proportion of voluntary admissions was 35 per cent; by 1948 it was 59 per cent (see, Jones, 1972, p. 256 and Goodwin, 1989, p. 45)

THE NATIONAL HEALTH SERVICE AND THE MENTAL HEALTH ACT, 1959

Local government was the major provider of services for the mentally ill until 1948 when the National Health Service was established (following the 1946 NHS Act). Now all the local authority mental hospitals (as they were called) were nationalised and became part of the NHS. They were transferred to specialist hospital authorities as part of the tripartite structure of the new Service—an arrangement which involved separate organisations and budgets for hospital, general practitioner and the remaining local authority health services. In relation to mental health services, the role of the latter was restricted to *mandatory duties* with regard to the initial care of patients and their removal to hospital, but only *permissive powers* with regard to prevention, care and after-care. But within four years of the establishment of the NHS, a report of the Central Health Services Council was listing the mental health services as one of the areas in which it was most necessary to find ways to overcome the disadvantages of the tripartite structure of the NHS. This criticism of the separation of responsibilities between hospitals, GPs and other community health services, and the limited powers to develop community care, may have been prompted in part by developments in the physical treatment of mental illness in the form of new drugs for the "treatment" of mental illness (see, for example, Roberts, 1967, p. 25).

In 1955 the Royal Commission on the Law relating to Mental Illness and Mental Deficiency was established; they reported two years later (see Royal Commission on the Law Relating to Mental Illness and Mental Deficiency, 1957). The recommendations included the introduction of new legal terminology (i.e. mentally ill, psychopathic, severely subnormal); the abolition of the Board of Control, with inspectorate functions to be taken over by the Ministry of Health, and the establishment of Mental Health Review Tribunals to take over the Board of Control's functions of investigating wrongful detention. It was proposed to end the special designation of mental hospitals with the Royal Commission recommending the legal confirmation of two established trends. Firstly that patients should be admitted to mental hospitals and mental deficiency hospitals in the same way as to other hospitals (compulsory detention would be used only where treatment was deemed necessary for personal or public safety but was refused). Secondly that no patient should be retained as a hospital in-patient when s/he has reached the stage at which s/he could return home if s/he had a reasonably good home to go to. At that stage the provision of residential care would become the responsibility of the local authority.

The subsequent Mental Health Act, 1959 led to the provision of community care becoming a duty for local authorities.

> "In fulfilment of the resolution of 26th January, the Minister had agreed to use his powers under section 28 of the NHS Act to make the provision of mental health care *mandatory* on local authorities." (Jones, 1960, p. 191).

In what proved to be an anticipation of subsequent debates there was considerable support for a key Royal Commission recommendation, that there should be a specific grant for capital development by local authorities in support of the new principles of community care. The Minister said this was not possible; the grant to mental health services was now part of the General Grant—a reference to a recent reform of local government finance which had abolished the system of specific, service-related grants. Neither the Royal Commission nor the Mental Health Act led to any changes in the organisational arrangements (the tripartite NHS) that had already been identified as a hindrance to policies of community care in relation to mental health services. Furthermore the Act "provided no additional resources to facilitate the development of community care services" (Goodwin, 1989, p. 41).

The recommendations of the Royal Commission and the enactment of the 1959 Act were broadly welcomed—perhaps in part because they did confirm well established trends. But a number of concerns were expressed; before the Bill became law McDougall encapsulated a number of these when observing that:

> "some may say that to change the right to stay in a modern, adequately equipped hospital, for the right to share the kind of services which some local authorities provide under their health and welfare services is a doubtful privilege . . . community care . . . a fine-sounding phrase . . . can be an almost intolerable burden on individual husbands, wives or parents involved . . . it also carries very considerable dangers if too much is put upon the community without adequate support from psychiatrists and social workers. 'Community care' could very easily become 'Community chaos' with a retrogression in public attitudes which might bring back the old cry of 'lock them up' again" (McDougall, 1959, p. 229).

Equally prophetic, but probably more well known, were the concerns expressed two years later by Richard Titmuss in a lecture delivered to the 1961 Annual Conference of the National Association of Mental Health. His lecture included the following comments.

> "We may pontificate about the philosophy of community care; we may feel righteous because we have a civilised Mental Health Act on the statute books; but unless we are prepared to examine at . . . (the) . . . level of concrete reality what we mean by community care we are simply indulging in wishful thinking . . . at present we are drifting into a situation in which, by shifting the emphasis from the institution to the community—a trend which, in principle and with qualifications, we all applaud—we are transferring the care of the mentally ill from trained staff to untrained or ill-equipped staff or no staff at all" (Titmuss, 1968, p. 106 and p. 109).

A year after these comments were made, the policy for community care for the mental health services took a very tangible step with the first plans to run-down the old asylums.

THE END OF THE ASYLUM

"There they stand, isolated, majestic, imperious, brooded over by the gigantic watertower and chimney combined, rising unmistakeable and daunting out of the country-side—the asylums which our forefathers built with such immense solidity" (Powell, 1961)

"we need to know whether the run down of the services we had—mainly in the shape of hospital beds—is in fact being compensated for by an extension of services we would like—small group homes, acute medical services of a high standard, and skilled counselling on human relations" (Jones, 1972, p. 345)

In 1962 the Hospital Plan was published (Ministry of Health, 1962). It projected a significant decrease in mental illness beds available per 1000 population by 1975, with an increasing proportion of this decreasing number of in-patients being located in the psychiatric units of the new District General Hospitals (see, for example, Maynard and Tingle, 1975, pp. 152–153). This Plan attracted contemporary criticism from a number of sources. For example, it was suggested that it:

"dismissed too lightly the increasing proportion of the elderly in the population . . . the Plan was slightly unrealistic in considering the 1954–59 period as normal; when it was, in fact, a stage of sudden advance whose pace could hardly be maintained, and in failing to take account of the probability that rehabilitation programmes had been directed at those long-stay patients who seemed the most hopeful prospects" (Roberts, 1967, p. 43; see also Tooth and Brook, 1961)

In addition it would be noted subsequently that the Plan

"made no directive as to what level of provision in the community should be, but simply assumed that the local authorities' plans would be carried out" (Maynard and Tingle, 1975, p. 156)

Despite the criticisms, the Plan remained in place and in 1968 the Report of the Chief Medical Officer said that District General Hospitals would totally replace the old mental hospitals, assuming that community services and geriatric services provided full support. However, between 1962 and 1970, a period over which the Hospital Plan proposed a 43.3 per cent reduction in mental hospital beds, the actual reduction was only 14.88 per cent (Maynard and Tingle, 1975, p. 153).

The case against the asylum rested on a powerful combination of explicit arguments relating to efficiency (e.g., the relative costs of institutional and community care) and needs (e.g., the proportions of institutional populations that did not need to be there) (see Carrier and Kendall, 1996, Chapter 13) against a background of ongoing concerns about the general resource implications of maintaining reasonable standards of traditional forms of institutional care (see, for example, Goodwin, 1989, pp. 39–41). By 1968 the first of a depressing series of enquiries into ill-treatment and neglect in long-stay institutions provided a further case against the traditional asylum rooted in human rights (see Robb, 1967; Martin, 1984).

In 1971 the DHSS Circular, *Hospital Services for the Mentally Ill*, Circular 71 (97) advised Regional Hospital Boards to plan for psychiatric services to replace the old hospitals. The then Secretary of State (Keith Joseph) commented that "psychiatry is to join the rest of medicine". Keith Joseph was also involved in the final stages of the health, personal social services and local government restructurings which had been under discussion since the mid-1960s. The outcome of these restructurings was a new pattern of two-tier local government, with responsibilities for all aspects of the personal social services, and an NHS completely separate from local government with responsibilities for all health services.

The 1974 restructurings tried to make a reasonably clear distinction between medical and non-medical areas of work, but problems arose because there were bound to be overlaps and difficulties in making this distinction in the care of people with mental health problems. Even the provision under Section 2 of the NHS Act (1977) for the establishment of Joint Consultative Committees could only partially impact on a fundamental administrative, budgetary and professional fragmentation of mental health services. A similar situation in the USA was accompanied by similar problems with incentives to externalise costs and internalise benefits; at the same time

"the diffusion of effective authority markedly increases the opportunities to block action, to separate aspiration from effective remedy, to stimulate agreement on the 'problem' to be solved rather than the remedy to be implemented" (Marmor, 1990, p. 141).

By 1975 when it had been expected that 13 mental illness hospitals would be closed, only one large hospital had been closed in England and Wales (and that became a mental handicap hospital). But despite the very slow process of closing the old asylums, there was already evidence of discharged mental hospital patients left without help and:

"sensational stories of psychiatric hospitals dumping their patients in the streets are regularly cropping up in the national and local press" (see *New Society*, 22.7.76, p. 184; see also Ball, 1972, p. 241).

The term "careless community" was being used to describe the circumstances that faced those decanted or diverted from the traditional asylum (Harrison, 1973). The comments over a decade earlier of McDougall and Titmuss were looking much more prescient than those authors would have wished.

In 1975 the government published a new White Paper *Better Services for the Mentally Ill* (DHSS, 1975). *Better Services* laid down norms of provision, attempting to match resources to needs. It included the observation that "the hallmark of a good service for the mentally ill is a degree of local co-ordination" (p. 10) and that "joint planning of health and local authority services is essential" (p. 86). The latter comment highlighted yet again the significance of inter-organisational co-operation, especially given that "it is not easy to draw an exact line between the functions of day centres . . . (managed by local authority Social Services Departments) . . . and those of day hospitals . . . (managed by the NHS)"; nor to define precisely "the point at which mental infirmity is severe enough to be beyond the scope of residential care" when the locus of responsibility would shift from the Social Services Department to the NHS (DHSS, 1975, p. 34 and p. 39). The White Paper principles were endorsed in the 1976 Consultative Document, *Priorities for Health and Personal Social Services in England* (DHSS, 1976) and the 1977 document *The Way Forward: Priorities for the Health and Personal Social Services in England* (DHSS, 1977). The former committed a rising proportion of NHS and personal social services budget to out-patient, day-patient, and day-care service, although the latter moderated the increase somewhat.

The Nodder Report (DHSS, 1978) argued for the creation of Psychiatric Management Teams, to bring some unity into the health and social services setting by making a team responsible for monitoring standards and quality of care. It was at this time that NETRHA published its first policy analysis for mental health services development (Mezey Report, NETRHA 1978). This was undertaken by a small panel of experts, led by a consultant psychiatrist. They argued that the choice of mental hospitals should be based on the strength of support for a changed community-oriented service among staff working within them (NETRHA, 1978; see also Carrier and Tomlinson, 1994, pp. 84–85).

The policy document *Care in Action* broadly confirmed the development of services as set out in the 1975 White Paper as follows.

"The aim is for people to be able to use the services they need with the minimum of formality and delay, and without losing touch with their normal lives" (DHSS, 1981a, p. 33).

It stressed the need for accessibility, non-separateness, and co-ordinated and complementary services. On local authority provision it noted that progress had been uneven and identified the aim to make satisfactory progress on closing those mental illness hospitals which were not well placed to provide a service reaching into the community and were already near the end of their useful lives.

By 1981 there was further evidence that these tasks were not being successfully undertaken in many areas. In June of that year a Government minister noted that 32 local authorities were still making no provision for mentally disabled people and seven provided no residential accommodation. The shift of the balance of care from the NHS to local authorities, and of resources to priority groups, was happening far more slowly than had been hoped for and intended. *Care in the Community* (DHSS, 1981b) addressed the issue of the long-stay population in all institutions—including those for elderly people and people with learning difficulties. Subsequent guidance enabled the Regional Health Authorities to make payments to local authorities in support of people moving out of NHS hospitals and in 1983 the DHSS made available £19 million to fund a number of locally based pilot resettlement projects (see Tomlinson, 1991, p. 16 and p. 17). It was in this same year that NETRHA announced a 10-year programme to close two of its psychiatric hospitals, Friern and Claybury. These were to become the main focus of the TAPS research and the subject of this book. These hospitals had been selected for closure through a set of what were called "quasi-objective" criteria rather than measures of staff support for change as recommended by the Mezey Report (NETRHA, 1978). The former ("quasi-objective" criteria) included the Yates indices of staff–patient ratios and other risk factors, as well as the scope of services provided by both the District General Hospital and the local authority Social Services Departments in the relevant catchment areas (NETRHA, 1982; see also Carrier and Tomlinson, 1994, p. 85). The initial costings were worked out by the then "Regional Team of Officers" on the basis of largely "new build" solutions. Initial planning expectations included significant transfers of patients between hospitals. In particular large numbers of patients were expected to move to local general or sub-general hospital sites. There is no doubt that this new build–extensive refurbishment solution can be attributed to the desire of key officers that the mentally ill should have facilities as good as those offered to all other client groups. As the general hospital facilities were the core of services for those with general medical problems and a high standard of accommodation was desired for these patients, then the same principle should be applied to those who had to put up with poor standards for many years (Carrier and Tomlinson, 1994, p. 87). It is notable that several years earlier the Royal Commission had already voiced concerns relating to the contribution of general hospital units to the care of mentally ill people, observing that:

"some DGH units have been selective, either in their admission policies or about those for whom they would continue to care, and the mental hospitals have had to receive those patients whom the DGH units have thought were unsuitable in the first place, or whom they had failed to cure" (Royal Commission on the NHS, 1979, para. 10.57, p. 137).

The NETRHA programme for the closure of Friern and Claybury and the re-provision of their services was seen as an opportunity to undertake an evaluation of the policy and its implementation. With funding help from the DHSS and the Kings Fund, the RHA established TAPS—The Team for the Assessment of Psychiatric Services. The resulting research agenda included examining the following services and groups: acute; long-stay non-demented; and psychogeriatric services; and the impact on patients, staff, relatives and members of the public.

Meanwhile the enduring theme of the limitations of policies for community care was returned to in a report of the House of Commons Social Services Committee:

> "We do not wish to slow down the exodus from mental illness or mental handicap hospitals for its own sake. But we do look to see the same degree of Ministerial pressure, and the provision of the necessary resources, devoted to the creation of alternative services. Any fool can close a long stay hospital: it takes more time and trouble to do it properly and compassionately" (Social Services Committee, 1985, p. xxii, para. 40).

During the time the above Social Services Committee were taking their evidence and coming to their conclusions, the Friern and Claybury programme was experiencing a particular problem. The consultant psychiatrists at Claybury Hospital were refusing to co-operate with the closure programme. As late as 1988 a group of these consultants were still challenging the RHA's closure plans for Claybury and putting forward their own alternatives (Carrier and Tomlinson, 1994, p. 85).

In 1986 the first "genuine" closure of a large mental hospital (i.e. not used for other long-stay residents) involved Banstead Hospital in Surrey, but only by decanting its residual patients to Horton Hospital. Other closures would follow in the period up to 1989 and one such closure (Powick) was the subject of a specific DHSS development project to replace the local mental hospital (see Tomlinson, 1991, p. 42, p. 47). The closure process for the hospitals in the Exeter area was regarded as particularly successful. The Exeter service prior to closure and reprovision has been described as representing "the worst kind of picture of mental health care, the very antithesis of care in the community" (Tomlinson, 1991, p. 57). However, by 1988 the new services for Exeter, based on community mental health centres and hostels for long-term clients, were adjudged to be working effectively and providing a superior quality by comparison with the previous regime (see Beardshaw and Morgan, 1990). Three outcomes of the Exeter reprovision programme could be seen as significant for Friern and Claybury. Firstly, that the psychogeriatric population appeared to be satisfactorily provided for in non-NHS facilities ranging from local authority homes to private care homes. Secondly, that the community mental health centres provided for a reasonably balanced proportion of long-term and short-term users. Thirdly, that the new community service suffered from a particular weakness in relation to employment and day-time activities—but that this reflected the impact of broader economic trends on those individuals with few marketable skills (see Carrier and Tomlinson, 1994, p. 88).

The next major national report on community care was published in 1985. This came from the Audit Commission who, reviewing a variety of community care schemes, concluded that all the successful schemes known to them involved "a radical departure from the generally accepted ways of doing things". In particular such schemes were characterised by at least six dominant features. Firstly, the presence of strong and committed local "champions" of change; this would be confirmed by the TAPS research which identified the crucial role of psychiatric hospital staff who are sympathetic to reprovision. "It is surely to the lack of product champions that much of the slower development of non-residential reprovision care and support services can be attributed" (Carrier and Tomlinson, 1994, p. 88). Secondly, a focus on action and not just the bureaucratic machinery for change; this meant taking risks rather than focusing strictly on conventional procedures. Thirdly, the existence of locally integrated machinery for service planning purposes was identified as vital if the patient was not to fall between the asylum / hospital provision and the enhanced social service responsibility for care. This was another Audit Commission feature which would be confirmed by the findings from the TAPS research; that central co-ordination is necessary to integrate planning work with providers, local authorities, users, carers, housing associations and other non-statutory agencies (Leff et al, 1995, p. 30). The latter point links with another feature emphasised by the Audit Commission—a partnership between statutory and voluntary organisations. The final two features identified by the Commission were a focus on the local neighbourhood and a multi-professional team approach (see, Audit Commission, 1985).

The Griffiths Report (published in March 1988) re-stated many of the themes of the Social Services Committee and the Audit Commission—"community care is a poor relation, everybody's distant relative but no-body's baby" (Griffiths, 1988, p. iv). Griffiths' answer was to identify a key role for local government (in the form of Social Services Departments) as:

"the designers, organisers and purchasers of non-health care services" (p. 1).

To some extent he was advocating an "internal market" in community care; certainly a purchaser/provider split, in which local authorities would be major purchasers rather than direct providers; as purchasers they would make:

"maximum possible use of voluntary and private sector bodies to widen consumer choice, stimulate innovation and encourage efficiency" (p. 1).

Griffiths also advocated a "Minister for Community Care" and a "ring-fenced" specific grant for community care services. His views on "ring-fencing" not only constituted a further vindication of views expressed during the debates on the 1959 Mental Health Act, but were also to be confirmed by a key finding in the Health Economics dimension of the TAPS study (see, Leff et al, 1995, p. 30).

While the comments and recommendations of the Audit Commission and the Griffiths report were being debated, the policy-making process for the closure of Friern and Claybury continued. A clear consensus had emerged that "reprovision" of the two asylums "by resettlement of the resident population was feasible", although "not within the cost constraints set out by the RHA" (Tomlinson, 1991, p. 79). However by 1990 only a handful of purpose-built units had been opened. The cost of following the new build/extensive rebuild option was significantly affecting the reprovision programme (NETRHA, 1990) and it was at this time that the programme as a whole had to be slowed down at Claybury Hospital in order that all efforts and available capital could be focused on Friern (Carrier and Tomlinson, 1994, p. 87). We should also note that by this time seven years had passed since the closure decisions were made, more than halfway through a planning and implementation time-scale which it has been suggested was "too long for staff to feel any responsibility for getting started or what they plan" (Korman, 1994, p. 16).

Following the reforms introduced by *Caring for People* (DoH, 1989) and the NHS and Community Care Act, 1990 (implemented from 1993) service developments such as those associated with the Friern and Claybury closures, can be seen as "both easier and more complex"; easier in so far as it is very clearly the responsibilities of the health care purchaser and the lead agency for community care to "decide upon appropriate replacement services"; more complex in so far as these agencies have to find suitable health and community care providers (Korman, 1994, p. 11). Furthermore, in one respect the situation was not changed; even after *Caring for People* the long standing division remained between health authorities (as purchasers of health care) and local government (as the lead agency for social care).

One outcome of TAPS research has been a series of recommendations related to the decision-making process and the economics of reprovision programmes. The most important of these are, for decision-making, that "overall accountability should remain with the health authorities"; and for the economic issues, the need to alter the funding balance,

"not only to move resources from hospitals to the community, but also from NHS budgets to the budgets of other agencies. The challenge for NHS purchasers and community care planners is to reallocate funds between agencies, for the financial burden of reprovision is not distributed equally or in a similar way to hospital-related costs. Resource flexibility is difficult to achieve but highly desirable" (Leff et al, 1995, p. 30).

Perhaps the challenge that TAPS has thrown down to health planners (decision-makers) and budget holders (treasurers) is how the NHS can retain overall accountability for this group of patients with the resource flexibility necessary for their long-term care in the community.

At the 5th TAPS Annual Conference in 1990 Stephen Dorrell (then Parliamentary Under-Secretary at the Department of Health) had been confident that treating "a much larger proportion of mentally ill patients within the community" and "the move toward a smaller and more humane scale of treatment for those patients was clearly not a 'leap in the dark' . . . (but) . . . the result of a shift in medical practice that has been fully considered and the implications of which will be properly followed up" (Dorrell, 1990).

It is the proper "following up" of the principles of policies for community care that has always been at the very centre of care for people with mental health problems. This is especially the case given the conclusions of the TAPS researchers that community care in general is not cheaper than hospital care. Although the savings from closing hospitals should be adequate in the long term to fund re-provision, this does require a strict "ring-fencing" of the funds so they can be transferred with the patients and the services. However the health authority managers' commitment to provide secure long-term resettlement for the patients under their care in the closing institutions may mean that:

"those with mental illness already in the community would not, at least initially, receive a development of services in accordance with either their own demands, or of professional assessment of their needs for support and activity. The same implication held for the demands and needs of their carers for such support and respite" (Carrier and Tomlinson, 1994, p. 88).

The complexities of planning reprovision, the commitment to funding the same, the role of professional opinions, and the political will all remain problematic dimensions of programmes like that for Friern and Claybury. As late as January 1992, almost nine years after the Friern and Claybury closure decisions were announced, the Regional Authority was still concerned about the

"poor understanding of the benefits of community care amongst the public and some staff and the reluctance through misinformation of some staff and patients to move from Friern" (NETRHA, 1992).

The persistence of such "poor understanding" is one explanation why all those concerned with the quality of mental health services continue to look forward to a time when the comments of McDougall (1959) and Titmuss (1961) become of purely historical relevance and lack the contemporary resonances that they still contain.

The TAPS research in this volume should be considered as part of the process of the "proper following up" of the principles of community care and the establishment of a "good understanding" of these principles. Such a "following up" is not simply for the intellectual excitement of the research process and the addition to knowledge, but because only through such long-term research can the key question "what happened to the patients?" be scientifically assessed, and the following statement be considered as a testable proposition;

"The concept of asylum has nothing inherently to do with large or isolated institutions. Asylums can be provided in a physical and psychological sense in the middle of a normal residential community; traditionally indeed, in the midst of a busy church. We must face the fact that some people need asylum" (Social Services Committee, 1985, para. 26, p. xvii).

This statement can stand as prologue to the TAPS research programme; the contents of this book might serve as its epilogue.

REFERENCES

Audit Commission (1985) *Making A Reality of Community Care*, HMSO, London.

Ball, D. (1972) Health, *New Society*, 3.8.72 (p. 241).

Beardshaw, V. and Morgan, E. (1990) *Community Care Works*, Mind Publications, London.

Carrier, J. (1990) Sociopolitical influences on mental health care policy in the United Kingdom, in Marks and Scott (1990).

Carrier, J. and Kendall, I. (1996) *Health and the National Health Service*, Athlone Press, London.

Carrier, J. and Tomlinson, D. (1994), in NETRHA (1994).

DHSS (1975) *Better Services for the Mentally Ill* (Cmnd.6233), HMSO, London.

DHSS (1976) *Priorities for Health and Personal Social Services in England: A Consultative Document*, HMSO, London.

DHSS (1977) *The Way Forward: Further Discussion of the Government's National Strategy*, HMSO, London.

DHSS (1978) *Organization and Management Problems of Mental Illness Hospitals* (Nodder Report), HMSO, London.

DHSS (1981a) *Consultative Document: Care in Action*, HMSO, London.

DHSS (1981b) *Care in the Community*, HMSO, London.

DoH (1989) *Caring for People : Community Care in the Next Decade and Beyond* (Cm.849), HMSO, London.

Dorrell, S. (1990) *Keynote Address* in NETRHA (1990).

Goodwin, S (1989) Community care for the mentally ill in England and Wales: myths, assumptions and reality, *Journal of Social Policy*, January 1989, pp. 27–52.

Griffiths, R. (1988) *Agenda for Action, A report to the Secretary of State for Social Services*, HMSO, London.

Harrison, P. (1973) Careless community, *New Society*, 28.6.73.

Hodgkinson, R. (1967) *The Origins of the National Health Service: The Medical Services of the New Poor Law* 1834–1871, The Wellcome Historical Medical Library, London.

Jones, K. (1955) *Lunacy, Law and Conscience*, Routledge and Kegan Paul, London.

Jones, K. (1960) *Mental Health and Social Policy*, Routledge and Kegan Paul, London.

Jones, K. (1972) *A History of the Mental Health Services*, Routledge and Kegan Paul, London.

Korman, N. (1994) in NETRHA (1994).

Leff, J., Knapp, M., Carrier, J., Trieman, N. (1995) Beyond the asylum. Reprovision for psychiatric hospitals: recommendations from TAPS/PSSRU research findings. *The Health Services Journal*, **105**, 28–30.

McDougall (1959) The Mental Health Bill, *Political Quarterly*, **30** 120–130.

Marmor, T. (1990) *The political and economic context of mental health care in the United States*, in Marks and Scott (1990).

Marks, I. and Scott, R. (1990) *Mental Health Care Delivery: Innovations, Impediments and Implementation*, Cambridge University Press, Cambridge.

Martin, J.P. (1984) *Hospitals in Trouble*, Blackwell, London.

Maynard, A. and Tingle, R. (1975) The objectives and performance of the mental health services in England and Wales in the 1960s, *Journal of Social Policy*, April, 151–168.

Ministry of Health (1962) *Hospital Plan for England and Wales* (Cmnd.1604), HMSO, London.

NETRHA (1978) *The Mezey Report.*

NETRHA (1982) *The Mental Illness Service in NE Thames RHA: A Policy Group Report,* NETRHA, London.

NETRHA (1990) *Better Out than In?* (Report from the 5th Annual Conference of the Team for the Assessment of Psychiatric Services), London.

NETRHA (1992) *The Closure of Friern Hospital and Development of Community-based Mental Health Services: Communication Strategy,* NETRHA, London.

NETRHA (1994) *Institution to Community : Friern Lessons Pack,* NETRHA, London.

Powell, E.J. (1961) Speech by the Minister of Health, the Rt Hon Enoch Powell. *Report of the Annual Conference of the National Association for Mental Health,* London.

Robb, B. (ed.) (1967) *Sans Everything,* Nelson, London.

Roberts, N. (1967) *Mental Health and Mental Illness,* Routledge and Kegan Paul, London.

Royal Commission on the Law Relating to Mental Illness and Mental Deficiency (1957), Report (Chair: Lord Percy of Newcastle), Cmnd. 169, HMSO, London.

Royal Commission on the NHS (1979), Report (Chair: Sir Alec Merrison), Cmnd. 7615, HMSO, London.

Scull, A. (1979) *Museums of Madness : the social organization of insanity in the nineteenth century,* Allen Lane, London.

Social Services Committee (1985), *Community Care with Special Reference to Adult Mentally Ill and Mentally Handicapped People,* Second Report from the Social Services Committee (Session 1984–85) Vol. 1, HMSO, London.

Taylor, D. and Taylor, J. (1989) *Mental Health in the 1990s: From Custody to Care?,* Office of Health Economics, London.

Titmuss, R.M. (1961) Speech to 1961 Annual Conference of the National Association of Mental Health.

Titmuss, R.M. (1968) *Commitment to Welfare,* George Allen and Unwin, London

Tomlinson, D. (1991), *Utopia, Community Care and the Retreat from the Asylums,* Open University Press, Milton Keynes.

Tooth, G.C. and Brook, E.M. (1961) Trends in the mental hospital population and their effect on future planning *The Lancet,* **1,** 710–713.

Unsworth, C. (1987) *The Politics of Mental Health Legislation,* Clarendon, Oxford.

Chapter 2

LESSONS FROM THE AMERICAN EXPERIENCE IN PROVIDING COMMUNITY-BASED SERVICES

Leona L. Bachrach
University of Maryland School of Medicine

Not only did 1995 mark the tenth anniversary of the TAPS initiative in England; it was also the fortieth anniversary of the year in which the United States achieved its peak enrollments in public psychiatric hospitals—its so-called "state mental hospitals." The resident count in those facilities has declined in each successive year.

This trend toward hospital depopulation in the United States reflects a series of complex decisions and events that have come to be known, collectively, as "deinstitutionalization." In this chapter I shall consider the relevance of American deinstitutionalization for mental health service delivery in the United Kingdom and elsewhere. I shall examine the ideological basis for, as well as the benefits and problems accompanying, that movement in the United States, and discuss six critical lessons reflecting its biopsychosocial legacy. I shall conclude with a plea for continued efforts to humanize the care of persons suffering from long-term mental illnesses.

RELEVANCE OF THE AMERICAN EXPERIENCE

It is well-known that the United States stands virtually alone in the western world in its failure to offer universal access to health care (Goldberg et al, 1995). At present an estimated 39 million Americans (Pear, 1993)—perhaps as many as 44 million (Bradsher, 1995)—possess no health insurance of any kind; and even for those who are insured, mental health services are frequently very limited or even nonexistent (Okin 1995a). It appears that the federal government's plans for health care reform, which appeared so promising only three years ago, are now at an impasse (Blumenthal, 1995); and although there is still hope that guaranteed general and mental health care will eventually be available to all Americans (Shalala, 1994), this is not currently the case.

What is perhaps less widely understood is that in the United States no single level of government determines basic health care policy (Bachrach, 1987). Instead, there are 50 separate state policies, each different from the others. What is more, the 50 state policies may themselves be modified, extended, or abridged by local governments, so that health and mental health services vary substantially even within the states, not only among them.

In addition, the United States contains numerous privately owned and operated mental health agencies that effectively make their own rules about service delivery: they determine what populations they will serve and how they will do so. Thus, the particular forms that mental health services take throughout the United States are highly variable (Freedman, 1990), a fact that makes it extremely risky to generalize about "American community mental health." Any generalizations one might wish to make are bound to have numerous exceptions.

In view of these circumstances readers may well wonder what relevance the American experience with deinstitutionalization might possibly have for the situation in the United Kingdom where an arguably more benign service delivery climate prevails (at least for the present). Why should service providers in the United Kingdom, or in other places where universal access to health care is still a part of national policy, be interested in the American deinstitutionalization experience?

The answer to this question lies in the fact that the problems associated with community-based care found in the United States are not limited to my country but are shared throughout the western world (Schmidt, 1992; Thornicroft and Bebbington, 1989); differences are often matters of degree, not substance. The United States appears, however, to have proceeded with the movement in a particularly aggressive manner (Bennett, 1978) and so is widely regarded as a "leader" in deinstitutionalization. It has, for better or worse, become customary for people in other places to look to the United States for direction and guidance in matters concerning service planning: a number of widely endorsed service delivery concepts are based upon our experiences and research, and Americans who travel abroad frequently find that many of their service "fads" have been adopted, perhaps without sufficient question, elsewhere.

Precisely why nations with widely differing health care philosophies, service delivery practices, and funding conventions should experience similar problems in community mental health initiatives is a most intriguing question and one that is certainly deserving of further study. Is there something about the biological aspects of mental illness that somehow transcends national boundaries and cultural differences, and leads to similar issues in service delivery? Or is the answer to be found instead in misdirected service delivery concepts? Whatever the case, I feel strongly that planners in other countries must be acquainted with our successes and our difficulties, as well as our concepts, if they wish to emulate our practices.

TOWARD AN UNDERSTANDING OF DEINSTITUTIONALIZATION

Despite widespread usage, the term "deinstitutionalization" lacks a standard definition. Indeed, the word has been interpreted in so many ways that it calls to mind the proverbial elephant: people are bound to judge this phenomenon according to which specific part of the beast they view and to how far away from the beast they stand. Deinstitutionalization is certain to look different to a patient who experiences the system at first hand or to a patient's relative, from what it does to a hospital-based psychiatrist, a community nurse, a case manager, a program evaluator, or a legislator.

A general definition of the term that allows for these various viewpoints, and others, is definitely in order. Accordingly, I would suggest that we define deinstitutionalization as *the replacement of long-stay psychiatric hospitals with smaller, less isolated community-based service alternatives for the care of mentally ill people.* According to this definition, deinstitutionalization is not limited to the reduction of psychiatric hospital censuses, even though this is a common understanding of the term (Bachrach, 1986, 1987). Rather, this definition extends beyond hospital depopulation to include the provision of alternative services. Downsizing or closing those hospitals is thus a critical part of deinstitutionalization, but only a part; it is not all of what that concept encompasses.

Indeed, early policy statements in the United States stressed three separate processes that deinstitutionalization would entail (Bachrach, 1976). First, patients already living in psychiatric hospitals would be released to alternative care facilities in the community. Second, potential new admissions to those hospitals would be prevented or diverted. And third, special community-based programs combining psychiatric and support services would be developed to meet the needs of a new, noninstitutionalized patient population. The third process was considered to be particularly important, for it was anticipated early in the community mental health movement that the altered life circumstances of mentally ill people would inevitably result in new configurations of service need.

DEINSTITUTIONALIZATION IN THE UNITED STATES

That the number of patients residing in American public psychiatric hospitals has declined dramatically since 1955 is illustrated by some basic statistics. There has been a drop of approximately 86 per cent in the number of resident patients in those facilities over the past four decades—from 560 000 people in

1955 to 77 000 people today (Bachrach, 1986; Center for Mental Health Services, 1995). The decrease in the resident patient rate over the same period is even more impressive, for in 1955, 339 of every 100 000 people living in the United States resided in public psychiatric hospitals. Today, only 31 of every 100 000 people are on those hospitals' rolls on any given day—a drop of well over 90 per cent in only four decades.

There are, according to our federal government, at least two-and-a-half-million long-term mentally ill people in the United States, most of them suffering from schizophrenia. In fact, this is a conservative number, for some estimates run as high as 2.8 million people (National Advisory Mental Health Council, 1993). Now, if only 77 000 of these individuals reside in psychiatric hospitals on any given day, that accounts for approximately 3 per cent of the total. Where are the other 97 per cent? The sad truth is that, often, we do not know where they are. Indeed, very often we do not even know *who* they are, even though it is virtually certain that many of them are in distress and in desperate need of help.

It thus makes sense, at least in retrospect, to ask what initially prompted us to promote deinstitutionalization in the United States. What gave Americans the idea that mentally ill people would be better served in the community than in hospitals? Part of the answer to this complex questions lies in the introduction and rapid spread of newly developed psychoactive medications following the conclusion of World War II (Havens, 1985; Langsley, 1980). With access to the new medications mentally ill people were becoming observably less symptomatic than they had previously been: they often appeared to function well with less intensive care.

However, certain philosophical and political considerations were at least as important as advances in psychopharmacology, if not more so (Bachrach, 1987; Langsley, 1980). A major boost was given to deinstitutionalization when President John F. Kennedy (1963) sent a message to Congress that heralded our first, and only, federally operated community mental health initiative. In that year Kennedy spoke of pursuing a "bold new approach" in mental health service delivery, three words that eventually became the by-words of the deinstitutionalization movement.

There were, indeed, several reasons that the President proposed and the nation largely supported change in this area. For one thing, the community mental health movement was undertaken during an era of unprecedented social consciousness and social reform in the United States (Hersch, 1972). It was at that time widely, even passionately, assumed that community care for mentally ill people would be more humane and more therapeutic than hospital care, and herein lay the rationale for the movement—a rationale that reflected justifiable concern for the well-being of mentally ill people, many of whom were living miserable lives inside psychiatric hospitals (Langsley, 1980). In addition, the rationale drew strength from another source: the assumption that community care would be less expensive—that is, more cost-effective—than hospital care.

Such a coalescence of ideologies is actually quite rare in American politics. In this instance, it granted permission to social reformers and fiscal reformers to become bedfellows, and so they did. Even though they were at times cautious and ambivalent, they were nonetheless loyal to each others' positions. Today, by contrast, social reformers and fiscal reformers in the United States tend to give each other very wide berth, and are far more likely to snipe at one another than to cooperate in common cause.

THE REALITIES OF AMERICAN DEINSTITUTIONALIZATION

As noted, the original intention when deinstitutionalization began in America was that three separate processes would play a critical part in the movement: patients would leave hospitals; new admissions would be blocked or restricted; and accessible, relevant new services would be developed in the community.

Have these elements of deinstitutionalization actually been realized over the past four decades? Some American communities have indeed done a fair-to-good job of implementing the three processes simultaneously; some have even done an excellent job (Cohen, 1990; Warner, 1995). However, if one attempts to assess the situation in the United States as a whole, he or she will probably conclude that the first two processes have proceeded far more rapidly than the third. That is to say, our hospital censuses throughout the country have been drastically reduced, and many would-be admissions to those hospitals have been blocked; but the critical third process of supplying adequate and accessible community alternatives to hospitalization has frequently lagged far behind. (I would note parenthetically that this is one reason that Americans often have trouble in making a summary judgment about deinstitutionalization after more than forty years. It is extremely difficult to evaluate a complex movement in which only some of what was intended has actually occurred.)

We may nonetheless conclude that the basic idea of community care appears to be valid for many persons who would formerly have resided in psychiatric hospitals. Our outcome research reveals that, in those communities where all three elements of deinstitutionalization have been concurrently implemented, the result has often proven beneficial to a great many people who suffer from mental illnesses. The quality of their care has improved substantially, and many individuals express much greater satisfaction with their life circumstances when those are contrasted with conditions inside psychiatric hospitals (Warner, 1995). In fact, some patients, in spite of their illnesses, have realized a certain degree of "normalization" in their daily activities. Some live independently and some are productively employed, achievements that were relatively rare in the days before deinstitutionalization. For these people deinstitutionalization must be regarded as a "plus."

However, these generalizations apply only to *some* mentally ill individuals.

Even in those places where community care has been thoughtfully conceived and adequately funded, some persons have fared poorly; and, given such a great investment of hope, effort, and clinical competence, we must ask ourselves why we have not witnessed more consistently positive outcomes in our community-based programs for mentally ill people.

Some portion of the answer to this vexing question undoubtedly lies in the fact that, over the years, patients' service needs have changed, often in ways not anticipated. For example, some so-called "new chronic" patients in the United States (Bachrach, in press)—in the United Kingdom these individuals are sometimes called "new long-term" patients (Shepherd, 1984; Wing and Morris, 1981)—have found it extremely difficult to sustain themselves in the community. Among other problems, their easy access to alcohol and other chemical substances has greatly exacerbated their symptoms and interfered with any progress they might have made, a circumstance largely overlooked in the early years of deinstitutionalization. Moreover, severe fragmentation of services, community resistance, and insufficient and inadequate housing opportunities have often conspired to create barriers to appropriate residential placement for these patients, even though it is widely acknowledged that housing is a critical element in the success of community-based care (Carling, 1993).

Further complications have arisen from the fact that nothing seems to stand still for long—a circumstance that makes it difficult to plan, justify, and sustain new programs. Old service structures are disappearing, service delivery practices are changing, and patients' needs are changing, even as political support for improving mental health care grows increasingly uncertain. Everything is in flux (Bachrach, 1991)!

I feel nonetheless that there is reason to be optimistic in the midst of this seeming chaos, for a new understanding of the complexities of community-based care for long-term mental patients has emerged. This is reflected in our support of some critical new service priorities.

For example, we have learned to focus (as we did not need to do when most patients were living in psychiatric hospitals) on providing a variety of *outreach interventions* that enable providers to go to patients where *they* are, not where we might wish or expect them to be (Cohen, 1990). We are also emphasizing the importance of improved *case finding* techniques, so that we may more easily find the people who are not being reached by the system of care. Too many individuals get lost in our fragmented service systems and must be located so that they may enter the system in the first place (Zealberg et al, 1993).

In addition, we are now stressing the need for productive *case management* efforts in which therapist-workers are charged with assisting patients in overcoming barriers to care (Harris and Bachrach, 1988). We are also striving to develop a wide variety of *specialized programs*—for example, vocational and psychosocial rehabilitation programs, psychoeducational efforts, and diversified housing programs—that respond to the new realities of patienthood (Cohen, 1990; Warner, 1995). The increasing prevalence of homelessness among mentally ill people in the United States tells us unequivocally how important it is that we consider such factors in service planning for long-term mental patients (Lamb et al, 1992).

We are, moreover, increasingly prepared to acknowledge that the care of mentally ill people is not merely a matter of social conscience and professional skill. It is also, unfortunately, very much a matter of politics. In the United States the move toward community care reached its highest expression during the 1960s, a time when human and civil rights were of great concern to many Americans. The process moved along with some successes, albeit with several false starts and bumps, throughout the 1970s. During the late 1970s a serious effort at mid-course correction was made when President Jimmy Carter convened the Presidents Commission on Mental Health (1978) and proposed important corrective legislation based on the Commission's Report. In response, Congress passed the Mental Health Services Act of 1980 (United States Congress, 1980). However, the Act was repealed soon after Ronald Reagan took office in 1981 (Okin, 1984). During the Reagan presidency, the federally funded community mental health program was essentially abandoned, and mandated federal funding for mental health services has now virtually disappeared. Major responsibility for programming today rests with the 50 states, even though state governments, in their need to respond to other special interest groups, largely lack the resources—and perhaps also the interest and will—to attend adequately to the needs of long-term mental patients (Kammer, 1995; Sowers, 1995; Wolpert, 1995).

The irony in this situation is that today we finally have a history of deinstitutionalization to guide us in future planning efforts. Experience has shown us that community care may indeed be more humane and more therapeutic than hospital care, but this happens only when certain preconditions have been met. We also have learned that sensitive and comprehensive mental health care is costly, no matter whether services are provided in a hospital or in the community; and that if we consider all the costs associated with responsible care, it is generally not accurate to say that community services will save substantial amounts of money (Kovaleski, 1993; Thornicroft and Bebbington, 1989). There are many hidden costs in community care, and these are frequently not factored into our studies of cost-effectiveness (Kirk and Therrien, 1975; Okin, 1995b).

My own judgment, in hindsight, is that our social reformers were perhaps too eager to ally themselves with fiscal reformers during the 1960s. They promised something they could not deliver—substantial cost savings—and the mental health community is still being held accountable for that promise. Not only has this claim detracted from the importance of quality of life concerns; it has also, more generally, severely damaged the credibility of mental health service planners.

THE LEGACY OF DEINSTITUTIONALIZATION: SIX LESSONS

To reiterate, a number of outcome studies document the fact that many mentally ill people in the United States today are living happier, more hopeful lives than they ever might have done in hospital-oriented systems of care; however, fewer people have shared in the benefits of deinstitutionalization than we would like. Again, a number of encouraging non-hospital programs have been developed for mentally ill people in selected American communities; however, these programs have not been so widespread as the architects of deinstitutionalization had anticipated; and it is undoubtedly safe to say that the majority of mentally ill Americans still lack the excellent care that has been identified with our "model" community programs.

In fact, some frankly troublesome events have been identified with deinstitutionalization. As noted, service fragmentation has been a serious issue. Instead of having all services available in a single place, patients must now be aggressive in navigating through a cumbersome series of disjointed program sites. Residential placement has posed especially difficult problems, for communities have generally been slow in developing an adequate array of housing opportunities (Bachrach, 1994; Carling, 1993). Further difficulties have arisen for relatives of mentally ill persons who, not infrequently, are overburdened by excessive responsibility in the care of disabled family members (Horwitz and Reinhard, 1995; Lefley and Johnson, 1990)—a problem exacerbated as parents age and face death. What will become of their nonhospitalized children?

Given these realities, how may I justify writing about a "legacy" of deinstitutionalization? A legacy, according to my dictionary, should be regarded as a bequest—as a gift of some consequence. What, exactly, can the gift of deinstitutionalization be?

I would argue that deinstitutionalization's legacy is simple but impressive. It is manifested in our *heightened awareness of the humanity and needs of mentally ill people*. And even though such a gift may not at first glance appear to be substantial in view of all the problems we face, I should like to go on record as saying that it really is quite remarkable.

To say this differently, deinstitutionalization has provided us with a *biopsychosocial* legacy, an adjective that implies the interaction of biological, psychological, and sociological events as they affect the lives of mentally ill people (Engel, 1977). Such a biopsychosocial view demands that we consider not only the biology of mental illness but also the sociological context of care and, most particularly, the special circumstances, needs, and hopes of individual patients, as we plan mental health services with them and for them (Hartmann, 1992). In the United Kingdom the biopsychosocial legacy has been most explicitly and eloquently described in Professor John Wing's contributions from the 1970s (Wing, 1978a, 1978b; Wing and Morris, 1981).

The essence of the biopsychosocial legacy may be depicted as a series of lessons whose observance is basic to the provision of humane and sensitive community mental health care. Included among these lessons are a broad view of the limits of deinstitutionalization, an understanding of the need for individualized treatments, accessible inpatient services, consideration of cultural factors, patient involvement in service planning, and flexiblity in systems of care.

Lesson 1—Deinstitutionalization involves more than changing the locus of care; it is a social process with secondary consequences

In addition to its being an important geographical event, deinstitutionalization is an ongoing process with subtle implications. More specifically, it is a vital process of social change—of movement away from one orientation in patient care to another that is radically different—that has had a profound influence upon the lives of mentally ill people. Today, deinstitutionalization affects those individuals who continue to use psychiatric hospitals by shortening their stays in those facilities and often by making discharge an end in itself that sometimes overrides clinical concerns. It also affects those people who do not use psychiatric hospitals but who might have done so in another era: the people whose very admissions have been prevented or diverted. Unfortunately, in the United States, some of these individuals receive no health or mental health services whatever.

The very process of change has thus created its own momentum. When understood as a process rather than a geographical event, deinstitutionalization may be seen to involve all elements of the service system; no agency is exempt. It consists of an ongoing series of accommodations and shifting boundaries that, not surprisingly, has generated disequilibrium in the system of care. These secondary consequences are, however, often overlooked by those who view deinstitutionalization more simply as a shifting numerical balance between inpatient and outpatient care.

We must no longer measure the success of deinstitutionalization in terms of reduced hospital populations, for when we do so we can easily lose sight of those mentally ill people who never enter hospitals in the first place (Bachrach, 1978). We can also lose sight of the many mentally ill persons who end up on the streets and in jails and other correctional facilities. The state of New York now reports more mentally ill people residing in state prisons and jails than in public psychiatric hospitals (Foderaro, 1994), a circumstance almost certainly duplicated in other states. Thus, Lesson 1 reminds us of the need to look beyond the depopulation of psychiatric hospitals toward some of the latent functions of deinstitutionalization (Bachrach, 1976) as we proceed with future service planning.

Lesson 2—Service planning must be individualized and tailored to the needs of specific individuals

Deinstitutionalization has clearly demonstrated the importance of highly individualized care for mentally ill individuals, who constitute a diverse and heterogeneous grouping of people (Sartorius, 1992). Some need pharmacological treatments, some individual or group psychotherapy or counseling, and some rehabilitation interventions. In most likelihood, any one individual will need some combination of all these, and often other, service modalities.

Mentally ill individuals also vary in the degree to which they are able to tolerate stress and unpredictability. And they vary as well in the kinds of programs that will best serve their needs—for example, whether they can live alone or would be better suited to congregate residential plans; whether they need intensive psychiatric interventions or would be better served by less invasive psychiatric care; and whether or not they are able to work, and, if so, whether they need sheltered or supported work or competitive employment opportunities.

In the days before deinstitutionalization service planners had a strong tendency to group all mentally ill people together and to ask, in effect, "What ought we to do with the 'mentally ill'?" However, deinstitutionalization has generated a focus on rehabilitation and individual need, and we are more likely today to rephrase this question to ask, "What may we do for *this particular person* who suffers from a mental illness?"—a conceptual shift of major proportions. Lesson 2 thus demands that we keep the individual differences among mentally ill people firmly in mind as we plan and provide diversified services. It is an extremely basic lesson, and honoring it is essential though admittedly difficult in times of limited resources when funding authorities demand that we simplify, not diversify, services.

Lesson 3—It is essential to facilitate access to hospital care for patients who need it, for as long as they need it

In the early years of deinstitutionalization many Americans believed that, could we but eliminate the countertherapeutic practices that had been exposed in some of our psychiatric hospitals, we would simultaneously eliminate the need for hospitals altogether. Unfortunately, much of our early community service planning proceeded on the assumption that we would never again require extensive resources for inpatient care. Experience has, however, demonstrated that, just as is the case for people who suffer from somatic illnesses, *some* mentally ill people *sometimes* require hospitalization. Precisely how many must be hospitalized and under what circumstances depends largely on what alternative services are available in any given community, for "trade-offs" are possible. Obviously, fewer people will require hospital care in those places that offer a complete array of excellent and integrated community-based services.

In any case, we know today that the community is not necessarily the most benign treatment site for all mentally ill people at all times; and that access to hospital care for those who need it, for as long as they need it, is absolutely essential to the success of deinstitutionalization. Lesson 3 underscores the importance of making distinctions among those people who do not require inpatient care and those who do, either briefly (usually briefly), or for a longer period.

Lesson 4—Services must be culturally relevant

We have often seen in the United States that mental health programs that meet with success in one time and place will encounter problems in another unless specific efforts have been made to adapt that program to local cultural realities (Bachrach, 1988). It makes good sense in the United States, for example, to plan services somewhat differently in urban and rural communities. Not only may there be major variations among these places in the array and quality of facilities; there are often differences as well in the effectiveness of social support networks. Often, there are marked discrepancies in attitude toward the use of mental health facilities as well (Sullivan et al, 1996).

Further, it makes good sense in the United States to plan services that respond to the distinctiveness of ethnically diverse populations (Garrison, 1978; Presidents Commission on Mental Health, 1978). I am acquainted with an Hispanic community in a southwestern state where it is considered good practice for a clinician or case manager to meet a patient or relative "by accident" in the local supermarket. But I know many other communities in which this kind of informality would be regarded as highly unprofessional and so would not serve the patient and his or her family at all well.

Cultural concerns are not, however, defined exclusively by urban or rural residence or ethnicity, for there are additional social factors to consider in service planning. For example, people who have spent many months, or even years, inside psychiatric hospitals may have learned to relate to caregivers in certain stereotyped ways that will affect the manner in which they approach and use the mental health system in the community (Schutt et al, 1993). This is true as well for individuals who have spent extended periods of time living in homeless shelters or sleeping rough on the streets (Lamb et al, 1992).

Lesson 4 thus underscores the fact that one-size-fits-all approaches is not appropriate for people who need mental health care, not only because each patient is different from every other as an individual, but also because each patient must be considered within a specific cultural context.

Lesson 5—Patients must be involved in service planning to the fullest extent possible

The experiences, values, and personal goals of individual patients must be acknowledged in the planning process (Heinssen et al, 1995; Sartorius, 1992); and this, in turn, requires that the person be informed about the nature of his or her illness, and about its symptoms, course, and possible consequences. Lamb (1976) has written that there is always an "intact portion of the ego" that the clinician can and must engage in order for care to be effective; this must be tapped and rewarded in treatment planning. "Ask the patient" is not an unreasonable guideline for service planning.

An extension of this lesson involves consulting with patients' families as well, whenever that is feasible. Relatives often have expert knowledge that is otherwise unavailable to service providers.

Before deinstitutionalization the concept that mentally ill people or their relatives could, or should, participate in service planning was not widely held. Deinstitutionalization has, however, given us an opportunity to explore the benefits of such involvement, and there is now widespread acknowledgment of its efficacy (Rogers, 1995).

Lesson 6—Service systems must be flexible and open to change

Just as much of yesterday's planning is no longer relevant today, today's service planning may well be inadequate for tomorrow's realities. We must thus be prepared to make adjustments and to alter our planning concepts as patients' needs change. This lesson is epitomized in the matter of housing (Goering et al, 1990). In the early days of deinstitutionalization, communities often provided one or perhaps two kinds of housing alternatives; but subsequent experience has demonstrated that we must offer a wide array of long-term, short-term, transitional, and crisis residences to respond to the service needs of a complex patient population. No single type of housing equally suits all mentally ill people. Some need highly structured residential settings, while others can live quite successfully in independent residences; those who best profit from the challenge of "high expectations" (Lamb and Goertzel, 1972) are best served by having clinical and auxiliary services (e.g., counseling, vocational training, social skills training, and medical and dental care) within the residential site.

In practical terms this means that we should not limit patients' housing choices to those alternatives that are available in the community at any given moment. Even though scarce resources may force us to make opportunistic housing assignments, these should be regarded as stop-gap measures until new programs can be developed.

Housing illustrates the need for flexibility in still other ways. It is not always in the patient's best interest to require that he or she move to a new residence in accord with some arbitrarily imposed time limit—as if, for example, six months in a transitional halfway house might be precisely what each patient needs. Some may need only three months in a halfway house, some may need five years, some may never be ready to leave, and some should probably not move into a halfway house in the first place (Bachrach, 1994). On the other hand, it is not always appropriate to force a patient into "permanent" housing, for some individuals have clinical needs, social histories, and personal preferences that make it desirable or even necessary for them to change residences with some frequency. Indeed, some American studies have shown that some homeless mentally ill people (though certainly not all) show more favorable clinical outcomes when they have been given the freedom to change residences, at least in the early stages of treatment (Dixon et al, 1993; Harris and Bachrach, 1990; Schutt et al, 1993).

Flexibility is thus a critical concept in residential planning, as it is in other service areas, and Lesson 6 represents a basic element in deinstitutionalization's biopsychosocial legacy. Allowing each mentally ill person access to those services that he or she needs, even when this contradicts preconceived ideology, is what makes community care more humane and more therapeutic (if not always more cost-effective) than hospital care.

CONCLUDING COMMENTARY

These six lessons, part and parcel of deinstitutionalization's biopsychosocial legacy, are, of course, not exhaustive; many others may be cited. One might, for example, point to the tremendous importance of a caregiver's establishing a permanent relationship with a patient, one that supersedes programmatic boundaries (Goering and Stylianos, 1988; Mosher and Burti, 1992). I believe that the United Kingdom is ahead of the United States in facilitating this kind of continuity of care (Bachrach, 1989). Alternatively, one might refer to the tremendous importance of developing more sensitive outcome measures to evaluate progress in community care (Bachrach, in press), instead of relying on traditional measures of patients' community tenure. Quality of care and quality of life are certainly better indicators of program effectiveness than are statistical summaries of geographical change.

I noted previously that community mental health care is potentially more humane and more therapeutic than hospital care, but that the potential is realized only in the presence of certain preconditions. The lessons of deinstitutionalization reflect those preconditions; and I am often struck by the fact that, although these lessons are now widely (if not universally) accepted almost without comment, they were virtually unknown in the days before deinstitutionalization!

Thus, as we Americans have sought to implement community care we have come to understand something that we should always have known: that mentally ill people are, first and foremost, human beings who do not experience their illnesses in a psychological or sociological vacuum. And we have learned that service planning that fails to acknowledge the biopsychosocial realities of people's lives will be incomplete, inappropriate, and at best only marginally successful.

Some readers may wish to argue that our deinstitutionalization programs in the United States have not consistently honored the biopsychosocial legacy, and I would not disagree. In fact, some may go so far as to say that, in the real world, these lessons are only rarely practiced. However, this does not alter the fact of the legacy. We now at least know something of the importance of biopsychosocial service planning and have a growing body of knowledge to assist us in the future as we attempt to fulfill the goal of humanizing care for mentally ill people. This places us several giant steps ahead of where we stood four decades ago.

The great American philosopher, George Santayana (1905), wrote at the beginning of this century, "Those who cannot remember the past are condemned to repeat it." As we approach a new century we are encountering unprecedented problems in service delivery. We are being asked to provide more and better care with fewer resources. I believe that we must meet these problems head-on by heeding the lessons of the past as best we can. Today we know much more than we did forty years ago; our challenge now is to keep the faith and put that knowledge to work in the service of mentally ill people.

REFERENCES

Bachrach, L.L. (1976) *Deinstitutionalization: An Analytical Review and Sociological Perspective*, National Institute of Mental Health, Rockville MD.

Bachrach, L.L. (1978) A conceptual approach to deinstitutionalization, *Hospital and Community Psychiatry*, **29**, 573–578.

Bachrach, L.L. (1986) Deinstitutionalization: what do the numbers mean?, *Hospital and Community Psychiatry*, **37**, 118–119.

Bachrach, L.L. (1987) Deinstitutionalization in the United States: promises and prospects. In L. L. Bachrach (ed.) *Leona Bachrach Speaks*, Jossey Bass, San Francisco, pp. 75–90.

Bachrach, L.L. (1988) On exporting and importing model programs, *Hospital and Community Psychiatry*, **39**, 1257–1258.

Bachrach, L.L. (1989) Some reflections from abroad, *Hospital and Community Psychiatry*, **40**, 573–574.

Bachrach, L.L. (1991) The 13th principle, *Hospital and Community Psychiatry*, **42**, 1205–1206.

Bachrach, L.L. (1994) Residential planning: concepts and themes, *Hospital and Community Psychiatry*, **45**, 202–203.

Bachrach, L.L. (in press) Deinstitutionalization: overview of promises, problems and prospects. In H. C. Knudsen and G. Thornicroft (eds), *Mental Health Service Evaluation*, Cambridge University Press, Cambridge.

Bennett, D. (1978) Community psychiatry, *British Journal of Psychiatry*, **132**, 209–220.

Blumenthal, M. (1995) Health care reform—past and future, *New England Journal of Medicine*, **332**, 465–468.

Bradsher, K. (1995) As 1 million leave ranks of insured, debate heats up, *New York Times*, 27 August, pp. 1, 20.

Carling, P. J. (1993) Housing and supports for persons with mental illness: emerging approaches to research and practice, *Hospital and Community Psychiatry*, **44**, 439–449.

Center for Mental Health Services (1995) *Additions and Resident Patients at End of Year, State and County Mental Hospitals, by Age and Diagnosis, United States, 1993*, Center for Mental Health Services, Rockville, Maryland.

Cohen, N.L. (ed) (1990) *Psychiatry Takes to the Streets: Outreach and Crisis Intervention for the Mentally Ill*, Guilford, New York.

Dixon, L., Friedman, N., and Lehman, A. (1993) Housing patterns of homeless mentally ill persons receiving assertive treatment services, *Hospital and Community Psychiatry* **44**, 286–288.

Engel, G.L. (1977) The need for a new medical model: a challenge for biomedicine, *Science*, **196**, 129–136.

Foderaro, L.W. (1994) For mentally ill inmates, punishment is treatment, New York Times, 6 October, pp. A1, B8.

Freedman, A.M. (1990) Mental health programs in the United States: idiosyncratic roots, *International Journal of Mental Health*, **18**, 81–98.

Garrison, V. (1978) Support systems of schizophrenic and nonschizophrenic Puerto

Rican migrant women in New York City, *Schizophrenia Bulletin*, **4**, 561–596.

Goering, P. N. and Stylianos, S.K. (1988) Exploring the helping relationship between the schizophrenic client and rehabilitation therapist, *American Journal of Orthopsychiatry*, **58**, 271–280.

Goering, P. , Durbin, J., Trainor, J., and Paduchak, D. (1990) Developing housing for the homeless, *Psychosocial Rehabilitation Journal*, **13**, 33–42.

Goldberg, M.A., Marmor T.R., and White, J. (1995) The relation between universal health insurance and cost control, *New England Journal of Medicine*, **332**, 742–744.

Harris, M. and Bachrach, L.L. (eds) (1988) *Clinical Case Management*, Jossey Bass, San Francisco.

Harris, M. and Bachrach, L.L. (1990) Perspectives on homeless mentally ill women, *Hospital and Community Psychiatry*, **41**, 253–254.

Hartmann, L. (1992) Presidential address: reflections on humane values and bio-psychosocial integration, *American Journal of Psychiatry*, **149**, 1135–1141.

Havens, L. (1985) Shooting ourselves in the foot, *Hospital and Community Psychiatry*, **36**, 811.

Heinssen, R.K., Levendusky, P. G., and Hunter, R.H. (1995) Client as colleague: therapeutic contracting with the seriously mentally ill, *American Psychologist*, **50**, 522–532.

Hersch, C. (1972) Social history, mental health, and community control, *American Psychologist*, **27**, 749–754.

Horwitz, V. and Reinhard, S.C. (1995) Ethnic differences in caregiving duties and burdens among parents and siblings of persons with severe mental illnesses, *Journal of Health and Social Behavior*, **36**, 138–150.

Kammer, F (1995) Block grants will worsen poverty, *New York Times*, 1 August, p. A15.

Kennedy, J.F. (1963) *Message from the President of the United States Relative to Mental Illness and Mental Retardation*, 88th Congress, First Session, House of Representatives Document no. 58, United States Congress, Washington.

Kirk, S.A. and Therrien, M.E. (1975) Community mental health myths and the fate of former hospitalized patients, *Psychiatry*, **38**, 209–217.

Kovaleski, S.F. (1993) D.C. mental health plan raises ire, *Washington Post*, 9 July, pp. D1, D5.

Lamb, H.R. (1976) *Community Survival for Long-Term Patients*, Jossey Bass, San Francisco.

Lamb, H.R. and Goertzel, V. (1972) High expectations of long-term ex-state hospital patients. *American Journal of Psychiatry*, **129**, 471–475.

Lamb, H.R., Bachrach, L.L., and Kass, F.I. (eds) (1992) *Treating the Homeless Mentally Ill: A Report of the Task Force on the Homeless Mentally Ill*, American Psychiatric Association, Washington.

Langsley, D.G. (1980) The community mental health center: does it treat patients?, *Hospital and Community Psychiatry*, **31**, 815–819.

Lefley, H.P. and Johnson, D.L. (eds) (1990) *Families As Allies in Treatment of the Mentally Ill: New Directions for Mental Health Professionals*, American Psychiatric Press, Washington.

Mosher L.R. and Burti, L. (1992) Relationships in rehabilitation: when technology fails, *Psychosocial Rehabilitation Journal*, **15**, 11–17.

National Advisory Mental Health Council (1993) Health care reform for Americans with severe mental illnesses: report of the National Advisory Mental Health Council, *American Journal of Psychiatry*, **150**, 1447–1465.

Okin, R.L. (1984) How community mental health centers are coping, *Hospital and Community Psychiatry*, **35**, 1118–1125.

Okin, R.L. (1995a) Parity is not enough, *Psychiatric Services*, **46**, 211.

Okin, R.L. (1995b) Testing the limits of deinstitutionalization, *Psychiatric Services*, **46**, 569–574.

Pear, R. (1993) Fewer now have health insurance, *New York Times*, 15 December, p. A24.

Presidents Commission on Mental Health (1978) *Report to the President from the Presidents Commission on Mental Health*, United States Government Printing Office, Washington.

Rogers, S. (1995) National Clearinghouse gets ready for the future, *Journal of the California Alliance for the Mentally Ill*, **6**, 9–10.

Santayana, G. (1905) *Reason in Common Sense*, Vol. 1, p. 284 (Dover edition, 1980), Dover Publications, New York.

Sartorius, N. (1992) Rehabilitation and quality of life, *Hospital and Community Psychiatry*, **43**, 1180–1181.

Schmidt, W. (1992) Across Europe, faces of homeless become more visible and vexing, *New York Times*, 5 January, pp. 1, 8.

Schutt, R.K., Goldfinger, S.M., and Penk, W.E. (1993) The structure and sources of residential preferences among seriously mentally ill homeless adults, *Sociological Practice Review*, **3**, 148–156.

Shalala, D.E. (1994) Health care reform isn't dead, *Washington Post*, 10 October, p. A23.

Shepherd. G. (1984) *Institutional Care and Rehabilitation*, Longman, London.

Sowers, W. (1995) The ethics of public sector managed care: civic responsibility or malignant neglect?, *Community Psychiatrist* (Newsletter of the American Association of Community Psychiatrists), Summer, pp. 1–2.

Sullivan, G., Jackson, C.A., and Spritzer, K.L. (1996) Characteristics and service use of seriously mentally ill persons living in rural areas, *Psychiatric Services*, **47**, 57–61.

Thornicroft, G. and Bebbington, P. (1989) Deinstitutionalisation—from hospital closure to service development, *British Journal of Psychiatry*, **155**, 739–753.

United States Congress (1980) *Mental Health Systems Act*, Public Law 96–398, October 7, United States Congress, Washington.

Warner, R. (ed.) (1995) *Alternatives to the Hospital for Acute Psychiatric Treatment*, American Psychiatric Press, Washington.

Wing, J.K. (1978a) The social context of schizophrenia, *American Journal of Psychiatry*, **135**, 1333–1339.

Wing, J.K. (1978b) Who becomes chronic, *Psychiatric Quarterly*, **50**, 178–190.

Wing, J.K. and Morris, B. (1981) Clinical basis of rehabilitation. In J.K. Wing and B. Morris (eds) *Handbook of Psychiatric Rehabilitation Practice*, Oxford University Press, Oxford.

Wolpert, J. (1995) Scrooges among us, *Washington Post*, 29 June, p. A21.

Zealberg, J.J., Santos, A.B., and Fisher, R.K. (1993) Benefits of mobile crisis programs, *Hospital and Community Psychiatry*, **44**, 16–17.

Chapter 3

THE MIXED ECONOMY OF PSYCHIATRIC REPROVISION

Martin Knapp*, Jennifer Beecham*† and Angela Hallam*†
*University of Kent; *†Institute of Psychiatry

INTRODUCTION

"Just as the history of institutions is an interplay between the medical profession, public morality and hard political economy, so too is the story of deinstitutionalisation" (Korman and Glennerster, 1990, p. 11).

The rundown of psychiatric hospital provision in England has a long history. Pharmaceutical and other clinical developments have facilitated the relocation of mental health care from hospital to the community, as have changes in professional and public attitudes to mental illness. It is also clear that economic considerations have long played their part. For example, although the stark economic realities of maintaining the psychiatric hospitals were brought home by the national economic difficulties of the 1950s and 1960s, the physical decline of the predominantly Victorian hospital stock had generated numerous problems somewhat earlier. In the early post-war years, however, it would have been perverse to have injected substantial capital sums into institutions which were not regarded by all psychiatrists as efficacious in the treatment of mental illness, or by a majority of public opinion as appropriate. The response at that time was not to develop community care but to lament the shortage of beds, psychiatrists and nurses, and the poor condition of the hospital fabric. Capital allocations to mental hospitals increased over the 1940s, and financial incentives were offered to attract psychiatric nurses, but neither was sufficient to improve standards to an acceptable level. The cost of improving the mental hospitals was seen as simply too great (Ministry of Health, 1962).

A similar argument surfaced in the 1970s, propelled onto the national policy stage by fiscal crises, and again in the 1980s by the Conservative government's value-for-money imperative. But the tenor of the argument in these latter years

Care in the Community: Illusion or Reality?
Edited by Julian Leff. © 1997 John Wiley & Sons Ltd.

now focused rather more on comparative costs: hospitals providing long-term care were believed to be more expensive than community services of comparable quality, so that the policy emphasis on community care gained support on financial grounds. Moreover, in this revival of the political-economic argument, there was the additional attraction that many hospitals were sitting on prime building land whose sale could—in keeping with the government's privatisation of other public assets—release quick injections of money into state coffers.

In the 1990s the economic arguments for the replacement of long-stay psychiatric hospital provision by community-based alternatives continue to be heard, but they might now be seen to be endowed with greater realism. The expenditure savings that could follow from hospital closure are generally recognised to be negligible or non-existent, and the short- and long-term challenges of developing cost-effective community alternatives are recognised to be less than straightforward, particularly for people with continuing or complex needs for skilled care and close support.

Much of the discussion of community care in Britain today is dominated by organisational and funding issues, encouraged by the changes introduced by the 1990 National Health Service and Community Care Act. Purchaser–provider separation and the developing internal health-care markets are proving especially influential, as is the growth of general practice fundholding. Two other aspects of the 1990 reforms—giving local authorities the lead role in community care and transferring social security funding of residential and nursing home care to social services departments—are also leaving their mark. In certain other respects, however, the changes introduced by the 1990 Act were foreshadowed in North London by the arrangements set in place in the reprovision programme for Friern and Claybury hospitals: the reprovision programme was obviously community-focused, it was characterised by plurality of both provision and funding, and process and care elements were regulated by regional personnel and clinicians, respectively.

We describe here the mixed economy of psychiatric reprovision—the multiplicity of provider arrangements, the funding mechanisms that support them and the regulatory framework that brings them together—in the context of local and national policy developments. In this way we can highlight policy and practice issues central to the success of community-based care.

THE MIXED ECONOMY OF REPROVISION

Both ideologically and practically, promoting the further development of a mixed economy of health and social care was central to the 1990 reforms. Consequently, system-wide implications of major policy initiatives such as closing a psychiatric hospital are now more likely to be couched in terms of the effects on a multiplicity of agents—statutory and independent—and in cognisance of broader societal expectations. At the same time, the 1990 Act required health and social care decision-making to become user-sensitive, bottom-up and needs-led, and of course market-influenced allocations are now more commonplace. Care management and care programmes are of growing importance at the interfaces between purchasers, providers and patients. In Britain in the 1990s, therefore, policy-makers, planners, purchasers and providers clearly need more and better evaluative and other information, and they need a "road map" through the fast-changing mixed economy.

Provision

Long-term psychiatric inpatient services are almost exclusively the responsibility of the NHS, while local authority housing and social services departments have been significant suppliers of accommodation for people with mental health problems not just since the establishment of the welfare state in the 1940s, but in the previous eras of public assistance institutions and workhouses. Within the UK mixed economy, the public sector plays the lead role.

The public sector today includes local authorities, NHS Trusts, directly managed hospital and community health services and general practitioner (primary care) services. Each is important in psychiatric reprovision, but mental health support seems to sit somewhat uncomfortably on the cusp between the social and health care systems, and many of the policy issues of the late 1990s revolve around the blurred or shifting boundaries between sectors. Moreover, since the establishment of the NHS in 1948, almost all health and social services for people with serious mental health problems have been provided or funded by the public sector. Not surprisingly, therefore, the resourcing and the direction of care have been heavily influenced by a combination of national economic welfare, government expenditure priorities, and the political importance (or unimportance) attached to mental health care.

However, one of the most marked features of the last two decades has been the rapid growth and influence of private and voluntary organisations, illustrated by these sectors' roles in hospital, nursing home and residential provision (Figure 3.1). This figure shows the declining role nationally of inpatient hospital care, the relative growth of psychiatric bed provision in general hospitals, the growth of community-based accommodation, and the importance in recent years of private sector hospitals and other facilities. The statistics in Figure 3.1 illustrate another pervasive trend of recent years: the declining importance of the NHS as a provider. The 1990 Act has thus reinforced a rebalancing of responsibilities within the public sector which has earlier origins. Of course, the trend towards community care has a longer pedigree than just the last two decades, so that the statistics summarised in Figure 3.1 tell only part of the story, but they neatly summarise some recent trends which will undoubtedly continue for some years.

Voluntary sector care for people with mental health problems, particularly through or inspired by religious bodies, predates state involvement by several

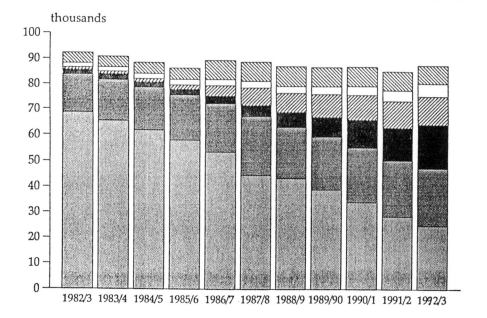

Local authority residential places

Voluntary residential places

Private residential places

Private and voluntary hospital beds

NHS other hospital beds

NHS psychiatric hospital beds

Figure 3.1   The changing balance of specialist accommodation 1982–1993

centuries (Kendall and Knapp, 1996 a,b). Today the voluntary sector is not only an important supplier of mental health services, but is active in campaigning, advocacy and research. Voluntary organisations are independent of government and, although they may earn profits, are bound by a nondistribution constraint—they cannot distribute profits to any owners. Most voluntary organisations active in the mental health field have charitable status, conferring certain tax advantages. Many are active in psychiatric reprovision in North London, and all place great emphasis on user involvement in decision-making. For example, MIND offers a range of services including accommodation (in most boroughs) and day care, in addition to its high-profile campaigns for the rights of people with mental health problems, and promoting research and service development. The Mental After Care Association (MACA) provides residential, day and domiciliary care, both in London and elsewhere, and has been an innovative provider throughout the reprovision process. Many smaller, local voluntary bodies have also been active providers and advocates.

Some voluntary organisations, particularly the smaller bodies, have found the new climate of formalised contracts with health and local authorities and the increased competition with the private sector to be challenging their traditional ways of working, their mission and, in some cases, their very existence. Nationally, the full voluntary sector contribution is not identified in Figure 3.1 (for example, in the independent hospitals category), but other statistics show that the sector maintained its share of registered community accommodation (called homes and hostels in government figures) at around 23 per cent of the total until 1990, since when it appears to have grown perhaps to as much as 35 per cent (Department of Health, 1995a).

The mixture of accommodation used by former Friern and Claybury residents is summarised in Table 3.1, and a very different picture of agency involvement can be seen for this reprovision programme. In North Thames, 28 per cent of all places are non-hospital beds provided by the NHS. Nearly 30 per cent of former hospital residents are living in voluntary sector community facilities (including consortium provision). Both percentages are higher than the national average (which is not exclusively reprovision, of course), due largely to the preferences embodied in the dowry transfers from hospital to community budgets (see below). In North Thames, very few readmissions to hospital resulted in placements outside the NHS (see Chapter 6). It can be seen that, as well as voluntary sector accommodation there have been joint or

Table 3.1 Community accommodation one year after leaving Friern or Claybury Hospital

Type of accommodation	Managing agency accommodation						
	NHS	SSD	Vol	Pri	Hsg	Consort	All
Residential home	76	40	59	36	0	11	222
Hostel	16	31	72	6	0	20	145
Sheltered housing	0	3	8	0	0	6	17
Staffed group home	0	5	17	10	0	13	45
Unstaffed group home	9	2	15	0	0	3	29
Foster care	0	16	0	0	0	0	16
Independent living	1	1	7	7	87	1	104
Hospital	60	0	0	0	0	0	60
Community in-patients	113	0	0	0	0	0	113
Total	275	98	178	59	87	54	751

Note: NHS = National Health Service. SSD = local authority social services department. Vol = voluntary organisation. Pri = private organisation or individual; Hsg = local authority housing department. Consort = consortium arrangement, jointly managed but led by voluntary organisation.

consortium initiatives between voluntary agencies (especially housing associations) and the NHS.

In recent years, the fastest growing sector nationally has been the private (for-profit) sector, which expanded its market share of community accommodation and simultaneously became a bigger provider of inpatient care, funded mainly through extra-contractual referrals. The private sector is constitutionally separate from government, but differs from the voluntary sector in its ability to earn and distribute profits. Reprovision patients made quite widespread use of private sector facilities, particularly residential care. Few of these people would have purchased the private sector services themselves, but would either have had them arranged by health or local authorities at the point of discharge from hospital, or by nurse proprietors of community facilities. The private residential facilities did not conform to common stereotypes of the commercial sector. Most were set up by individuals with nursing or social work qualifications, often former Friern or Claybury nurses providing valued continuity of care for people they had known as inpatients. (Indeed, some of the new nurse proprietors chose the hospital residents who would move with them from hospital, subject to the approval of clinicians.) In other words these were not large corporations managing a string of facilities across the country, but small enterprises often with the character of family businesses.

In addition to residential accommodation and inpatient treatment, the independent sectors offer day care and other specialist services. When monitoring the services received by former long-stay patients, we found that between 13 and 24 per cent of the members of annual "leaver cohorts" 2 to 6 used voluntary day care facilities. On average, the costs of this service suggest regular attendance once or twice a week. Nationally, there are no statistics on total numbers of day centres or places, but the number of voluntary day centres which received financial support from English local authorities numbered 600 in 1992 and 1180 in 1994 (49 000 and 76 500 places respectively), representing 14 per cent of total local authority purchases in the latter year (Department of Health, 1995b). This is an increase on the voluntary sector's share of total provision in the 1970s (Edwards and Carter, 1979).

There is another and often forgotten sector on the provider side of the mixed economy—the informal sector—principally composed of individual carers (relatives and others), who often represent first-line support, and upon whom the greatest care burden may fall. The 1990 Act sought to provide more support for family and other carers, through respite and other services, and by encouraging health and local authorities to involve them more fully in decision-making. In fact, few reprovision clients moving from Friern or Claybury were supported more than minimally by their families, for the simple reasons either that their needs made it necessary for them to move from hospital into quite highly staffed community accommodation, or because they had been resident in hospital for so long that they had lost contact with relatives. Only a small proportion were married.

Purchasing

Total community provision of accommodation for people with mental health problems increased threefold between 1975 and 1990, and has continued to grow since. As with residential and nursing home care for elderly people in the 1980s—which was the long-term care sector whose uncontrolled growth caused the government most anxiety, particularly because of its enormous impact on social security spending and the public sector borrowing requirement—the growth of independent provision was directly linked to the rather loose pre-reform fiscal environment. In the case of a hospital run-down programme, the demand was channelled through NHS managers, which is one reason why the private sector did not dominate the market in North Thames.

The 1980s provide a clear example of the ways in which patterns of provision are heavily influenced by the patterns of purchasing. In the wider mixed economy there are many purchasing routes, including privately financed insurance, health care financed by employers, and services purchased on behalf of patients by relatives or friends. For reprovision patients the purchasing variety was less, and not surprisingly dominated by public sector purchasing on behalf of citizens, mandated by democratic processes, and funded predominantly from central and local taxation.

Although health authorities make a substantial input to community care, their percentage share of funding is now a lot less than it was in hospital where almost 100 per cent of costs fall to them. In the community, non-NHS agencies carry some of the costs burden and are not always reimbursed by the NHS, although there were so-called dowry mechanisms in force to transfer revenue from hospital to community budgets, and capital funding schemes to jump-start new community facilities. Such arrangements could be found in almost every health region, but their implementation in the former North East Thames region was one of the most generous. Voluntary organisations (and occasionally other bodies) may use voluntarily donated funds to subsidise the services they offer, including some of those they sell to the state, and private sector providers may choose or be forced to cross-subsidise one line of business from another.

The funding of accommodation in the reprovision programme illustrates the diversity (Table 3.2). There is still a predominance of public sector funding, but rather than a single source (the hospital budget) we now see a number of routes by which public money supports former long-stay hospital inpatients. Much more of the burden now falls on clients, subsidised through their social benefit entitlements. (All members of the sample had moved into community residences by April 1993, and therefore their funding was a DSS rather than local authority responsibility; if they do not move to another facility, their DSS entitlements are preserved rights.) Private sector residential accommodation, for example, relies almost entirely on client contributions for its income. Both voluntary sector organisations and consortia rely heavily on the health sector and client contributions (Hallam et al, 1994). Housing corporation funds are yet another

Table 3.2 Funding of community accomodation by cohort

Source of funding (%)	Cohort							
	1	2	3	4	5	6	7	8
District health authority	4.16	54.14	74.90	60.45	59.65	61.43	64.44	80.69
Local authority social services department	22.83	8.14	3.33	2.17	9.16	3.58	4.55	2.41
Voluntary organisation	0.06	4.45	1.23	0.30	0.00	0.00	0.00	0.00
Local authority housing department	2.59	0.46	0.00	1.70	0.73	0.47	0.60	0.00
Housing association	0.35	3.69	2.26	1.93	4.10	3.92	2.13	2.38
Local authority forgone local taxes	1.09	1.03	0.80	1.36	2.10	1.68	1.60	0.26
Housing benefits	1.43	0.80	0.00	0.57	1.64	0.80	1.03	0.06
Client contribution	67.49	27.29	17.48	31.52	22.62	28.12	25.65	14.20

Note: Relates to accommodation facility costs only; not total cost of care.

source (now tending to be supplemented with private sector money) which, alongside the local authority housing department, provide subsidised accommodation.

The picture changed over time as successive groups of people moved from the two hospitals. The analyses showed that the small NHS contribution to accommodation costs for the first leavers rose substantially at cohort 2, reached 75 per cent at cohort 3 and subsequently levelled out at around 60 per cent until cohort 8, when it peaked at 81 per cent. By contrast, funding from local authority social services departments fell sharply after cohort 1 and contributed less than 10 per cent towards accommodation cost for all subsequent cohorts. Amounts paid by clients themselves, which made up 67 per cent of the cost for cohort 1 members, also dropped at cohort 2 and never again rose higher than 31 per cent. Table 3.2 indicates that client contributions are lowest for cohorts where NHS funding makes up more than 70 per cent of accommodation costs.

Regulation

As well as purchasing and providing there is a third dimension of the mixed economy which overlays the interrelationship between purchasers and providers: this is regulation (in a broad sense). Public sector influence over mental health service providers is exercised indirectly, for example through corporate or charitable-sector tax policies and through public-sector hegemony in setting professional training curricula and in shaping public expectations. More direct and more interesting influences come via formal regulations through contracts, and from law-making and other central government policy prescriptions, including powers to call for reports and issue directives.

Although formal contractual links were comparatively rare where facilities and services for reprovision patients were concerned, regional personnel could veto districts' plans for community-based reprovision services, and the responsible consultants had to agree to patients transferring to community services. Contracts have now become more influential in the broader context of health and social care (Wistow et al, 1996). There is also provider self-regulation through codes of practice, such as that developed by independent-sector providers of home care, by professional associations such as the BMA, and by British Standards Authority accreditation in residential care. Finally, there is regulation through the courts, to which users and carers might apply when public authorities are alleged to have failed to fulfil their statutory responsibilities.

CURRENT MIXED ECONOMY ISSUES

In Britain today a great many agencies and professions are actively involved in mental health care delivery, funded from a variety of sources. The 1990 NHS and Community Care Act encouraged the mixed economy by separating purchasers from providers, and by promoting market forces. We have seen that community reprovision from Friern and Claybury embraced many key elements of this developing mixed economy. Although the formal care systems and services set in place in North London (and nationally) are still heavily dominated by public expenditure, there is clearly marked plurality of both purchasing and provision. The 1990 Act also facilitated the formalisation of linkages between public sector purchasers and public and independent sector providers through contracts, but—because most reprovision patients had moved from hospital before April 1993, their main source of funding for accommodation was—and remains—social security support, so that the contract culture has yet to bite in these cases.

The 1989 White Paper setting out the government's intentions for health service reform, *Working for Patients*, stressed two objectives: to give patients, wherever they live in the UK, better health care and greater choice of the services available; and greater satisfaction and rewards for those working in the NHS who successfully respond to local needs and preferences (Secretaries of State for Health, 1989, para. 18). The future development of mental health services in Britain is difficult to predict because so many social and economic forces exert so many diverse influences. It is, however, inconceivable that a change of government would reverse the dehospitalisation trend of the past 50 years, so that we can expect more psychiatric hospital closures, more challenges in the community for service providers, members of the general public and service users themselves, and probably more variation in the mixed economy of care. Private and voluntary sector providers are likely to assume larger roles and acquire bigger market shares. The increasingly blurred boundaries between the compartmentalised public sector responsibilities for health care, social care and housing present further policy challenges (Beecham et al, 1996). Fiscal pressures (because of the ageing population) will lead to greater reliance on private sources of finance for some services and treatments, which will need careful integration into the current set of incentives.

None of these expectations for the next 10 or 15 years is particularly controversial or novel, but each requires a substantial "change agenda" and considerable policy preparation. For example, larger provider roles for the independent sectors will need to be monitored in ways which not only ensure high quality community-based care at an affordable price, but also encourage forms of market behaviour which will not jeopardize health or local authorities' long-term abilities to secure appropriate care for their populations. To take another example of the changing mental health care agenda, general practitioners—especially those who are fundholders—are becoming increasingly important purchasers of mental health care. Their roles in relation to discharged long-term psychiatric hospital inpatients may be limited, but their more general influences on the care system must be recognised and responded to.

These policy needs remind us that the developing mixed economy of mental health care is both opportunity and challenge. It is the means by which to secure diversity and quality of support, and it is the framework within which an increasingly pressed public finance system can look to extend the sources of finance. But it also changes the orientation and content of public administration. It places new burdens on purchasers to manage flows of money to secure the right services in the right place at the right time. In the search for better organisation and funding arrangements, a road map such as that presented here can indicate not just the stage of development of the care system but also its antecedents and its future shape. However, within this environment of change, users' welfare (broadly defined) and freedom of choice must be the primary foci.

REFERENCES

Beecham, J.K., Knapp, M.R.J. and Schneider, J. (1996) Policy and finance for community care: the new mixed economy. In M. Watkins, N. Harvey, J. Carson and S. Ritter (eds) *Collaborative Community Mental Health Care*, Arnold, London.

Department of Health (1995a) Residential accommodation statistics 1995, *Statistical Bulletin*, Department of Health, London.

Department of Health (1995b) Community care statistics 1994, *Statistical Bulletin*, Department of Health, London.

Edwards, C., and Carter, J.C. (1979) Day services and the mentally ill. In J.K. Wing and R. Olsen (eds) *Community Care for the Mentally Disordered*, Oxford University Press, Oxford.

Hallam, A.J., Beecham, J., Knapp, M.R.J. and Fenyo, A.J. (1994) The costs of accommodation and care: community provision for former long-stay psychiatric hospital patients, *European Archives of Psychiatry and Clinical Neuroscience*, 243, 301–310.

Kendall, J. and Knapp, M.R.J. (1996a) *The Voluntary Sector in the UK*, Manchester University Press, Manchester.

Kendall, J. and Knapp, M.R.J. (1996b) Financial, political and social realities of the voluntary sector. In P. Asconas (ed.) *Meeting the Escalating Costs of Social Needs: A Moral and Spiritual Challenge*, Macmillan, London, forthcoming.

Korman, N. and Glennerster, H. (1990) *Hospital Closure*, Open University Press, Buckingham.

Ministry of Health (1962) *A Hospital Plan for England and Wales*, Cmnd 1604, HMSO, London.

Secretaries of State for Health (1989) *Working for Patients*, Cm 555, HMSO, London.

Wistow, G., Knapp, M.R.J., Hardy, B., Forder, J., Kendall, J. and Manning, R. (1996) *Social Care Markets: Progress and Prospects*, Open University Press, Buckingham.

Part II

Perspectives on Community Care: Patients, Staff and Public

Chapter 4

RESIDENTIAL CARE FOR THE MENTALLY ILL IN THE COMMUNITY

Noam Trieman

Team for the Assessment of Psychiatric Services (TAPS)

Since 1983, when the decision was taken by NETRHA to close two of its psychiatric hospitals, about 100 residential facilities have been established in the area of north London. These constitute a range of living arrangements, provided for every long-stay patient who was discharged from hospital. Seventy eight per cent of the patients were placed in sheltered accommodation in the form of residential homes and staffed group homes. The rest of the patients, being less disabled, were discharged to unstaffed group homes (7 per cent), or lived independently in council flats (11 per cent), or with their families (4 per cent).

Table 4.1   Setting to which first discharged

Cohort	Living alone		Unstaffed		Staffed	
	N	%	N	%	N	%
1	9	20.4	1	2.3	34	77.3
2	19	16.3	8	6.8	90	76.9
3	15	12.6	9	7.6	95	79.8
4	17	22.1	7	9.1	53	68.8
5	20	14.8	12	8.9	103	76.3
6	7	10.8	7	10.8	51	78.4
7	10	18.8	2	3.8	41	77.4
8	1	1.8	0	0	54	98.2
ALL	98	14.7	46	6.9	521	78.4

Patients from psychogeriatric wards (EMI) were reprovided for in nursing homes or purpose-built community-based EMI units (see Chapter 7). A residual group of 120 long-stay patients, who were still at Friern hospital a year before it closed, consisted of severely disabled patients, relatively young and of

Care in the Community: Illusion or Reality?
Edited by Julian Leff. © 1997 John Wiley & Sons Ltd.

Footnote: *Figures refer to total population, 1984 (in thousands)*

Figure 4.1   Location of Friern and Claybury Hospitals and their catchment areas in London

shorter duration of stay. Sixty-four patients, More than half of this residual group, were regarded as too "difficult to place" in community homes. Instead they were transferred to specialized rehabilitation units within other hospitals (see Chapter 13). The other patients, being less behaviourally problematic than the former, were nearly all placed in staffed group homes.

The network of residential facilities in north London, as well as nationwide, is characterized by wide diversity in terms of the levels and types of support, financial and administrative arrangements, social environment and the quality of care. Studying these crucial aspects of community residential care was an integral part of the TAPS research project.

Basic environmental features of each setting were formally assessed by the use of two schedules: The Environmental Index (EI) (O'Driscoll and Leff, 1993) and the Living Unit Environmental Schedule (LUES) (Wing, 1989). The EI rates the degree of autonomy available for an individual within his/her living environment, and also the availability and accessibility of amenities (shops, pubs etc.) in the neighbourhood. The LUES rates the suitability of the living unit as a home in terms of comfort, state of repair and attractiveness of appearance.

From the range of residential settings in the area of north London, a representative sample of ten houses was selected (Table 4.2) for an in-depth study (Lewis and Trieman, 1995), aiming to gain an insight into the features and practices of various community homes. In addition two pilot studies (Dayson, 1992; Lee-Jones et al, 1994) have looked at the social milieu within two types of group homes. Data regarding the availability and the use of amenities in the community were accumulated as part of the economic evaluation of the reprovision programme.

The broad scope of this research, combined with data obtained in the course of numerous visits to care facilities by members of TAPS, enables us to form a comprehensive view of residential care in the community.

THE RANGE OF RESIDENTIAL FACILITIES

Community care for the majority of the long-term mentally ill rests upon the provision of structured and supportive residential facilities (Cutler, 1986; Pepper, 1985). Clearly the variety of needs can be met by the availability of a spectrum of facilities (see appendix). Two major models of housing have emerged over the last three decades: the custodial-type and the alternative (Trainor et al, 1993). Large custodial settings include residential (boarding) houses, nursing homes and specialized units. Alternative housing refers to a range of smaller settings, including hostels, group homes and sheltered housing. By and large a quality of life gradient exists across all these living arrangements, and likewise, a gradient of the residents' satisfaction.

Group homes, offering different levels of support, are the most common type of residential arrangement in the UK, as they are in the USA (Randolph et al, 1991). Much of the success of the group home is attributable to a combination of qualities:

"a homelike environment, emotional support from staff, social skills development and on-site supervision."

PROGRESSIVE AND REGRESSIVE MODELS OF RESIDENTIAL FACILITIES

The Friern hospital reprovision programme relied on a network of small-size residential and group homes which proved to be adequate for most of the long-stay patients. On average the number of residents in a living unit was six. This size of a group is containable within the dimensions of a normal home.

From an economic point of view, larger settings might be more cost effective. Such settings are more practical to manage where high nursing input is needed. Indeed, nursing homes for the elderly, "special needs" units and some residential houses are densely populated. The capacity of community EMI units and specialized units may often exceed 20 places.

Though not much systematic data is available, there seems to be a growing trend in the current reprovision programmes to replace the hospital with fewer, larger-size residential settings, instead of multiple small-size group homes. This emerging trend might potentially jeopardize one of the valued qualities of community care, namely the opportunity to normalize living conditions. If this proves to be a general trend, it runs the risk of a throwback to what Lamb (1979) called "new asylums in the community".

The fragmentation of the large psychiatric hospital into multiple small and dispersed residential units raises the need for more integrative models of residential care which are capable of providing a more structured environment without compromising the intimate quality of a home. This calls for some creative models of residential facilities. Some variations have already emerged:

1. A cluster of several two-person flats, all in one building with a communal room and office.
2. Three living units within a terrace or neighbouring houses. One group home is staffed while the other two are merely supervised.
3. Four autonomous group homes built in close proximity to a day centre/common office.
4. A group home with a few "satellite" flats in the neighbourhood administered and regularly visited by members of staff from the "mother" house.

All these are examples of "macro structure", also known as "core and cluster" settings, consisting of a few small residential units, which are self-contained, yet physically and administratively linked. Besides the organizational advantages, such models of accommodation manage to create a sense of cohesiveness and some flexibility in caring for mixed groups of residents.

WHO PROVIDES WHAT?

The private sector, currently the largest provider of residential care in the country (Faulkner et al, 1993), was more involved at the initial stages of the reprovision programme for Friern and Claybury, providing mostly residential homes, or board and lodging type accommodation. During the later stages, the contribution of the statutory agencies exceeded that of the private sector, and the district health authorities and local social services became the main providers of residential care. The voluntary sector provided a complementary range of accommodation, as well as day centres, social clubs and a few vocational projects. Cross-agency projects have increasingly become a common arrangement, taking the form of consortia between housing associations, statutory and voluntary agencies.

There were no clear indications that different providers targeted any specific type of patient or particular form of residential care. Overall, the

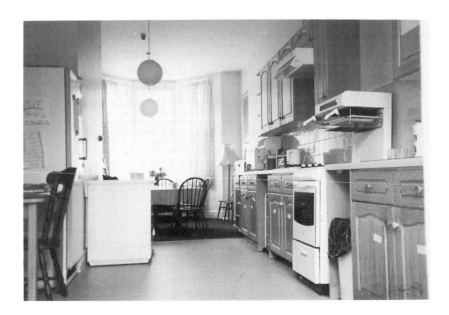

Figure 4.2, 4.3 A typical group home for former Friern patients—interior

continuum of services for Friern and Claybury represented a considerable overlap of different agencies involved in the course of the reprovision programme. Specialization was apparent only at the extremes, i.e. residential homes or specialized units run by NHS trusts, and independent accommodation, mostly within council flats, being the domain of the local authority social and housing departments.

THE PHYSICAL ENVIRONMENT: HOSPITAL VS COMMUNITY SETTING

The physical layout of a living environment has substantial impact on the life style of its residents. The construction of the Victorian asylums, more than 100 years ago, was regarded at that time as highly progressive. The massive complex of buildings provided spacious ventilated halls and many on-site amenities like workshops, a church, shops etc. Outside the building was a farm and a large well-tended garden, surrounded by high walls. The whole design reflected the original objective of segregating mentally ill people from society: hence the asylum was remote and self-sufficient.

In the course of the last few decades psychiatric hospitals have changed considerably, and have become less restrictive and more interactive with the community. Nevertheless, some basic features of the old asylums have not changed to this day: the large dormitories, where ten people are sleeping next to each other and only a curtain marks their living territory, the maze of corridors, the "no entry" doors, the administrative offices, all creating a rather strange "industrial" setting which lacks any sense of a normal home environment. It is all too symbolic that the empty site of Friern hospital was first used in 1993 to make a horror film . . .

The alternative residential facilities in the community are by concept, much as they are by design, modelled as closely as possible on "ordinary" homes. Many of these houses are converted properties situated in quiet residential streets, near shopping and other public facilities. The houses are indistinguishable architecturally from the houses on either side of the street and rarely bear a sign. The interior of each house has communal rooms such as kitchen, living rooms, bathrooms, and single (sometimes shared) bedrooms.

Housing characteristics such as privacy (having a single room), ordinary domestic features, a well-kept place appearance, are all indicators of what we commonly call "quality of life". No wonder that these characteristics are bound to influence our own subjective perception of the suitability of a place as a home. The majority of community accommodations visited by TAPS researchers were regarded by them as acceptable, and a considerable number of houses were seen as excellent homely environments. Conversely, facilities with greater similarity to hospital care, such as large residential homes, were much less appealing. An alarming finding was that many council flats were neglected, some of which had deteriorated to the level of poor physical conditions.

AUTONOMY AND RESIDENTIAL CARE

The gaining of autonomy by mentally ill people within a homely living environment is a value regarded as a cornerstone in the ethos of deinstitutionalism. Autonomy means less regulation, more freedom of movement and freedom of choice. These indices were formally measured and the picture is unequivocally clear: while hospital wards were invariably restrictive by the nature of their structured management (scoring on average 26 out of a maximum 55 points on the EI restrictiveness scale), the community homes scored just under 10. This dramatic difference indicates that patients who moved to live in the community have gained greater freedom in all aspects of their lives (see Chapter 5).

As might be anticipated, community homes which were occupied by patients discharged in a later stage of the reprovision programme, were more restrictive (higher EI score) than those established in the early stage of the reprovision programme, presumably reflecting the greater dependence of the residual inpatients.

Community settings for the elderly mentally ill were usually the most restrictive (see Setting A, Table 4.2). These nursing homes or EMI units have obviously been designed to manage greater physical and cognitive disabilities, therefore had to introduce stricter supervision.

Figure 4.4   The majestic façade of Friern Hospital

Figure 4.5   Claybury Hospital. In the background the characteristic water tower

It is of interest that repeated EI measurements for community homes five years after the initial assessment, reveal a trend towards more restrictiveness, which may be interpreted either as a realistic adaptation to a growing disability of the residents, or as an indication of the diminished expectations of care workers.

Anecdotally, in some houses where residents were initially encouraged to manage many of the household tasks by themselves, the care workers soon realized that it would be more sensible for them to prepare the meals for the residents or employ a cleaner to tidy up their rooms. These sort of late reactions may account for the above trend.

We must bear in mind that restrictions imposed on residents by a certain management policy should not be judged *a priori* in absolute terms of good or bad. Excessive autonomy might well be indistinguishable from sheer neglect. In principle, a good quality environment should aim to adjust its regulations to the differing levels of disability, while striving to achieve the minimal possible level of restrictiveness.

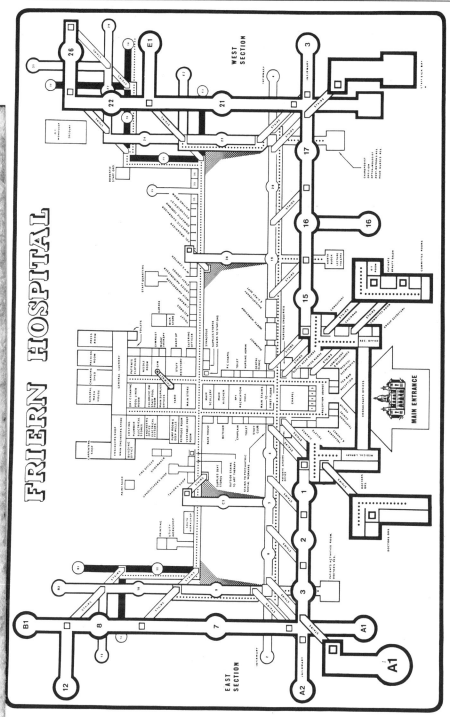

Figure 4.6 Layout of Friern Hospital

Figure 4.7   The long, wide corridors of Claybury Hospital

Indications are available that this standard is widely achieved within the residential settings studied by TAPS, regardless of which managing agency is involved. It was evident that houses run by voluntary bodies which vigorously advocate liberal policies are in practice not less restrictive than comparable houses run by other agencies. Moreover, it has been a common finding that regulations and restrictive measures are implemented in a selective and flexible way.

OBJECTIVES, OPPORTUNITIES AND ACTUAL PRACTICES

Despite the involvement of various agencies in administering different types of houses, the daily management styles for chronically ill people within the supported housing are basically not very different. The care provided corresponds

Figure 4.8 A home for the mentally ill, indistinguishable from neighbouring houses

Table 4.2 A sample of residential homes in north London

House	Agency which runs house	Type of home	Number of residents	Staffing levels
A	Local authority	Group home for older adults	8	24 hours
B	Social services	Group home	6	24 hours
C	Voluntary organization	Cluster flats (× 5)	2	part-time
D	Health authority	Group home (× 4)	5	24 hours
E	consortium	1-bedroom flats (× 5)	1	unstaffed (supervised daily)
F	Voluntary organization	Group home	5	unstaffed
G	Private landlady	Board and lodging with care	4	24 hours
H	Private proprietor	Hostel (× 3)	6	24 hours
I	Voluntary organization	Group home	8	24 hours
J	Private landlady	Adult fostering	1	part-time

above all to the level of clients' dependency, rather than to conceptual or ideological principles.

The bulk of residential houses in the community, regardless of who manages the house, try to facilitate opportunities for the residents to gain independence and encourage them to participate in the running of the house. Aspects of life such as privacy, freedom and responsibility seem to be advocated more strongly in houses run by voluntary agencies, but in practice these values seem to be equally respected in most places.

Residents are commonly encouraged to accept responsibility for self-medication. When the need arises, the function of supervising medication is undertaken by most houses, with a somewhat lower profile in houses run by voluntary organizations. This sector of providers is also less inclined to employ nurses, in line with the concepts of normalization and de-medicalization of its care provisions.

Most residents within the residential homes manage their own money, which they regularly receive as a disability allowance. Staff generally manage the household budget, which is needed to cover elementary necessities and sometimes holidays or outings.

Meeting the basic needs of the residents is the focus of care in most settings, along with efforts to improve social functioning, and to encourage the resident to get involved in his neighbourhood, namely shopping, visiting friends, going to a pub, social club etc.

A flexible task-oriented approach is employed, mainly within the domestic living space. Not much emphasis seems to be directed towards engaging the residents in formal or structured activities (e.g. occupational therapy or work) either in or out of the house. While indoor organized occupation is probably not practical and less advisable in a small homely setting, it is the scarcity of community facilities offering rehabilitation and work schemes that should be regarded as a gap in the care services (see Chapter 13). Moreover, there are some indications that even the existing recreational facilities such as day centres or social clubs are not utilized to their full capacity. A previous TAPS study (Knapp et al, 1993) showed that higher usage of non-accommodation community services is more common in types of settings which encourage more independence and offer fewer services on site, such as unstaffed group homes. Lower use of community services was particularly apparent in settings like hostels, nursing and residential homes. The reason for that stems basically from a low motivation on behalf of the highly dependent users, combined with a liberal and cautious approach taken by the mental health workers, who refrain from exerting too much pressure on the residents.

Studies in the US (Shern, 1989) have also revealed that the accessibility of recreational and rehabilitation facilities will to a great extent determine their usage, and that some patients in the community will not use the available services even if those are just across the street. A system composed of multiple small-sized residential settings, scattered throughout the region is inherently faced with this kind of problem. In this respect, there seems to be some advantage for residential models, such as settings C and D, Table 4.2), in which a few living units are located in close proximity to a day centre.

THE SOCIAL ENVIRONMENT

Some factors are likely to determine the distinctive nature of the social environment within the houses. One factor is staff-related, referring to the degree of staff involvement, staff support and expression of anger (Downs and Fox, 1993) (see Chapter 10). The other factor is resident-related, which is predetermined by the original mix of residents.

The most common arrangement in houses in the community is a mixture of male and female residents. The age range is usually very wide, except for the residents of the older adult placements. Beyond these demographic features, there seems to be no clear concept of what is the best social mix for a group of residents living under the same roof. Although there is no conclusive evidence that richer social networks can protect against relapse of illness and readmission (Sokolovsky et al, 1978; Gooch and Leff, 1996), nobody will dispute that having a mutually supportive clique of residents, or simply friends, means a better quality of life within the living environment.

In the course of the reprovision programme for Friern hospital, special care was taken to preserve existing social links between patients while moving them to the community. This wise policy was not always feasible. It is inevitable that reprovision schemes that consistently aim to move the more able people first, as happened in Friern, may impoverish socially the later established homes. Likewise community schemes that aim in due course to move able people from group settings into more independent accommodation, could result in a deleterious effect on the social mix of the remaining residents. This might, in addition, distance the mover from any protective effect of his former social milieu (Dayson, 1992).

An observational study conducted at Friern hospital (Dunn et al, 1990) demonstrated patterns of social interactions and roles undertaken by the mentally ill people. It identified four prototypes of role players, notably the "helper" type who is the more socially able person within a group and tends to facilitate interaction between members of that group.

A comparison between social networks of two group settings (A and B) in the community (Dayson, 1992; Lee-Jones et al, 1994) showed that while a group of twelve residents in setting A had only sparse contacts and no natural hierarchy of leadership, the other group of five residents within setting B formed strong reciprocal relationships. One of its residents emerged in the role of a pseudo-staff member, contributing enormously to the vitality and cohesion of that particular group. The impoverished social network in setting A was associated with an inadequate social mix of residents, poor physical environment, a high staff:patient ratio, and low morale among the staff.

It is concluded that a policy segregating the most socially withdrawn people will inevitably create a breed of gloomy low-morale care facilities. In other words, a more advisable policy would be to encourage heterogeneity of social ability in the process of grouping residents together, and subsequently to provide special training for residential staff in order to reduce the expression of critical attitudes towards the residents.

COPING WITH BEHAVIOURAL PROBLEMS

Most of the behavioural problems exhibited by the ex-long-stay patients can be dealt with successfully within ordinary group homes. The most usual problems encountered routinely were poor hygiene, lack of motivation and poor social skills. Nevertheless it is evident that challenging behaviours such as aggression, substance abuse or arson are not considered tolerable in most residential settings, and in fact these are often specified among the exclusion criteria for acceptance. This policy partially explains the fact that apart from occasional friction between residents, no serious disruption is evident in the day-to-day routine of most houses. Contrary to fears that many long-stay patients may drift into unacceptable behaviour once they move to a relatively non-structured setting, this has not been demonstrated in any of the settings observed by TAPS. Residential solutions for patients with special needs will be discussed elsewhere (see Chapter 13).

PERMANENCE OF LIVING ARRANGEMENT

A crucial question concerning residential facilities for mentally ill people is whether the objective is to provide a permanent home or a transitory accommodation. The latter option is based on a somewhat over-optimistic assumption that the patients would progressively become more independent and would "graduate" to less supportive homes. That model, also known as the linear continuum housing, prevailed in the US for some time (Ridgeway and Zipple, 1990) but soon gave way to a realization of the need for permanent supported housing (Carling, 1993; Fields, 1990).

The prevailing policy for the reprovision of Friern and Claybury patients was to provide a permanent home for each individual. This approach stems mainly from the recognition of the fixed disabilities of most long-term patients, and the continuous need for a supportive environment regardless of how vigorous the rehabilitation efforts are. The National Audit Commission (1994) reasoned that:

> "Long-term or permanent housing is the goal for most people, since frequent moves between temporary placements are very disruptive. It is better to adjust the

level of staff support when necessary, than to make people move on as their needs change."

A study of the pathways 281 patients followed in the community (Trieman and Kendal, 1995) revealed that 61 per cent were still living in their original placement five years after they left hospital. Most houses retained places for residents readmitted to hospital for as long as six months or more. These findings prove that the majority of the hospital long-term patients (excluding those with multiple disabilities and challenging behaviour) have been settled successfully in their new placements and eventually found themselves a home.

WHAT DO THE RESIDENTS WANT?

The advantages of a permanent residential arrangement are becoming even more meaningful in view of the wish of the overwhelming majority of residents to stay in their present accommodation in the community (Anderson et al, 1993: Leff et al, 1996). A negligible proportion of residents stated a preference to return to hospital. It should be noted however, that if given the opportunity, many would choose to live in their own house or apartment rather than in a group home (Tanzman, 1993). This is particularly applicable to the younger group of users, who are less institutionalized. The needs and voice of these users will need to be considered in planning future residential facilities.

REFERENCES

Anderson, J., Dayson, D., Wills, W., Gooch, C., Margolius, O., O'Driscoll C. and Leff, J. (1993) The TAPS Project 13: Clinical and social outcomes of long-stay psychiatric patients after one year in the community. *British Journal of Psychiatry*, **162** (suppl 19), 45–56.

Carling, P.J. (1993) Housing and support for persons with mental illness: emerging approaches to research and practice. *Hospital and Community Psychiatry*, **44**(5), 439–449.

Cutler, D.L. (1986) Community residential options for the chronically mentally ill. *Community Mental Health Journal*, **22**, 61–73.

Dayson, D. (1992) The TAPS Project 15: The social networks of two group homes: a pilot study. *Journal of Mental Health*, **1**, 99–106.

Downs, M.W. and Fox, J.C. (1993) Social environments of adult homes. *Community Mental Health Journal*, **29**(1), 15–23.

Dunn, M., O'Driscoll, C., Dayson, D., Wills, W. and Leff, J. (1990) The TAPS Project 4: An observational study of the social life of long-stay patients. *British Journal of Psychiatry*, **157**, 842–848.

Faulkner, A., Field, V. and Lindesay, J. (1993) Residential care provision in mental health: The current picture and future uncertainties. *Journal of Mental Health*, **2**, 57–64.

Fields, S. (1990) The relationship between residential treatment and supported housing in a community system of services. *Psychological Rehabilitation Journal*, **13**, 105–113.

Gooch, C. and Leff J. (1996) Factors affecting the success of community placement: The TAPS Project 26. *Psychological Medicine*, **26**, 511–520.

Knapp, M., Beecham, J., Hallam, A. and Fenyo, A. (1993) The TAPS Project 18: The costs of community care for former long-stay psychiatric hospital residents. *Health and Social Care in the Community*, 2(4), 193–201.

Lamb, H.R. (1979) The new asylums in the community. *Archives of General Psychiatry*, **36**, 129.

Lee-Jones, R., Chahal, K.K. and Dayson, D. (1994) The TAPS Project 32: Social networks of two group homes—five years on (unpublished paper).

Leff, J., Gooch, C. and Trieman, N. (1996) The TAPS Project 33: A prospective follow-up study of long-stay patients discharged from two psychiatric hospitals. *American Journal of Psychiatry*, **153**, 1318–1323.

Lewis, A. and Trieman, N. (1995) The TAPS Project. 29: Residential care provision in north London: a representative sample of ten facilities for mentally ill people. *International Journal of Social Psychiatry*, 41(4), 257–267.

National Audit Commission (1994) *Finding a place—a review of mental health services for adults*. HMSO, London.

O'Driscoll, C. and Leff, J. (1993) The TAPS Project. 8: Design of the research study on the long-stay patients. *British Journal of Psychiatry*, **162** (suppl. 19), 18–24.

Pepper, B. (1985) Where (and how) should young adult chronic patients live?—The concept of a residential spectrum. *Tie Lines*, 2(2), 1–6.

Randolph, F.L, Ridgeway, P. and Carling, P.J. (1991) Residential programs for persons with severe mental illness: a nationwide survey of state-affiliated agencies. *Hospital and Community Psychiatry*, **42**(11), 1111–1115.

Ridgeway, P. and Zipple, A.M. (1990) The paradigm shift in residential services: from the linear continuum to supported housing approaches. *Psychosocial Rehabilitation Journal*, 13(4), 11–32.

Shern, D.L., Surles, R.C. and Whizer, J. (1989) Designing community treatment systems for the most seriously mentally ill: a state administrative perspective. *Journal of Social Issues*. 45(3), 105.

Sokolovsky, J., Cohen, C., Berger, D. and Geiger, J. (1978) Personal networks of ex-mental patients in a Manhattan SR Hotel. *Human Organization*, 37, 5–15.

Tanzman, B. (1993) An overview of surveys of mental health consumers' preferences for housing and support services. *Hospital and Community Psychiatry*, **44**(5), 450–455.

Trainor, J., Morrell-Bellai, T., Ballantyne, R. and Boydell, K. (1993) Housing for people with mental illness: a comparison of models and examination of the growth of alternative housing in Canada. *Canadian Journal of Psychiatry*, 38(7), 494–501.

Trieman, N. and Kendal, R. (1995) The TAPS Project. 27: After hospital, pathways patients follow in the community. *Journal of Mental Health*, 4, 423–429.

Wing, L. (1989) *Hospital closure and the resettlement of residents*. Aldershot: Gower.

APPENDIX:

Various Types of Residential Care Facilities are Classified as Follows:

Continuing care provisions

These facilities are usually, but not necessarily, hospital-based. They provide 24 hour nursing care with full medical cover, long- and medium-term accommodation and a slow-stream or intensive rehabilitation, depending on the particular client group. In general such provisions cater for highly disabled patients who would not be accommodated in any ordinary group home. These patients need help with everyday self care, physical and psychiatric care, and they often exhibit challenging /socially unacceptable behaviour. Types of provisions: *rehabilitation ward, hospital hostel,* and registered *nursing home* (highly staffed).

Supported housing

This class of facilities comprises relatively small-sized community-based houses, adjusted to a gradient of support needs. This range of provisions caters for the vast majority of the former long-stay patients. The houses provide support with everyday living (finances, domestic tasks, self care, travel etc.) and facilitate access to rehabilitative and social community facilities. They are medically covered by the primary care services (GP, CPN).
Types of provisions:

- Maximum support facilities in the form of a *residential care home* or a *nursing home* (continuous staff cover by day and night, *six* or more residents).
- Medium support facilities in the forms of a *hostel* (continous or regular staff cover by day, on call night staff cover, *six* or more residents). A *staffed group home* (continous or regular staff cover by day, waking or sleeping or on-call night staff cover. Between two and five residents).
- Low support facilities in the forms of an *unstaffed group home* (two to five residents, *ad hoc* or no day staff, on call or no night staff cover). *Adult foster home* (one to three residents living within an established household, support by day and on-call at night). *Sheltered housing* (continuous or regular staff cover by day, waking or sleeping or on-call night-staff cover. Individual units in a larger complex).

Assisted/independent accommodation

These forms of facilities are provided for ex-patients who have both the desire and capacity to manage their basic affairs, though they occasionally need some practical support or monitoring.
The common forms of such accommodation are *independent* or *supervised flats* (*ad hoc* or no day staff, on-call or no night staff cover).

Chapter 5

THE OUTCOME FOR LONG-STAY NON-DEMENTED PATIENTS

Julian Leff
Team for the Assessment of Psychiatric Services (TAPS)

There are different definitions of long-stay patients, ranging from stays of six months to two years. The choice of time period is of course arbitrary, depending on the purpose of the enquiry. Studies of admission wards tend to use the lower limit of six months. We were concerned with the long-stay population of an institution so chose one year as our defining period. We also wished to exclude patients suffering from Alzheimer's disease, since their outlook and their needs for care differ considerably from those of patients with functional disorders such as schizophrenia and manic-depressive psychosis. Consequently we excluded from this sample patients over the age of 65 with a dementing condition. This was not always an easy decision, since some patients who had been admitted decades earlier with a diagnosis other than dementia, had reached an advanced age in the hospital and were considered by the staff to have developed dementia. This group of patients, dubbed somewhat ironically "the graduates", has been the subject of a special study by TAPS (see Chapter 7).

Our main aim was to compare the quality of life of patients when they were cared for in Friern and Claybury hospitals with that in the community homes to which they were discharged. The term "quality of life" has entered the professional vocabulary, but remains difficult to define and covers a wide variety of areas of activity and experience (Lehman et al, 1986). When we began this study in 1985, we spent a great deal of time choosing a batch of schedules that we considered would adequately represent the patients' quality of life in both hospital and community settings. Knowing that the study was likely to take many years to complete, we were sensible of the danger of selecting assessments that would look antiquated and inadequate when we came to analyse the data. Some areas of enquiry we deemed important were well covered by existing instruments, which we adopted. For others, no suitable instrument existed and we had to develop our own customised

Care in the Community: Illusion or Reality?
Edited by Julian Leff. © 1997 John Wiley & Sons Ltd.

assessments. We will present the batch of schedules in some detail as this is necessary for an understanding of the results.

THE TAPS SCHEDULES

Personal Data and Psychiatric History (PDPH)

Data for this schedule, which we constructed, are obtained from the case notes and include the patient's age, sex, marital status, duration of stay in hospital, and diagnosis. Total length of stay could be difficult to calculate if the patient had a thick file of case notes and many admissions over several decades. At the extreme end of the range, one patient had had over 20 admissions. By contrast, six patients had had a single admission which lasted over 60 years. Ascertaining the hospital diagnosis could also be problematic. For some of the longer stay patients, the changes of diagnosis over the years reflected the history of psychiatry. If the diagnosis was unclear because of conflicting information in the notes, the patient's consultant was asked to provide a current diagnosis.

Present State Examination (PSE)

This standardised assessment of the mental state was developed by Wing et al (1974) and has been used in a multitude of studies. The interview covers the previous month. The 140 items can be summed to give a total score, or may be presented as subscores on psychotic symptoms (delusions and hallucinations), abnormalities noted during the interview (speech and behaviour), and neurotic symptoms of a specific and non-specific type. We ran into a problem with the administration of this schedule in that we could not complete the interview with one third of the patients. This was because they were mute, talked incomprehensibly, or got up and walked away. For these patients it was only possible to complete the speech and behaviour section of the PSE. It might be supposed that this represents the loss of a large amount of important data, but in practice the account from the staff of the patients' behavioural problems (see below) covers the same areas as the PSE.

Social Behaviour Schedule (SBS)

The SBS was developed by Sturt and Wykes (1986) for use with a hospital population. A member of staff is interviewed about the patient's behaviour in the preceding three months. The schedule covers 20 areas of behaviour including personal hygiene, the expression of delusions, and the ability to initiate conversation. The frequency and severity of problems in each of the areas is recorded.

We found that the SBS gave good coverage of the problems commonly encountered in hospital. However, once we started interviewing patients who had moved into the community, we discovered that important areas of behaviour were not enquired about. These included the ability to use public transport, to claim benefits, and to prepare meals. Consequently we had to construct a new schedule to supplement the SBS, a description of which follows.

Basic Everyday Living Skills (BELS)

The purpose of this schedule is to assess the patients' performance of activities for which no opportunity existed in the hospital. It is also possible that some community settings may not have provided full opportunity to perform all activities included in the BELS. Hence for each activity, a rating is made of the opportunity to perform it.

Social Network Schedule (SNS)

This interview is conducted with the patient to elicit the individuals with whom the patient has been in contact in the past month. For each individual identified, the patient is then asked whether they would be missed, whether contact is welcome, whether they are considered to be a friend, and whether the patient would confide in them. Initially we supplemented the patients' accounts with interviews with staff members. However, it soon became apparent that the staff overestimated the social meaning of contacts on the ward and knew nothing of social activity off the ward. Therefore we have not used SNS data provided by the staff.

The reliability of patients' reports of the size of their social network has been established by an observational study in which a research worker sat in the patients' club over several months and observed the interactions between patients (Dunn et al, 1990).

Environmental Index (EI)

This has been developed from the Hospital/Hostel Practices Schedule and measures the degree of restrictiveness of the care setting. An enquiry is made of a member of staff about such regulations as the times of meals, going to bed, and visiting, and the availability of a locker for personal possessions.

Patient Attitude Questionnaire (PAQ)

The patients are the people most affected by the closure of psychiatric hospitals and yet their views have been ignored, as illustrated by the fact that no suitable instrument existed for recording their opinions. Professionals may have dismissed this kind of enquiry on the grounds that people suffering from chronic psychoses could not give consistent answers. In order to check on this, we gave the PAQ to 40 patients on two occasions six months apart. We found that they gave identical answers to two-thirds of the questions. In many instances, their answers had changed in line with alterations in their circumstances. Only 15 per cent of their answers could be discounted as stemming from delusions or other irrational thinking (Thornicroft et al, 1993).

The schedule includes questions on what the patients like and dislike about the care they receive, and where they would prefer to live.

Physical Health Index (PHI)

In hospital, patients' physical health is closely monitored by junior psychiatric staff and the nurses. We were concerned that once patients were living in the community, their physical health might suffer, particularly as people with schizophrenia tend to be unusually tolerant of physical pain and discomfort. Consequently we wished to assess their physical health before and after discharge. There were insufficient medically qualified researchers in TAPS to conduct physical examinations on every patient. Instead we relied on case notes and information from staff members. The PHI is divided into sections according to the various bodily systems (O'Driscoll and Leff, 1993). For each system the amount of medical and nursing care received by the patient is recorded.

DATA COLLECTION AND ANALYSIS

The complete batch of schedules generates more than 500 items per patient. Collecting baseline data on the initial sample of 770 patients occupied a group of researchers two years. Although they were trained to an acceptable level of inter-rater reliability initially, it was recognised that drift might occur in the course of time. Therefore we held joint rating sessions of patients in the hospital every two weeks throughout the study.

The methods of analysis differed according to whether the data were continuous or categorical. Parametric statistics were applied to continuous data that were normally distributed. If they were not normally distributed, a logarithmic transformation was executed to attempt to induce normality. If this failed, the data were dichotomised and treated as categorical. For dichotomous variables, percentages and their 95 per cent confidence intervals were compared at the two time points. For both kinds of data a matched analysis was carried out using cases having complete data at baseline and at one year follow-up.

It was not possible to collect complete data sets on every patient at both time points, since some patients refused to cooperate with one or more parts of the interview. This led to the omission of some patients from the analysis of each schedule, hence introducing a possible bias. To take this into account, the general estimating equation (GEE) approach of Zeger and Liang (1986) was used in addition to the matched analysis. This utilises all available data and makes an allowance for missing data. If the GEE produces a different result from the matched analysis, it indicates that the findings of the latter apply only to the selected group of patients with complete data, and cannot be generalised to the whole sample of patients.

THE SUCCESS OF THE ONE YEAR FOLLOW-UP

In 1985, when TAPS was established, we carried out a survey of the patient populations of Friern and Claybury hospitals, each of which contained about 900 patients at the time. A total of 770 patients met the study criteria and subsequently received a baseline assessment. However, the completion of this task, arduous as it was, did not mark the end of our initial assessments. To our surprise, our baseline sample continued to grow at an alarming rate due to patients being admitted to the acute wards and then staying in hospital for over a year, hence qualifying as long-stay. This was a result of a policy of keeping the admission wards open up to the time of closure in order to sustain a high level of clinical activity and maintain morale. By the time Friern hospital closed in March 1993, our sample had grown to 1166, the "new long-stay" patients comprising one third of it. We noticed that the accumulation of these patients was faster at Friern than at Claybury hospital. This prompted us to study the factors that might be associated with the build-up of new long-stay patients. We found a strong association with the Jarman Index of the health districts in the two catchment areas (Thornicroft et al, 1992). This indicates that the more socially deprived districts will generate larger numbers of new long-stay patients, an important consideration for planners.

During the course of this study, NETRHA found that its resources were insufficient to pursue the reprovision of both hospitals simultaneously. The decision was taken to postpone the closure of Claybury hospital indefinitely. Therefore TAPS ceased to follow-up Claybury discharges after 1990. Thus the TAPS follow-up sample comprises Claybury discharges up to 1990 and the entire long-stay population of Friern hospital, a total of 737 patients.

A flow chart is presented in Figure 5.1 which shows the attrition of the sample between baseline and one year follow-up.

The 671 patients followed-up represent 94.6 per cent of the 710 who had not died within the year or moved away from London, a very satisfactory success rate. This figure includes 64 patients who were considered unsuitable for discharge to community homes when Friern hospital closed. These "difficult-to-place" patients constitute 13.8 per cent of the Friern long-stay population and are the subjects of a special study which is described in Chapter 12. They are not included in the data presented here, which only concern patients discharged to the community.

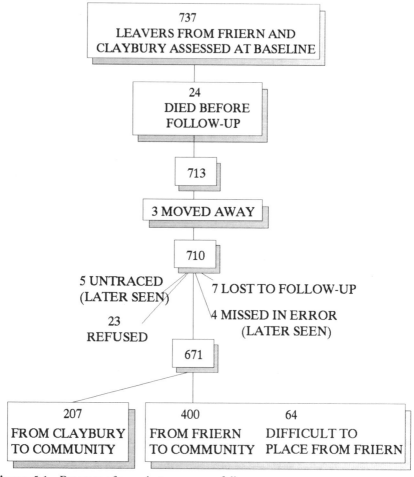

Figure 5.1   Progress of sample to one year follow-up

WHAT WAS THE BASELINE SAMPLE LIKE?

When considering the characteristics of the baseline sample it must be remembered that it consists of a mixture of old long-stay patients, who are the remnants of a process of discharge which has been ongoing for 30 years, and new long-stay patients who have been admitted relatively recently. The mean age of the sample was 53.4 years, and their median length of stay was 53 months, with a range from one year to 62 years. The patient with the longest duration of stay was a man aged 82 on discharge. The median score on the PSE was 9, the median number of problems of social behaviour was 4, and the median number of people in the patients' social networks was 8. It is informative to give more details about the patients' social networks since this has a direct bearing on the aim of integrating them into the normal community. One fifth of the patients knew no-one they would call a friend, over two-thirds included no member of staff in their networks, three-quarters were not in contact with any relative, and over 90 per cent had no contacts in the community other than relatives. These findings do not augur well for social integration.

The patients discharged in the course of one year are termed a cohort. Thus there are eight cohorts of patients between 1985 when the study began and 1993 when Friern hospital closed. A preliminary study of the first three cohorts suggested that the most able patients were being selected for discharge earlier (Jones, 1993). Analysis of data for all eight cohorts confirmed this finding. It is particularly evident when we consider problems with negative symptoms from the SBS. The scores for cohorts 1–8 in sequence are: 1.59, 1.55, 2.10, 2.01, 2.28, 2.35, 2.53, 2.93. These figures show a linear increase over time, with a line of best fit accounting for 92 per cent of the variance. This suggests a highly systematic selection of each subsequent cohort on the basis of negative symptoms as perceived by the staff caring for the patients.

DEATH, SUICIDE, CRIME AND VAGRANCY

These are the outcomes that are of greatest concern to the public and the media (see Chapter 10). As can be seen from Figure 5.1, 24 patients died during the follow-up year. Three of these deaths occurred among the group of difficult-to-place patients, leaving 21 deaths among patients discharged to community homes. This gives an annual death rate of 3.24 per 100. This rate was compared with the mortality rates for the general population standardised for age and sex. The ratio of the patients' death rate to that of the general population was 1.4, a non-significant excess, although it is worth noting that the number of deaths was small, resulting in a wide confidence interval (95 per cent C.I. 0.87–2.14). The deaths included two possible suicides, one a man who died in a fire in his flat, the other a man who jumped in front of a lorry, which swerved and missed him, and who died later in hospital of pneumonia.

All contacts with the police during the follow-up period in the community were recorded. Only two patients were imprisoned, one for over a year for attempted rape. This was a young man with a diagnosis of inadequate personality, who was discharged to bed and breakfast accommodation. On his way from the hospital to the address, he touched the breasts of a woman in the street. He was arrested and convicted of attempted rape, and was still in prison at the time of the one-year follow-up. The other patient was a man living in independent accommodation, who stopped his medication, became increasingly paranoid, and threw a cup of tea over a stranger in a cafe. The police were called and found that he was carrying a knife. He was imprisoned briefly before being transferred to a psychiatric hospital. This is the only incident which was potentially dangerous for a member of the public.

Five other patients were admitted to a psychiatric hospital on police orders under the Mental Health Act, three for assaults (with no weapon involved) and two for abusive behaviour. Patients were more often the victims of crime than perpetrators. Three were mugged, three were involved in road traffic accidents, two were victimised at work, and one was stolen from, amounting to nine victims in all.

The number of mentally ill people living on the streets in British cities has risen visibly in recent years, but this does not appear to be caused by the discharge of long-stay patients from psychiatric hospitals. We were unable to trace only seven of the 737 patients in our sample, and assume that they became vagrants. One of them was later readmitted to hospital from no fixed abode, confirming our supposition. Four of the untraced patients had previously led a vagrant life before becoming long-stay in the psychiatric hospital. No patient was lost from a staffed home, and there were no transient periods of homelessness for residents of these facilities (Trieman and Kendal, 1995). In retrospect, it was an error of judgement to place patients with a history of vagrancy in unstaffed accommodation.

One measure of the stability of discharged patients in the community is their liability to be readmitted. Of the 671 patients followed up at one year, 102 (15.2 per cent) had been readmitted at some point to a psychiatric ward. Young men who were new long-stay were most likely to be readmitted (Gooch and Leff, 1996). The majority of readmitted patients were discharged back to their original community home (Trieman and Kendal, 1995). However, some readmitted patients remained in hospital for over a year, hence qualifying as long-stay again. These patients, who amounted to 6 per cent of the original sample, obviously constitute a serious problem for community care. The implication of this readmission rate for the provision of acute beds is explored in Chapter 13.

CLINICAL OUTCOME

It would have been too cumbersome to analyse the hundreds of items of data collected. Furthermore many significant differences would have emerged by chance. Therefore 66 items were selected which either summarised a number of variables or were of obvious clinical importance. Those items showing a significant ($p < 0.05$) difference over time are displayed in Tables 5.1 and 5.2, which present summary statistics at each time point, together with paired differences and associated t or chi-square statistics as appropriate.

Table 5.1 1 year follow-up of long-stay patients discharged from Friern and Claybury Hospitals continuous variables

Variable	Baseline (time 1)			1 yr follow-up (time 2)			Paired differences (complete data only)			Null hypothesis (no differences)		
	N	Mean	95% C.I.	N	Mean	95% C.I.	N	Mean difference	95% C.I.	t	d.f.	p
PSE												
Total score: log (anti-log)	631	2.34 (9.38)	2.27 to 2.41 (8.68 to 10.13)	532	2.26 (8.58)	2.18 to 2.34 (7.85 to 9.38)	506	2.34 − 2.27 = 0.07	−0.11 to 0.15	1.74	504	<0.085
SBS												
Total score	664	4.43	4.18 to 4.68	557	4.24	3.97 to 4.51	553	4.61 − 4.26 = 0.34	0.03 to 0.65	2.17	551	<0.035
EI												
Restrictiveness total score	661	26.15	25.7 to 26.6	535	9.92	9.22 to 10.6	527	26.34 − 9.93 = 16.40	15.60 to 17.20	42.6	525	<0.0001
BELS												
Community score	395	6.78	6.28 to 7.28	517	8.06	7.64 to 8.48	285	6.18 − 7.48 = −1.29	−1.80 to −0.78	5.02	283	<0.0001
Domestic score	395	12.30	11.30 to 13.30	515	17.51	16.40 to 18.60	284	11.65 − 16.90 = −5.25	−6.89 to −3.61	6.32	282	<0.0001
SNS												
Total named	505	9.81	9.09 to 10.5	392	10.53	9.79 to 11.30	326	10.33 − 11.30 = −0.97	−2.02 to 0.077	1.83	324	<0.07
Sum of friends: log (anti-log)	505	1.19 (2.29)	1.11 to 1.27 (2.03 to 2.56)	392	1.43 (3.18)	1.34 to 1.52 (2.82 to 3.57)	326	1.19 − 1.54 = −0.35	−0.47 to −0.23	5.90	324	<0.0001
Sum of confidants: log (anti-log)	505	0.97 (1.64)	0.89 to 1.05 (1.44 to 1.86)	392	1.04 (1.83)	0.95 to 1.13 (1.59 to 2.10)	326	0.98 − 1.12 = −0.14	−0.25 to −0.026	2.41	324	<0.02

Table 5.2 1 year follow-up of long-stay patients discharged from Friern and Claybury Hospitals categorical variables

Variable	Baseline (time 1)			1-yr follow-up (time 2)			Paired differences (complete data only) * excludes "ambivalence" etc			Null hypothesis (no differences)	
	N	%	95% C.I.	N	%	95% C.I.	N	Difference (percentage points)	95% C.I. of difference	X^2 d.f. = 1	p
PSE											
Negative symptoms	651	60.4	56.6 to 64.1	545	55.2	51.1 to 59.4	533	$62.1 - 55.2 = 6.94$	1.89 to 12.0	7.27	<0.007
PAQ											
Like of permissiveness	651	3.8	2.50 to 5.62	560	20.5	17.2 to 23.9	550	$4.18 - 20.4 = 16.2$	12.4 to 20.0	70.35	<0.0001
Desire to remain	610	25.1	21.6 to 28.5	410	73.7	69.4 to 77.9	308*	$33.4 - 82.5 = -49.0$	−55.7 to −42.3	205.5	<0.00001
Helpfulness of medication	572	52.6	48.5 to 56.7	399	69.2	64.6 to 73.7	358	$55.9 - 72.3 = -16.5$	−22.5 to −10.5	28.70	<0.0001
BELS											
Problem with medication	376	90.2	86.7 to 93.0	491	67.4	63.4 to 71.6	262	$91.6 - 74.8 = 16.8$	11.6 to 20.2	36.80	<0.0001
PHI											
Impaired mobility	657	6.5	4.71 to 8.71	516	20.5	17.1 to 24.0	507	$7.3 - 12.0 = -5.3$	−8.2 to −2.5	13.61	<0.0002
Incontinence	657	10.5	8.16 to 12.8	518	20.1	16.6 to 23.5	509	$11.2 - 19.4 = -8.2$	−11.4 to −4.5	19.92	<0.0001
SNS											
Acquaintances (70)	505	19.4	16.0 to 22.9	392	28.8	24.3 to 33.3	326	$17.2 - 32.5 = -15.3$	−19.5 to −10.1	32.75	<0.0001
Relatives (70)	505	55.2	50.9 to 59.6	392	48.0	43.0 to 52.9	326	$57.4 - 48.8 = 8.6$	2.4 to 14.5	8.20	<0.005
Service contacts (70)	505	7.9	5.72 to 10.6	392	16.3	12.7 to 20.0	326	$7.7 - 18.1 = -10.4$	−14.9 to −5.1	15.95	<0.0001
SBS											
Positive symptoms	664	42.9	39.2 to 46.7	558	51.6	47.5 to 55.8	554	$44.8 - 52.0 = -7.22$	−12.0 to −2.43	8.74	<0.004

Psychiatric Symptoms

Patients' mental state remained remarkably stable over the follow-up period. In particular there was no change in the score for delusions and hallucinations. However, the score on negative symptoms decreased significantly. In all, 7 per cent of patients lost their negative symptoms entirely. This small, but highly significant, change has important practical and theoretical implications. On the practical side, negative symptoms do not respond well to antipsychotic drugs, so that their response to a change in the social environment is encouraging, particularly since negative symptoms are a major impediment to rehabilitation. On the theoretical side, this finding is a confirmation of Wing and Brown's (1970) finding that negative symptoms were closely related to the level of social stimulation in psychiatric hospitals. Our result demonstrates that the increased social stimulation that follows from discharge into community homes also improves negative symptoms.

Social Behaviour

There was a significant improvement in problems of social behaviour after a year in the community. However, before ascribing this to the patients' experience in the community homes, it is necessary to present some results from an earlier phase of the study. For the first five years it was possible to match patients who were discharged with others who were likely to remain in hospital for a further year. We aimed at close matching on a number of variables including age, sex, length of stay, and number of social behaviour problems. The matched comparison revealed that patients who remained in hospital showed a similar improvement in social behaviour to those who were discharged (Leff et al, 1996). This finding shows that rehabilitation in hospital can be as effective as in the community.

One subscore of the SBS showed a significant deterioration over time, namely positive symptoms. The proportion of patients with these symptoms increased by 7 per cent over time. We had expected to find indications from the PSE that the transition to community living would lead to a deterioration in patients' mental state. As we have already described, this was not picked up by the researchers giving the PSE. However it was noticed by staff in daily contact with the patients.

Everyday Living Skills

Significant improvements were observed in domestic skills and in community skills. Relatively little was done to replace the thriving industrial therapy department at Friern, which in its heyday employed 120 people. Instead, the majority of patients in the community were expected to take an active part in the maintenance of their homes. It is not surprising, therefore, that their domestic skills improved. Community skills included budgeting, use of public transport, competence at claiming social security benefits, and use of public amenities such as parks. It may seem obvious that these would improve with the increased opportunities to practise the relevant skills in the community. But it must be remembered that almost all these patients lived on open wards in the hospital and were free to walk through the main gate and take a bus to any destination. The fact that they did not do so can be attributed to the invisible psychological barrier that separated the institution from the outside world.

One unexpected change in this area was concerned with problems of compliance with medication. These decreased significantly after a year in the community. Possibly this may have been aided by a programme run by the pharmacy department in the hospital to teach as many patients as possible to be responsible for their oral medication before their discharge.

Restrictiveness of the Environment

The total score on the Environmental Index dropped dramatically from over 26 in the hospitals to just under 10 in the community homes. This reduction occurred in all subsections of the EI indicating much greater freedom in all aspects of the patients' lives. However, we noted that the EI scores in the community homes occupied by the later cohorts were higher than for the earlier cohorts, suggesting that the staff were responding to the greater dependence of the later discharges by imposing more restrictions.

Patients' Attitudes

Of the three schedules administered to the patients, this was the most acceptable, judging by the response rate. Patients evidently appreciated the greater freedom in the community, since a liking for permissiveness was mentioned spontaneously by 20 per cent at follow-up compared with only 4 per cent in hospital. Initially, only one third of the sample wished to stay in hospital, whereas the great majority (over 80 per cent) desired to remain in their community homes. An unexpected finding was an increase over time in the proportion who found their medication helpful. This was not related to changes in medication over time, which rarely occurred, with less than 1 per cent of patients discontinuing medication.

Physical Health

It was reassuring to find that, in general, patients' physical health did not deteriorate during the year in the community, nor was there any change in the medical and nursing care received. However, two areas of physical disability showed a highly significant worsening over time; incontinence and impaired mobility. In both cases, patients who deteriorated were significantly older

($p < 0.01$) than those who were free of these problems. These changes, which are probably an inevitable accompaniment of ageing in an elderly population, need to be anticipated in planning community homes for long-stay patients. At the very least, some homes should contain ground floor bedrooms for patients who become incapable of climbing stairs.

Social Life

A relatively low proportion of the sample completed the SNS, 76 per cent of those with data at baseline and 70 per cent at follow-up. There is evidence from the SBS that patients who refused the SNS were more socially disabled than those who cooperated with the interview. Consequently the SNS data may present an overly optimistic view of the social life of the whole sample. To check for a possible bias, attention needs to be paid to the results of the general estimating equations (GEE).

There was a marginally significant increase in the total size of patients' networks ($p < 0.07$). The GEE, based on 571 patients rather than 326, indicated a more clearly significant change ($p < 0.035$). There was a significant increase in the number of people considered by the patients to be friends, which was confirmed by the GEE. On average, each patient gained one extra friend over the follow-up year. The value of this has to be judged in relation to the small size of their social networks, 11 people on average. A small number of the friendships were made with neighbours. There was also an increase in the number of confidants (the most intense form of relationship) but this was not confirmed by the GEE, indicating that only a selected group of patients benefited in this way.

It is possible for patients to be living in the community but not to be socially integrated with ordinary people. If this were the case, all their social contacts, including the most meaningful, would be confined to providers and users of mental health services. Patients would be within the community but not part of it, encapsulated in a world dominated by mental illness. To see whether this was the case, we defined a category of social contact, termed an acquaintance, who was involved in neither providing nor receiving psychiatric care. We found that there was an increase in the proportion of patients who knew at least one acquaintance, from 19 per cent in the hospital to 29 per cent in the community. We were interested in the source of these acquaintances, and found that most were met at social clubs, including those run by churches, or were neighbours, or relatives and friends of carers. It was reassuring to find that some patients had made social contact with ordinary members of the public, but they still represent only a small minority of those discharged. Part of the problem is likely to lie in the social disabilities resulting from the combination of chronic schizophrenia and institutionalism. However, public attitudes undoubtedly form a barrier to the social integration of patients and need to be addressed (see Chapter 10).

We also recorded contacts with people providing a service to the general public, mainly shopkeepers. These increased significantly, a matter of some importance to patients, since the observational study in the patients' club at Friern had taught us the value of the exchange of goods and services in the maintenance of social bonds (Dunn et al., 1990). From anecdotal reports, it became evident that local shopkeepers had learned to cope with the sometimes eccentric shopping habits of the patients.

The sole negative finding from the SNS was a significant decrease in contacts with relatives. This is disappointing, as one of the reasons for relocating patients in the districts from which they were originally admitted was to facilitate visits by relatives. We have no explanation for this unexpected consequence of relocation to the community which requires further study.

Conclusions from the One Year Follow-up

This comprehensive study of reprovision for the long-stay patients from Friern and Claybury hospitals has shown major benefits and few disadvantages after one year in the community. The main advantages for the patients were a decrease in negative symptoms, an increase in living skills, much more freedom, and a richer social life. The great majority of patients responded to these positive changes by expressing a wish to stay in their community homes. On the down side, staff perceived an increase in patients' psychotic symptoms, and fewer patients had visits from relatives. Increases in immobility and incontinence were almost certainly a consequence of ageing, and unrelated to the move to the community. An advantage for the staff was that there were fewer problems concerning compliance with medication.

The fears commonly expressed by the media and the public that discharged patients would kill themselves or others, or be exposed to the neglect of a life on the streets, were not borne out by our results. It could be argued that a one year follow-up is too brief to serve as an adequate test of community care for long-stay patients, many of whom have been ill for decades. We see this as a cogent objection and for that reason have mounted a five year follow-up of this sample. To date we have followed up the first four cohorts of discharges.

The Success of the Five Year Follow-up

The first four cohorts of discharged patients numbered 359 individuals. By the one year follow-up, seven people had died, six moved away from London, and six were lost to follow-up. The flow chart in Figure 5.2 shows what happened to the 340 patients who were still accessible after one year in the community. After five years TAPS was able to follow up just over 80 per cent of the patients who could have been interviewed.

As with the one year follow-up, we will first consider the outcomes that give rise to most public concern

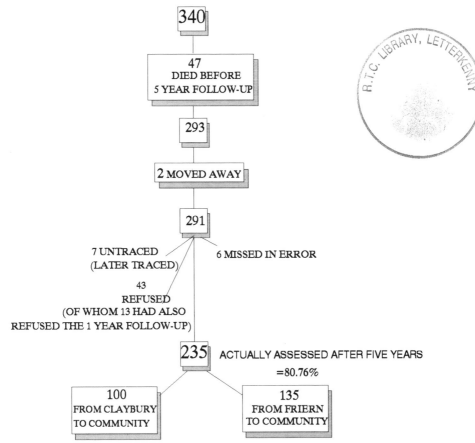

Figure 5.2   Success rate in following up cohorts 1–4 between 1 year and 5 years after discharge

Death, Suicide, Crime and Vagrancy

Over the whole five years, there were 54 deaths. The expected number of deaths for a sample of the general population matched with the patients on age and sex is 29.5. Hence the patients show a rate which is 1.83 times that expected, representing a significant excess (99 per cent confidence limits, 1.25–2.58). This could be interpreted as showing that the move into the community exerts a damaging effect on some patients' health. However, other studies have found an excessively high death rate among patients suffering from severe psychiatric disorders, even when suicide is excluded. Furthermore, in an earlier phase of our study when discharged patients were matched on age, sex and other variables with patients who remained in hospital, the death rates of the two groups did not differ. Taking all this evidence into account, it seems likely that discharge into the community does not carry an increased mortality.

Among these four cohorts there were no suicides in the first year of follow-up, but five patients (1.5 per cent) killed themselves during the next four years. The lifetime risk of suicide in schizophrenia is 10 per cent so that the rate we found is not surprising. Furthermore, two of the suicides occurred in hospital during a readmission. Thus it appears that the risk of suicide is not increased by living in the community.

The crime rate for this sample of patients over the five years of follow-up was low. Three patients committed theft and another three assaults, one on his mother, one on another patient, and one on a carer. Patients were much more often the victims of crime than the perpetrators. Patients were stolen from on six occasions, one once, one twice, and one three times. Six patients were burgled, and three were assaulted, one by a boyfriend, one by another patient, and one by a stranger, who also raped her. This list of crimes against patients suggests that they are particularly vulnerable in the community and need some protection against the dangers of city life.

We noted above that seven patients were lost from all eight cohorts during the first year of follow-up. Six of these were lost from the first four cohorts to be discharged. No further losses occurred from this sample in the next four years in the community. This indicates that the greatest risk of residential instability is in the first year following discharge, which is when professionals need to be at their most vigilant.

CLINICAL OUTCOME

Psychiatric Symptoms

There was very little change in scores on the PSE. In general, patients' mental state remained remarkably stable over the entire five years. However, there was a significant reduction in negative symptoms. As can be seen from Figure 5.3, most of this reduction occurred in the first year.

Social Behaviour

There was a significant downward trend in the number of severe problems over the five years. However, this was not confirmed by the GEE, indicating that only a selected group of patients improved. In presenting the data for the one year follow-up, we noted an increase in patients' anxiety as perceived by the staff. It can be seen in Figure 5.4 that this anxiety subsides over the next four years, returning to its baseline level. This indicates that the move into the community is disturbing for the patients in the first year, but that they are able to adjust to the change over the next few years.

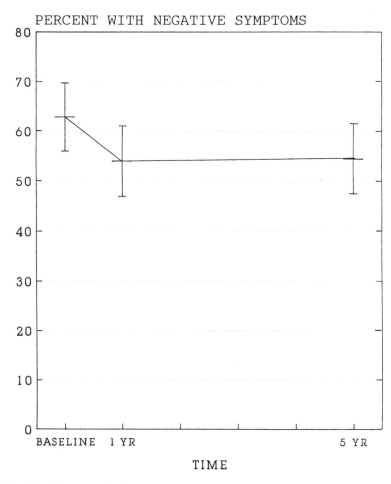

95% Confidence Intervals

Figure 5.3 Cohorts 1–4 at three time points: negative symptoms (PSE)

Everyday Living Skills

There was a significant improvement in patients' community skills in the first year, as noted above for all eight cohorts, and a further small improvement over the next four years. Unfortunately, the gain in domestic skills noted at one year declined by the five year follow-up, although was still above the baseline level. This may have been a consequence of staff becoming tired of chivvying the patients to perform their domestic chores. The proportion of patients showing problems in compliance with medication decreased significantly from 87 per cent to 78 per cent over one year, and showed a further decline to 68 per cent by five years. This change would obviously lighten the burden on staff.

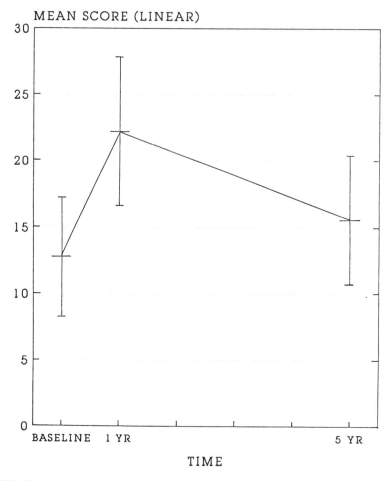

Figure 5.4   Cohorts 1–4 at three time points: anxiety score (SBS)

Restrictiveness of the Environment

The dramatically lower level of restrictiveness in the community homes compared with the hospital wards was sustained throughout the five years after discharge. This is understandable since there was no deterioration in patients' mental state or behavioural problems over time which might have prompted staff to tighten up the rules. On the contrary, some patients lost their negative symptoms and all improved their domestic and community skills.

Patients' Attitudes

Despite the lack of change in restrictions after the first year in the community, patients' liking for freedom continued to grow over the five years, as shown in Figure 5.5. This indicates that it took some years for a proportion of the patients to appreciate the more relaxed environment in their new homes, which would have been evident as soon as they moved in. By the fifth year, 40 per cent of patients spontaneously mentioned freedom as one of the features of their home they liked.

We noted above that at one year over 80 per cent of patients wanted to remain in their community homes. This proportion remained stable over the next four

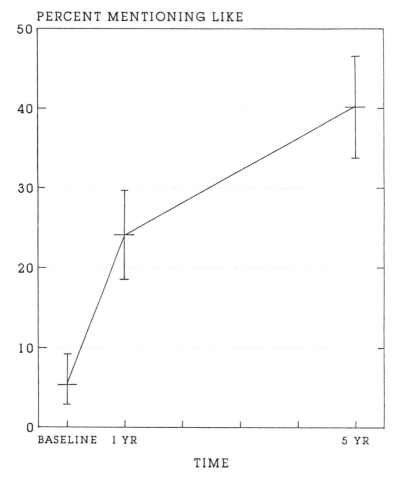

95% Confidence Intervals

Figure 5.6 Cohorts 1–4 at three time points: need for physical nursing care (PHI)

years. Of the 21 patients who wished to leave their community homes, only three wanted to return to hospital. Patients' view of medication as helpful also remained stable over the longer follow-up.

Physical Health

Over the five year period there was a linear increase in the proportion of patients with impaired mobility and a similar picture for incontinence. By the end of this period, 19 per cent of patients had problems with mobility and 21 per cent were incontinent. As a result, the need for physical nursing care increased significantly

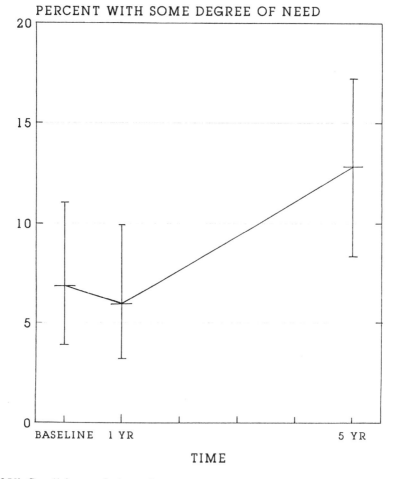

95% Confidence Intervals

Figure 5.6 Cohorts 1–4 at three time points: need for physical nursing care (PHI)

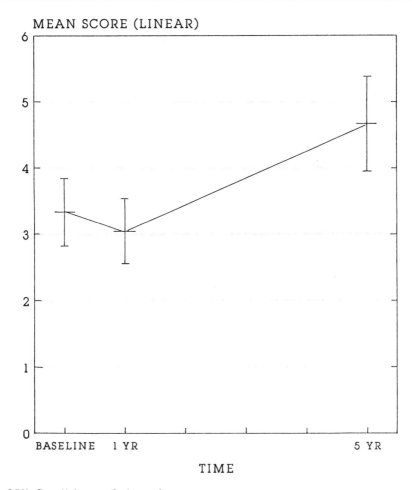

MEAN SCORE (LINEAR)

95% Confidence Intervals

Figure 5.7 Cohorts 1–4 at three time points: confidants in social network (SNS)

between the first and fifth year follow-up. The increase in these problems was a natural consequence of the ageing of the patients. When planning homes for long-stay patients, their future needs for additional nursing care and for ground floor bedrooms have to be taken into account.

Social life

For the patients in this sample there was no change in the size of the social network. The increase in the number of friends noted at one year was sustained over the whole follow-up period. The number of confidants remained steady during the first year, then increased significantly over the next four years, as can be seen from Figure 5.7. It is to be expected that it takes longer for patients to acquire confidants, the most intense form of social relationship, than to make friends.

The increases in acquaintances and service contacts that occurred in the first year were sustained throughout the next four years, but were not further augmented. The disappointing reduction in contact with relatives in the first year continued during the whole follow-up period, resulting in a decline from an average of 1.6 relatives in contact with each patient to 1.2.

CONCLUSIONS

The benefits of the move from hospital to community care for this sample of long-stay patients clearly outweigh the disadvantages. There was evidence from the staff of a transient increase in anxiety in response to the move. Otherwise patients' mental state remained stable over five years apart from a reduction in negative symptoms in the first year. There were improvements in social behaviour problems and daily living skills. Life in the community was much freer, to which patients responded with increasing appreciation. Their social life became enriched by more meaningful relationships, some of which were forged with ordinary citizens, including neighbours.

Fears expressed by the public and media concerning deaths, suicide, crime and homelessness were not supported by our findings. The only negative results were the increase in immobility and incontinence, attributable to the passage of time rather than relocation, and the reduction in contacts with relatives. The latter finding needs exploration to see whether it can be avoided in future programmes. Probably the most important change we recorded was in patients' attitudes to their care environment. They are, after all, the recipients of the services provided, so that the satisfaction of their needs should be the paramount consideration. The fact that over 80 per cent of the patients wished to remain in their community homes both one year and five years after leaving the psychiatric hospital speaks volumes.

REFERENCES

Dunn, M., O'Driscoll, C., Dayson, D., Wills, W. and Leff, J. (1990) The TAPS Project. 4: An observational study of the social life of long-stay patients. *British Journal of Psychiatry* **157**, 842–848.

Gooch, C., Leff, J. (1996) Factors affecting the success of community placement. The TAPS Project. 26 *Psychological Medicine*, **26**, 511–520.

Jones, D. (1993) The TAPS Project. 11: The selection of patients for reprovision. *British Journal of Psychiatry*, **162** (suppl. 19), 36–39.

Leff, J., Dayson, D., Gooch, C., Thornicroft, G. and Wills, W. (1996) The TAPS Project. 19: Quality of life of long-stay patients discharged from two psychiatric institutions. *Psychiatric Services*, **47**(1), 62–67.

Lehman, A., Possidente, S. and Hawker, F. (1986). The quality of life of chronic patients in a state hospital and in community residences. *Community and Hospital Psychiatry*, **37**, 901–907.

O'Driscoll, C. and Leff, J. (1993) The TAPS Project. 8: Design of the research study on the long-stay patients. *British Journal of Psychiatry*, **162** (suppl. 19), 7–17.

Sturt, E. and Wykes, T. (1986) The Social Behaviour Schedule: a validity and reliability study. *British Journal of Psychiatry*, **148**, 1–11.

Thornicroft, G., Margolius, O. and Jones, D. (1992) The TAPS Project. 6: New long-stay psychiatric patients and social deprivation. *British Journal of Psychiatry*, **161**, 621–624.

Thornicroft, G., Gooch, C., O'Driscoll, C. and Reda, S. (1993) The TAPS Project. 9: The reliability of the Patient Attitude Questionnaire. *British Journal of Psychiatry*, **162** (suppl.19) 25–29.

Trieman, N. and Kendal, R. (1995) The TAPS Project. 27: After hospital: pathways patients follow in the community. *Journal of Mental Health*, **4**, 423–429.

Wing, J.K. and Brown, G.W. (1970) *Institutionalism and Schizophrenia; A Comparative Study Of Three Mental Hospitals 1960–1968*. Cambridge University Press, London.

Wing, J.K., Cooper, J.E. and Sartorius, N. (1974) *The Measurement and Classification of Psychiatric Symptoms*. Cambridge University Press, London.

Zeger, S.L. and Liang, K.Y. (1986) Longitudinal data analysis for discrete and continuous outcomes. *Biometrics*, **42**, 121–130.

Chapter 6

COSTING CARE IN HOSPITAL AND IN THE COMMUNITY

Jennifer Beecham*, Angela Hallam*†, Martin Knapp‡†, Barry Baines§, Andrew Fenyo* and Michelle Asbury
*University of Kent; †Institute of Psychiatry; ‡London School of Economics; §Alba Associates

INTRODUCTION

The question of cost is central to the government's policy to close all long-stay hospitals in England by the year 2000 (Department of Health, 1992). Relocation to community-based care is being accomplished in increasingly cost-conscious policy and practice environments, intensified as local health and social care markets develop. There have been incremental reductions to budgets over a number of years, and incentives not to overspend have been introduced through the central government's allocative procedures alongside demands to assess and respond to unmet needs within the population. Some policy initiatives, often to be funded from existing resources, have been introduced (the care programme approach is a recent example) and other changes in practices, such as case management, have their own budgetary influences. The operational split between purchasing and providing services not only generates a demand for accurate cost information and makes it imperative that costs and service provision are far more closely linked, but also carries its own managerial and administrative costs.

Each of these factors is encouraging, or forcing, purchasers and providers to consider the resource implications as services are planned, commissioned and evaluated. It has become increasingly important that issues of cost-effectiveness are addressed at each stage of mental health care planning, purchasing and providing. Is it better to spend this "mental health pound" on service A or service B? Will a greater improvement in clients' outcomes result from providing staff support in one type of setting or in another?

A few years before the 1990 NHS and Community Care Act reforms, but at

Care in the Community: Illusion or Reality?
Edited by Julian Leff. © 1997 John Wiley & Sons Ltd.

a time when the new cost-consciousness was beginning to take hold, the (then) North East Thames Regional Health Authority (NETRHA) commissioned an economic evaluation of reprovision from the Personal Social Services Research Unit (PSSRU) as part of the regional research programme to monitor the impact of the move from Friern and Claybury hospitals to community-based care. The size and comprehensiveness of the data set compiled under this ten year evaluation and close collaboration with TAPS have made it possible to address numerous cost-related questions and to explore a range of policy issues, some of which are summarised in this chapter: the services used in the community; the costs associated with reprovision; comparison of hospital and community care costs; and associations between the costs, needs and outcomes.

UNDERLYING PRINCIPLES

The theoretical framework and principles which underlie the economic evaluation build directly on previous research programmes at the PSSRU and the broad health economics tradition. The methodology employed is summarised briefly here, and more details can be found in Knapp and Beecham (1990) and Knapp (1995a, Chapters 1 and 4).

Four basic rules guided and structured our work. First, costs should normally be measured comprehensively, and include all components of care packages, or should employ partial measures advisedly (see, for example, Burns et al, 1993). A new research instrument—the Client Service Receipt Inventory (CSRI)—was developed in 1986, designed to collect individualised information on the frequency with which named services were used and the duration of each contact (Beecham and Knapp, 1992; Beecham, 1995). Details of services used in the month prior to interview were recorded, although a twelve-month retrospective period was allowed for less commonly used services (such as out-patient attendances or dentist appointments) and changes in accommodation to be recorded.

Two main procedures were used to cost or price each service. Accommodation, hospital and day care services were expected to account for a large proportion of the total cost of care packages and their unit costs were carefully and individually calculated by adjusting published or routinely collected facility accounts. Particular attention was paid to services at Friern and Claybury Hospitals, the costs of which would be required as a comparator for community care costs. The planned level of detail to be obtained, and therefore the accuracy of the pricing, was lower where the service was likely to contribute less to total cost, such as input from field social workers, nurses, psychiatrists, or chiropodists. Here, national statistics or estimates from other studies were used. In all cases prices were calculated to approximate the long-run marginal costs of care, including the opportunity costs of all capital employed. (For a discussion of long-run marginal opportunity costs see Knapp, 1993; Beecham, 1995.)

The final step in applying this first principle was to combine a unit price for each service with data on the individual's level of service receipt (as recorded on the CSRI), thus producing an individualised total package cost spanning service and agency boundaries.

The second evaluative principle was to examine inter-client service use and cost differences carefully. Why are costs or outcomes different for one user when compared to another? Without closer examination of cost variations, evaluations can give only incomplete guidance to care providers and purchasers looking to target available treatment resources on assessed needs in order to improve efficiency or equity. The third principle was that the evaluation should aim to make comparisons between placements and care arrangements on a careful like-with-like basis, often with the help of statistical standardisation. The reprovision evaluation relied on before–after comparisons, matching (for some comparisons between hospital and community care) and statistical controls (for comparisons between the various community care settings).

The final principle was to look at cost findings in the context of the outcome results and evidence of the needs of users. Do better outcomes follow from higher levels of spending, once other factors have been held constant? What are the user characteristics and needs which push up or reduce costs? The project-specific application of these principles and the interpretation of the results produced by our analyses are discussed below.

THE STUDY POPULATION

The personal and clinical characteristics of study members, described and distinguished with reference to annual cohorts can be found in Chapter 5. The distribution of members in the costed sample between cohorts is given in Figure 6.1. Our study sample includes 711 people who were long-stay patients at Friern or Claybury Hospital and who, if over 65, did not have a diagnosis of dementia. Several people, however, have fulfilled the study criteria more than once, thus the full costed sample comprises 751 leavers. Within this sample, costs have been interpolated for people who declined to be interviewed in the community, where there were unavoidable delays in data collection and those for whom financial information on their accommodation facility was not made available (218 people in the costed sample). The analyses in this chapter examine data collected during the twelfth month after discharge for members of all eight cohorts of long-stay patients to leave Friern and for people in the first five cohorts to move from Claybury.

The development of effective community services to replace long-term hospital inpatient care takes time and involves professional and political risks. These risks are likely to be reduced if patients whose service needs are

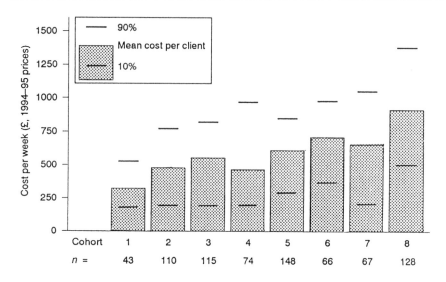

Figure 6.1   Clients and community care costs by cohort

comparatively easy to meet are the earliest to leave hospital. Arranging a reprovision programme in this way, however, carries numerous organisational and financial implications (see, for example, Knapp, 1995b) and Figure 6.1 shows the impact of this discharge policy at Friern and Claybury on the pattern of total community care costs. The more severe mental health problems of the later cohorts (see Chapter 5) generally increase the costs of providing community-based support. This relationship between greater needs and higher costs is particularly noticeable in Cohort 8. This group was the last to leave Friern Hospital and included some people hospital staff had identified as requiring the intensive levels of support only to be found in hospital or hospital-like facilities (see Chapter 13). Indeed, the mean cost of care for this group was half as much again as the mean community care cost for other people leaving hospital in the same year (Hallam, 1996).

SERVICE RECEIPT

Accommodation Arrangements

Throughout the hospital closure programme, accommodation arrangements received particularly close attention from both planners and researchers. Administrative arrangements attached to the special finance mechanism ("dowries") linked hospital resources to the clients who were targeted to move and much planning energy went into ensuring a range of accommodation facilities was available for former hospital inpatients. (This finance mechanism allowed a sum of money, equal to the average revenue cost of a hospital bed, to be transferred from the hospital budget to the district health authority responsible for the client and thence to the community services provider.) Accommodation arrangements are central to one's style and quality of life. From an evaluative perspective, our interest stemmed from the large impact these arrangements were likely to have on the total costs of community care and the way different types of accommodation facilities would link with other community-based services.

Most people moved to addresses within the eight (former) health authorities in London for which the two hospitals had traditionally provided inpatient facilities, but the variation in accommodation arrangements (and consequently their costs) was enormous. To facilitate analysis, standardised definitions were developed to distinguish accommodation types by the level of staffing and number of places. Table 6.1, for example, shows that 30 per cent of the study clients moved to the larger residential or nursing homes and 15 per cent to community inpatient facilities. By comparison, 12 per cent of people were living independently with no on-site staff support, usually in flats or houses rented from the local authority. We should not, of course, be surprised at the number of people living in highly-staffed homes, as many of the study members have numerous and complex needs.

Accommodation facilities were also distinguished by the agency responsible for managing the unit, an increasingly important perspective in the development of a mixed economy of care (Wistow et al, 1996 and see Chapter 3). One year after discharge, almost half of the clients were still resident in facilities managed by health authorities (NHS), including hospital wards and community inpatient facilities. Only 8 per cent of clients moved into privately managed units. Commonly, these private sector facilities had more than four resident places and 24-hour staff cover—conditions laid down by the pre-1993 Department of Social Security (DSS) regulations governing residents' entitlement to boarders (income support) allowances which funded many of these placements. These homes were often set up by individual hospital nurses rather than provided as part of a larger profit-generating organisation. Seven people were living independently in privately-owned flats or houses. Voluntary (not-for-profit) organisations managed a range of accommodation types, supporting 24 per cent of the sample, and also jointly managed consortium arrangements. A large part of consortium income was derived from the health sector but these arrangements also allowed access to extra income through the pre-1993 DSS boarders allowances. Under consortium arrangements, there was a trend towards smaller and less highly staffed units than health authorities otherwise provided.

Use of Other Services

Accommodation and on-site support provide a central focus for community care. However, use of services based outside the accommodation unit also plays an important role in maintaining clients' wellbeing and quality of life. Over the

Table 6.1 Clients' accommodation arrangements—one year after leaving Friern or Claybury Hospital

	Managing agency for accommodation[1]						
Type of accommodation[2]	NHS	SSD	Vol	Priv	Hsg	Consort	All
Residential home	76	40	59	36	0	11	222
Hostel	16	31	72	6	0	20	145
Sheltered housing	0	3	8	0	0	6	17
Staffed group home	0	5	17	10	0	13	45
Unstaffed group home	9	2	15	0	0	3	29
Foster care	0	16	0	0	0	0	16
Independent living	1	1	7	7	87	1	104
Hospital	60	0	0	0	0	0	60
Community inpatients	113	0	0	0	0	0	113
Total	275	98	178	59	87	54	751

Notes:
1. NHS = National Health Service. SSD = local authority social services department. Vol = voluntary organisation. Priv = private organisation or individual; Hsg = local authority housing department. Consort = consortium arrangement, jointly managed but led by voluntary organisation.
2. *Residential or nursing home*: continuous staff cover by day; waking night staff cover; $\geqslant 6$ places.
   Hostel: continuous or regular staff cover by day, sleeping-in or on-call night staff cover; $\geqslant 6$ places.
   Sheltered housing: continuous or regular staff cover by day; waking or sleeping or on-call night staff cover, individual living units in a larger complex.
   Staffed group home: continuous or regular staff cover by day; waking or sleeping or on-call night staff cover; $1 <$ places < 6.
   Unstaffed group home: ad hoc or no day staff; on-call or no night staff cover; $1 <$ places < 6.
   Foster care: regular foster family support by day; on-call night support; client(s) move into an established household.
   Independent living: ad hoc or no day staff; on-call or no night staff cover.
   Hospital: clients transferred to alternative hospital settings on an individual basis, or readmitted from community placements.
   Community in-patients: planned reprovision facility in hospital setting; or community facility in which residents remain registered as hospital in-patients.

eight years of the evaluation, use of some fifty discrete service types has been recorded and of course, there is considerable diversity of provision within each service category. Not all clients have tapped into this range of service provision, but ten services were used by 20 per cent or more of the people for whom data were collected with the CSRI. Table 6.2 lists these most common services and the percentage of each cohort using the service. Apart from accommodation, only the general practitioner and community psychiatry services (this category excludes hospital outpatient clinics) were used by more than 50 per cent of the

Table 6.2 Service utilisation by cohort

| | Percentage of cohort using service in year since discharge[1] | | | | | | | | |
| | | | | Cohort | | | | | |
Service[2]	1	2	3	4	5	6	7	8	All
Accomodation facility	100	100	100	100	100	100	100	100	100
Hospital inpatient	18	22	5	17	21	21	20	5	15
Hospital outpatient	39	15	25	40	22	46	41	13	26
Hospital day-patient	50	21	20	19	25	27	15	18	23
Community psychiatry	39	54	76	45	70	65	41	52	58
Nursing services	37	31	21	28	34	50	31	18	29
Chiropody	37	30	40	28	63	58	36	35	41
GP	76	69	96	79	80	88	85	45	74
Dentist	21	21	29	15	28	18	28	35	26
Optician	24	9	18	15	24	21	15	29	33
Field social work	55	41	21	23	16	4	26	14	24
Social services day care	26	34	20	23	9	8	15	8	17
Voluntary organisation day care	5	23	21	13	24	21	8	2	15
Sample size	38	87	82	47	87	48	38	106	533

Notes:

1. For people for whom we have completed CSRIs. The sample is therefore biased against those people readmitted to hospital (for whom, generally, inpatient utilisation is higher and other utilisation lower).

2. Not all services are listed, see text.

former long-stay patients, each contributing less that 1 per cent to the total cost of users' packages.

Displaying the data by cohort highlights some of the changes in service use over the period of the evaluation, allowing us to explore how service-providing organisations are responding to the demands of service relocation. For example, the number of people using day services (in particular those provided by social services departments) has been falling as successive cohorts have moved from hospital. The contact rates for field social workers also decrease over time and by Cohort 6, only 4 per cent of leavers had seen a social worker in the twelve months after their discharge during 1990–91.

This fall in the use of services could be indicative of two trends. First, it may reflect scarcity of resources within the provider organisations, which reduces their capacity to meet clients' needs. A number of outside influences could be exerting pressure on budgets. For example, the input from social services departments appears to rise at Cohort 7, so the key to understanding the downward trend might be found during the years following the discharge of people in Cohort 6. During this period (1991–92), local industrial disputes and the early stages of implementation of the 1990 NHS and Community Care Act and the 1989 Children Act may have reduced the availability of resources for this client group.

Second, the decline in service use might reflect changes in the service delivery mode; perhaps more of the services are provided *within* the accommodation unit. For example, a number of purpose-built, highly staffed NHS units, planned at the beginning of the reprovision programme, came on-stream for Cohort 3 leavers. The high levels of on-site nursing support may have enabled more severely disturbed residents to remain in their community residences, thus contributing to the fall in the number of people with short admissions to hospital. Similarly, many of the final group to leave Friern (Cohort 8) moved to units with high nurse-resident ratios, and again a fall from the otherwise constant readmission rates can be seen.

Three further points can be made from our exploration of the service use data. First, it is clear that changing the locus of care to the community has not eliminated the need for hospitals *per se*: 48 per cent of all clients whose service receipt details were collected at interview had used hospital-based services during the year since the index discharge. Second, contact with the criminal justice system has been minimal: just 6 per cent of the 533 people for whom we have full service receipt details had been in contact with the police (see also Chapter 5). Third, the high contact rates with general community-based health services serve as a reminder that people with mental health problems still need general health care. These services can be provided at a relatively low cost in terms of overall care packages, but may place high burdens on health professionals (Kendrick et al, 1991).

THE COSTS OF COMMUNITY CARE
Costs Descriptions

Using the methods described above, unit costs were calculated for each service and combined with the service receipt data to produce costs for individuals' full community care packages. Figure 6.1 shows the comprehensive weekly costs of care one year after leaving hospital (after adjusting for inflation). These costs include those absorbed by accommodation-related services and the provision of *all* service components that make up clients' individual community care packages. The height of each bar represents the average care cost for each cohort. There is a general trend of increasing costs as successive cohorts move from hospital, although the average costs of people in Cohorts 4 and 7 dip below those calculated for the previous cohorts. (Cohort 4 members were found not to be as dependent as Cohorts 3 or 5; Hallam et al, 1994.)

It is, of course, misleading to think that *all* people in the earlier cohorts are less expensive to care for than *all* people in later cohorts, for these are general trends rather than sure-fire truths to be applied to the planning of a reprovision programme. To illustrate this, Figure 6.1 also shows the range of costs within each cohort where the smaller horizontal lines show the 10th and 90th percentiles for each cohort. The trend of rising costs is still clear but, for example, "low cost" clients can be found through to Cohort 4 and also among some of the last people to leave hospital (Cohort 7). The mean cost for Cohort 4 is one of the lowest, yet the 90th percentile is one of the highest (and it was a member of Cohort 5 who was the most expensive of all to support). Moreover, despite the very high costs found for Cohort 8 members, even at cohort 4 there were 10 per cent of people whose community care packages cost more than £970 per week.

The variation in care package costs was also explored using the standardised accommodation categories to illustrate (among other things) the impact of placement arrangements on the total costs of care. It should come as no surprise that the most expensive care packages were received by those people from all cohorts who live in community inpatient facilities (mean care package cost, £913 per week), followed by residents of other highly staffed units (such as residential or nursing homes) whose mean care package cost was £716 per week. We would expect these facilities to accommodate people with high levels of needs and who require relatively intensive levels of support, which in turn raise costs. For clients in these facilities, accommodation costs make up approximately 90 per cent of the total costs of care. Generally, as the level of support provided on-site diminishes, so does the proportion of total cost which is absorbed by the accommodation facility. Independent accommodation, where clients rarely have on-site staff support, is the least costly of the arrangements. If outside service receipt did not make a substantial contribution to the total cost of these clients' packages, it might indicate problems with access to services (rather than lack of need). For people living independently, in unstaffed group homes and in adult fostering arrangements, more than 30 per cent of the average service package cost was for non-accommodation services.

These findings make it abundantly clear that community care is not cheap. They also show how important it is to explore the variations around the "average" cost of reproviding hospital care; Figure 6.1 shows the cost variation between cohorts but there was also up to a 90 per cent cost difference *within* cohorts. Some people presented particularly severe problems to those planning their rehabilitation and required expensive support packages. On the other hand, many clients could move to much less formal environments.

COMMUNITY–HOSPITAL COST COMPARISONS

Hospital–Community Comparisons

Claybury hospital has yet to close and its residents were not included in the study after August 1990 (Cohort 5). This part of the evaluation, therefore, used only costs data pertaining to Friern hospital and its former residents. For comparison with the costs of community-based care, the most appropriate year for the hospital costing is 1985–86, since this was the year before the number of long-stay beds in the hospital began to decline under the regional policy of reprovision. It is also the year that people in Cohort 1 moved from the hospital.

When inflated to 1994–95 prices, the 1985–86 weekly cost of care in Friern was £595 per patient. This hospital cost is not a notional figure. It is the real cost of running the hospital and hence also indicates the *real* saving once the rundown programme had been completed. It includes the direct revenue costs of running the hospital and the capital valuation of the site once it had been sold. (A number of different assumptions were made as to site values without altering our overall conclusion.) The figure also includes indirect costs, such as the social security payments to inpatients which allow them to purchase cigarettes and toiletries, and the costs of field social work and volunteer inputs which will be saved or redeployed within community settings.

However, there are two reasons why this cost may *under*-estimate the true long-run, steady state cost of running Friern Hospital. First, earlier cuts in maintenance expenditure (estimated at £6.5 million in 1984; Weller, 1985) mean that considerable sums of money would have to be spent on the fabric of the hospital for it to remain open. However, our calculations suggest that unless these costs amounted to £42 per inpatient per week (1994–95 prices), it would not alter our conclusion. Second, the hospital costs also exclude forgone payments of property rate/council tax, a cost—probably small—falling to the local authority.

Until data relating to the final cohort of Friern leavers were included, the overall costs of community-based care were broadly similar to the global costs of hospital care. However, with the inclusion of the reprovision costs for Cohort 8, the figure for the hospital cost (£595 per patient week) now compares with £665 per week in the community (standard deviation £321), averaged over all former Friern long-stay patients. If we treat the hospital cost as fixed, the difference between the two is statistically significant ($p < 0.01$).

Given the TAPS outcome results summarised in earlier chapters and the small difference between the hospital and reprovision costs, a commonly posited hypothesis about community care can be rejected. The replacement of hospital with community services does not require substantial additional resources if the quality of life of former long-stay in-patients is to be at least maintained. On the other hand, provision of community-based care does not appear to *save* money. The Secretary of State for Social Services (1985) said "A good quality community-orientated service may well be more expensive than a poor quality institutional one. . . . The aim is not to save money but to use it responsibly" (p. 1–2). Planners of reprovision services should, in particular, be prepared to reserve resources for a small group of hospital residents who can be identified as having special needs (see Chapter 13). They are often among the last people to leave hospital and require more intensive and more costly support than earlier leavers.

EXPLAINING COST VARIATIONS

Predicting the Costs of Community Care

Service planners and purchasers need to know in advance how to structure and finance community support for people with long-term mental health problems. Economic analysis can assist by examining the statistical associations between subsequent community care costs and the characteristics of sample members *before* they leave hospital. Earlier examinations of these links provided the basis for some tentative national extrapolations, first by the House of Commons Health Committee in 1991 and then by ourselves (Knapp et al, 1992).

For this work, multivariate statistical analyses were used to tease out the simultaneous influences on costs of demographic characteristics, pre-hospital experiences and the TAPS "baseline" assessments. (Chapter 5 gives details of the schedules used. Information on the research background and theoretical bases for these analyses can be found in Knapp, 1995a.) Ordinary least squares estimation was employed using average cost per week of community support for each individual as the dependent variable, and clinical and other characteristics were introduced into the regression equations singly and in multiplicative combinations (including higher powers) to capture possible non-linear effects.

The "best" prediction equation to date, for the full sample, is given in Table 6.3, "explaining" 21 per cent of the observed variation in community cost. This is a lower percentage of variance explained than the 39 and 35 per cent achieved with smaller samples of early leavers (Knapp et al., 1990, 1995) but the increase in sample size has meant greater heterogeneity among the sample members and

Table 6.3 Community reprovision: cost predictions from hospital baseline

Predictor	Coeff't	Sig
Age (in years)	+1.5	0.128
Single (1 = single; 0 = other)	+32.1	0.107
Reason for original admission: transfer from other psychiatric facility	+67.6	0.003
inability to cope	−58.7	0.016
Legal status on admission (1 = formal; 0 = informal)	−36.2	0.026
Number of previous admissions	+4.2	0.004
Percentage of life spent in hospital	+5.5	0.001
Total previous time in psychiatric hospital	−0.6	0.005
Negative symptoms score (PSE)	+29.3	0.000
Attention-seeking behaviour (SBS)	−40.1	0.072
Laughing and talking to self (SBS)	+65.2	0.001
Acting out bizarre ideas (SBS)	+51.3	0.048
Personal appearance and hygiene (SBS)	+30.9	0.078
Needs for daily nursing care (PHI)	+50.5	0.005
Other medication for physical illness (PHI) (1 = yes; 0 = no)	+56.3	0.001
High disabilities score (PHI) (1 = high; 0 = low)	−63.0	0.072
Constant term	+261.2	0.000

Notes: The sample size fell from 751 people to 570 because of missing data.
$R^2 = 0.212$; adjusted $R = 0.189$; F statistic = 9.3 ($p < 0.0001$).

there have been quite marked changes in local policy and practice over the eight-year period. There would also have been a "time lag effect", for baseline assessments completed in 1983–86 will not always accurately measure the characteristics of individuals who moved from hospital in (say) 1989. Disease progression and ageing could have increased patients' dependency, whilst rehabilitation and other inpatient services could have reduced it.

Table 6.3 shows that demographic information exerts only a limited influence on costs: neither age nor gender prove to be significant but costs are higher for people who never married. Three of the reasons for original admission to hospital (transfer from another psychiatric facility, inability to cope and admission to hospital under the Mental Health Act) are associated with the much later community reprovision costs, but their effects are not easy to interpret and the data may have referred to circumstances prevailing many years earlier. Easier to understand perhaps, is the effect of people's history of hospital care. A greater proportion of life spent in hospital and a greater number of previous admissions to hospital increased the costs of support packages in the community, suggesting that prolonged institutionalisation increases the need for community support services. The contrary effect found for people who spent longer periods in *previous* psychiatric hospitals is small.

The influences of the clinical factors on cost are particularly interesting. People with more negative symptoms (a measure constructed from the Present State Examination scores) have higher than average costs. Higher scores on the Social Behaviour Schedule reflect higher staff-reported ratings of abnormal behaviours and, with one exception, imply higher costs. The negative effect of attention-seeking behaviour could be indicative of a therapeutic response, or may be related to social network size and gregarious behaviour. Two indicators of physical health needs (number of areas in which daily nursing care is required and taking medication for physical illness) are both associated with higher costs. Diagnosis had no obvious effect on cost once the above factors had been taken into account, reflecting other research findings on the predictive power of diagnostic-related groups (cf. English et al, 1986; McCrone and Strathdee, 1994).

Costs and Outcomes

A central part of any economic evaluation should be to look at costs alongside outcomes. Reporting on all eight cohorts of leavers, but excluding people identified as "difficult to place", the outcomes evaluation found that community reprovision appeared to have been beneficial to the former long-stay patients. Clients' mental health generally remained stable and a moderate decrease in negative symptoms was detected. Clients' domestic skills improved, and they appreciated the increased freedom in their community homes. On average, each had gained one extra friend during the year, and there was also an increase in the number of clients who made social contact with ordinary members of the public, particularly local shopkeepers (Leff et al, 1996 and see Chapter 5).

We might reasonably conclude, therefore, that the levels of expenditure on community reprovision revealed by our research have produced encouraging outcomes for clients, including an overall reduction in the frequency of aggressive behaviour for the group of people identified as difficult to place within the usual range of community facilities. But not every client fared equally well, nor were costs identical. It is, therefore, important to examine whether there were any associations between costs and outcomes *at the individual level*.

Individual outcomes (changes in welfare) were calculated as the differences between the hospital and community scores and subscores on each of the TAPS assessment instruments. Significant correlations ($p < 0.01$) were found between costs and eight measures from the Present State Examination, and between costs and the size of social networks. The results imply that higher costs are associated with improvements in symptoms but reductions in the overall size of social networks. Scores from the Social Behaviour Schedule were also significantly linked to costs ($p < 0.05$). These associations are encouraging for reprovision practice, but warrant further analysis to establish more clearly the underlying causal relationships.

CONCLUSION

Summarised considerably, the main conclusions from the PSSRU's economic evaluation of psychiatric reprovision are set out in Box 1. The reprovision of

Box 1 Summary results from the economic evaluation of reprovision

- Community care packages comprise many services, provided by a range of public, voluntary and private agencies. All the clinical, social and other support services provided by long-stay hospitals should be reprovided in the community to meet former residents' continuing needs.

- The variety of accomodation types and services used by former hospital residents reflects their different needs and demands.

- Accommodation, often provided by health authorities, dominates the costs of community reprovision. However, appropriate distribution of funds between providing agencies and organisations is essential to ensuring sufficient community-based services exist and are accessible.

- Average costs in the community are higher for later cohorts than for earlier leavers as closure programmes typically resettle easier (less dependent) people first. There is, however, considerable cost variation within each annual cohort.

- Community care costs are marginally but significantly greater than hospital costs. This increase is particularly apparent for a group of people who left Friern hospital in its final year and who required intensive packages of support.

- Adequate funding is obviously crucial to enable reprovision not just in the long term but also *before* patients move out of hospital to ensure necessary support services are in place.

- There are marked variations in community care costs between individual clients. A proportion of these cost variations can be attributed to differences in the clients' characteristics before they left hospital.

- Higher expenditure on community services appears to promote improvements in clients' mental health but may also be associated with a reduction in the number of people with whom they have regular contact.

long-stay services from Friern and Claybury hospitals was a well-planned and well-financed programme, and the research evidence suggests it has been a successful approach.

The descriptions of the service receipt and costs data can inform planners' and purchasers' decisions regarding the range and quantity of community-based services required by former inpatients. Clearly, providing new places to live is important, but so is access to the many non-accommodation services found to be used by study members. The costs used in this study are calculated to include the resource implications of setting up new facilities for future leavers and for those diverted from hospital care. Thus, the comprehensive costs of support packages reflect the medium- and longer-term financial implications during a hospital closure programme.

The costs analyses suggest that a reprovision programme which promotes an acceptable quality of care (no change or improvement in client outcomes) need not cost substantially more than hospital-based care but will require input from many different agencies. The resources freed from hospital closure should, therefore, be distributed between all organisations and providers in respect of the services they provide. However, the close link maintained in the reprovision programme between patients and the mechanism to finance their community care ("ring-fenced" dowries) has facilitated better care coordination and ensured that few people "slip through the net".

Finally, the level of resources required to support individuals in the community varies considerably but is linked in part to patients' characteristics and needs whilst they are still in hospital. Such information can aid the planning of financial allocations *between* long-stay hospital residents so that a budget based on average hospital costs can be disbursed in recognition of people's characteristics and needs. This can help ensure that there are sufficient resources to provide for the later (and often the most challenging) patients while earlier leavers continue to receive support packages that respond to their needs.

REFERENCES

Beecham, J. (1995) Collecting and estimating costs, in M.R.J. Knapp (ed.) *The Economic Evaluation of Mental Health Care*, Arena, Aldershot.

Beecham, J. and Knapp, M.R.J. (1992) Costing psychiatric interventions. In G.J. Thornicroft, C.R. Brewin and J.K. Wing (eds), *Measuring Mental Health Needs*, Gaskell, London.

Burns, T., Raftery, J., Beadsmoore, A., McGuigan, S. and Dickson, M. (1993) A controlled trial of home-based acute psychiatric services. II: Treatment patterns and costs, *British Journal of Psychiatry*, **163**, 55–61.

Department of Health (1992) *The Health of the Nation*, Cm 1523, HMSO, London.

English, J., Sharfstein, S., Scheri, D., Astrachan, B. and Muszyaski, L. (1986) DRGs and general hospital psychiatry: the APA study, *American Journal of Psychiatry*, **143**, 131–139.

Hallam, A. (1996) Costs and outcomes for people with special psychiatric needs, *Mental Health Research Review*, Centre for the Economics of Mental Health at the Institute of Psychiatry in London, and Personal Social Services Research Unit, University of Kent at Canterbury.

Hallam, A., Beecham, J.K., Knapp, M.R.J. and Fenyo, A.J. (1994) The costs of accommodation and care: community provision for former long-stay psychiatric hospital patients, *European Archives of Psychiatry and Clinical Neuroscience*, **243**(6), 304–310.

Kendrick, T., Sibbald, B., Burns, T. and Freeling, P. (1991) The role of general practitioners in the care of long-term mentally ill patients, *British Medical Journal*, March 2, 508–510.

Knapp, M.R.J. (1993) Background theory. In A. Netten and J. Beecham (eds), *Costing Community Care: Theory and Practice*, Ashgate, Aldershot.

Knapp, M.R.J. (1995a) (editor) *The Economic Evaluation of Mental Health Care*, Arena, Aldershot.

Knapp, M.R.J. (1995b) Community mental health services: towards an understanding of cost-effectiveness. In P. Tyrer and F. Creed (eds), *Community Psychiatry in Action*, Cambridge University Press, Cambridge.

Knapp, M.R.J. and Beecham, J.K. (1990) Costing mental health services, *Psychological Medicine*, **20**, 893–908.

Knapp, M.R.J., Beecham, J., Anderson, J., Dayson, D., Leff, J., Margolius, O., O'Driscoll, C. and Wills, W. (1990) Predicting the community costs of closing psychiatric hospitals, *British Journal of Psychiatry*, **157**, 661–670.

Knapp, M.R.J., Beecham, J.K., Gordon, K. (1992) Predicting the community costs of closing psychiatric hospitals: national extrapolations, *Journal of Mental Health*, **1**, 315–326.

Knapp, M.R.J., Beecham, J., Fenyo, A., Hallam, A. (1995) Community mental health care for former hospital in-patients; predicting costs from needs and diagnoses, *British Journal of Psychiatry*, **166** (suppl. 27), 10–18.

Leff, J., Trieman, N., Gooch, C. (1996) The TAPS Project. 33: A prospective follow-up study of long-stay patients discharged from two psychiatric hospitals. *American Journal of Psychiatry*, **153**, 1318–1323.

McCrone, P. and Strathdee, G. (1994) Needs not diagnosis: towards a more rational approach to community mental health resourcing in Britain, *International Journal of Social Psychiatry*, **40**, 79–86.

Secretary of State for Social Services (1985) *Community Care: Government Response to the Second Report from the Social Services Committee*, Cmnd 9674, HMSO, London.

Weller, M.P.I. (1985) A mental hospital's share, *Lancet*, **1**, 984–985.

Wistow, G., Knapp, M.R.J., Hardy, B., Forder, J., Manning, R., Kendall, J. (1996) *Social Care Markets: Progress and Prospects*, Open University Press, Buckingham.

Chapter 7

THE PSYCHOGERIATRIC POPULATION: IN TRANSITION FROM HOSPITAL TO COMMUNITY-BASED SERVICES

Noam Trieman* and Walter Wills[†]
*Team for the Assessment of Psychiatric Services (TAPS); [†]Dementia Relief Trust

Psychiatric hospitals in the UK have traditionally served as asylums for elderly mentally ill people. A large proportion of this population were old "functionally ill" patients, who had spent many years in hospital. The features of their original illness were often superseded by pervasive social withdrawal and neglect of self-care, which made them highly dependent. Many of those patients had developed over the years severe cognitive disability. Another major group of elderly inpatients comprised those who suffered from various forms of senile dementia. The so called "organic" patients were usually admitted to hospital in an advanced stage of their illness to be cared for until their death. The massive representation of psychogeriatric patients, still evident to this day in psychiatric hospitals, reflects the cardinal role the asylum has played since its inception as a non-selective provider of shelter and total nursing care for the elderly.

The ongoing process of running down psychiatric hospitals has generated alternative types of care environment for the elderly patients, ranging from nursing homes to community-based EMI units. While the mental hospital used to be an all-encompassing container for mixed populations, care facilities in the community, by virtue of size and variability, could potentially provide for distinctive needs, previously overlooked. Moreover the transition to the community has created a unique opportunity to improve the quality of life for these people.

TAPS mounted a special research project to evaluate the effects on the psychogeriatric population of closing hospitals, with the aim of seeing whether, in practice, care in the community is beneficial for elderly people. Four different studies, conducted between 1988 and 1993, took place in twelve different sites:

Care in the Community: Illusion or Reality?
Edited by Julian Leff. © 1997 John Wiley & Sons Ltd.

two psychiatric hospitals, Claybury and Friern, and ten community-based facilities which replaced the hospital psychogeriatric wards.

PROFILE OF THE PSYCHOGERIATRIC POPULATION IN THE OLD MENTAL HOSPITAL

Surveys of psychogeriatric populations in the two hospitals were conducted by TAPS in the years 1988–89. At Friern, a pilot study (Anderson, 1990) examined 89 long-stay patients located within four EMI wards. The majority (4/5) of the patients suffered from organic disorders, of which 70 per cent were Alzheimer-type dementia. One fifth of the patients within the EMI wards were originally diagnosed as having a functional illness (mostly schizophrenia). Functional diagnosis was more common among patients who were relatively younger and stayed longer periods in hospitals. Although the total group of patients was markedly impaired in cognitive terms, the following variables were independently associated with better performance: being male, younger age, and previous functional diagnosis. Male subjects with original functional disorders had also exhibited less behaviour disability. It was evident that the organic patients were to a large extent more disabled both behaviourally and cognitively than the functional patients.

These findings appeared to suggest that an "instant" profile of disability among psychogeriatric populations could be drawn simply by looking at gender and the initial diagnosis. However, the validity of this conclusion was confined to EMI wards and was not applicable to the rest of the hospital psychogeriatric population. This was due to the entirely different distribution of elderly patients elsewhere, in which the majority of the "functional" patients were situated in continuous care wards and none of the "organic" patients were to be found there. It is concluded that planning alternative services in the community should not be based on the profile of disabilities prevailing in EMI wards. Instead, accurate planning should take account of the needs profile of the *whole* hospital psychogeriatric population.

In view of this, a subsequent study of a whole hospital population was conducted at Claybury hospital in 1989 (Anderson and Trieman, 1995). Of 214 long-stay patients aged 70 and above, two thirds were originally diagnosed as suffering from a "functional" illness. The other third had "organic" disorders. Nearly all the patients were assessed for cognitive functioning by using the Mini-Mental State Examination [MMSE] (Folstein et al, 1975). Levels of behavioural disability were assessed by using the Modified Crichton Royal Behavioural Rating Scale [MCRBRS] (Wilkin and Jolley, 1979).

As expected, the "organic" patients were significantly more disabled both in regard to cognitive and behavioural functioning than the rest of the sample, the majority of whom suffered from schizophrenia. The "organic" patients (mostly suffering from Alzheimer-type dementia) had poor social skills and were totally dependent on staff in almost every aspect of basic self-care. The "functional" patients, although considerably disabled, were relatively less severely affected.

Nearly all of the organic patients had a very severe form of dementia (often a zero MMSE score). In comparison, while the "functional" patients almost invariably exhibited some cognitive deficit, it was less profound. A striking finding was that half of the "functional" patients exhibited severe cognitive impairment. In fact they appeared to have a mixed type of morbidity (hence the term "mixed group"), in which dementia had apparently superseded the features of the original illness.

The association of cognitive deficit with schizophrenic illness is well documented (Kraepelin, 1919; Bleuler, 1950; Goldberg et al, 1988; Greb and Cancro, 1989). Neuroanatomical studies (Johnstone et al, 1976; Andreasen et al, 1990; Pearlson et al, 1989) have confirmed structural changes in the brains of schizophrenic patients. Neuropsychological studies (Cutting, 1979; Goldstein and Zubin, 1990; Gold and Harvey, 1993) provide evidence of memory and attention disorders in schizophrenia. Despite this evidence there is much variability among individuals in the extent of the cognitive deficit and the life time course of cognitive decline (Heaton and Drexler, 1987; Ciompi, 1987; Hyde et al, 1994). It is still undetermined whether the dementia is strictly an integral feature of the disease, or is superimposed on it (Prohovnik et al, 1993). Alternatively it may be an apparent dementia due in part to "institutionalisation" (Wing and Brown, 1970).

Our findings suggest that the degree of cognitive disability in the so called "functional" inpatients is even higher than previously recognized. Notably there is a gradient of cognitive and behavioural disability along a functional-mixed-organic continuum. In general, although unequivocal severe cognitive disability is very common among the hospital psychogeriatric population, it exerted little influence on the type and location of care. In effect, elderly inpatients were considerably more likely to be nursed on an EMI ward if they exhibited severe behavioural problems. These findings confirm those of the pilot study conducted at Friern hospital (Anderson, 1990). As we shall see later, cognitive level, in common with original diagnosis, exerted a minimal impact on the selection of patients for reprovision in the community. This fact raises two intriguing questions: Is it right to mix "organic" with "functional" patients in one environment (considering the different potential for behavioural change)? Should we not take account of cognitive functioning in the process of reprovision (considering the potential for cognitive change)? These issues will be addressed later.

THE QUALITY OF LIFE FOR ELDERLY MENTALLY ILL PATIENTS: A COMPARISON BETWEEN HOSPITAL WARDS AND COMMUNITY SETTINGS

After deciding to close Friern and Claybury hospitals, NETRHA enunciated a policy that "residential provision for the elderly will be in small, homely units of not more than 24 people". The rationale behind this was evidently to avoid as much as possible some of the negative features of institutional care by limiting the size of the alternative facilities. Other than that, no recommendations were made about how to create a homely atmosphere.

One of the TAPS psychogeriatric studies (Wills and Leff, 1996) examined the characteristics of community facilities for the elderly in comparison with the hospital EMI wards, aiming to determine whether indeed the former facilities provide a superior quality of life to the hospital.

An immediate obstacle in assessing the quality of life of patients with dementia is the impossibility of obtaining their subjective view. The research was therefore designed to employ a multi-perspective approach which could illuminate different domains relating to quality of life. The following comparisons were made between hospital and community facilities:

1. Characteristics of the care facilities: staff, residents and physical environment.
2. Systematic observations of social interactions, daily routine and practices within the different settings.
3. The staff's views regarding the social climate, their role and job satisfaction.
4. The relatives' views regarding the quality of care (a proxy for the unobtainable patients' attitudes).

The Characteristics of the Care Facilities

The care facilities selected for this study included six psychogeriatric (EMI) wards at Friern hospital and four community facilities, representing a spectrum from hospital-like to domestic-type residences. These comprise two NHS trust community facilities, one of which was converted from a large house to a nursing home for 22 people with dementia. The second facility is divided into two subunits, each for 18 residents, on the site of a former maternity hospital. Two other facilities, run by social services, comprise a modern single storey residence, purpose-built for a group of 24 residents (divided into two subunits). The other facility is a three storey residential conversion for seven residents.

Physical layout

The community facilities provide single rooms for most residents, in striking contrast to conditions in the EMI hospital wards, where a group of between four and ten patients shared a rather congested dormitory. The physical and architectural features of the care environments were formally evaluated by the Multiphasic Environmental Assessment Procedure (MEAP) (Moos and Lemke, 1984). The following aspects were examined: Privacy and comfort of the living space; homely atmosphere; furniture and decoration. The community settings were typically superior to hospital in respect to each of those aspects.

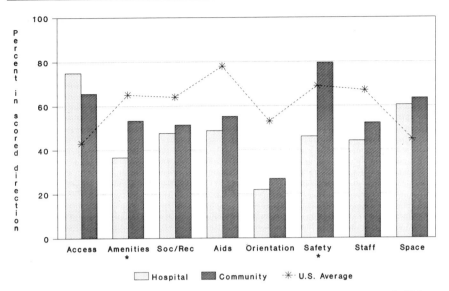

Figure 7.1 Physical and architectural features of psychogeriatric care facilities—community versus hospital. *Amenities: difference in means: −16.8; 95% confidence intervals −26.9 to −6.6; $p < 0.01$. *Safety: difference in means: −33.5; 95% confidence intervals −47.7 to −19.3; $p < 0.01$.

Only the fourth setting, also the largest of the four, was no different in its layout from the EMI hospital wards.

Similar advantages of the community settings were evident in regard to physical and safety amenities (like prosthetic aids, hand rails, barriers, visual cues to help orientation). Access to the facilities was notably better in the hospital, especially when compared to the social services community facilities which had no provision for wheelchairs. Overall the standard of the amenities in the community was slightly below the formal American norms for such facilities (see Figure 7.1).

The staff

The NHS community-based facilities had a 1 : 4 staff–patient ratio whereas the social services facilities had a 1 : 2 ratio in the smaller residential home and a 1 : 5 ratio in the purpose-built unit. Notably, while the average staff–patient ratio in the community was not different from hospital, it was observed that the actual presence of staff in the community was more compatible with the numbers reported.

About half of the staff in the hospital and in the NHS trust homes had a nursing qualification, while only 17 per cent of the staff in social services facilities were nurses by profession. The majority (45 per cent) of staff members in these latter facilities were social services qualified care officers.

In general, community staff had fewer years experience of working with psychogeriatric patients than hospital staff. Interestingly, the largest proportion of unqualified staff was found in the hospital rather than in the community.

The residents

Nearly 70 per cent of the patients within the six EMI hospital wards were women, while the median age for the whole group was 80. Of these, 78 per cent were diagnosed with some form of senile dementia, while the remaining 22 per cent had a prior diagnosis of a functional illness (often referred to as "graduates", since these patients have grown old within the system of care and have eventually achieved geriatric status).

The residents within the community facilities had similar demographic features to the hospital sample. They also had the same profile of cognitive disability, mostly of a severe degree. As in assignment to hospital wards, neither the level of cognitive functioning nor the original diagnosis constituted the core criteria for placement in the community (see page 111).

In general, members of the hospital group were physically more handicapped and presented more behavioural problems than their counterparts in the community.

Policy and daily practices

The care policies in the community were less structured than those in hospital. Procedures and routine practices such as ward rounds, care programmes and keeping daily records were vaguely defined, and apparently had not been regarded as essential. Daily activities were much less organized in the community, and likewise, occupational therapy and physiotherapy were practised on a smaller scale than in hospital. Facilities run by social services provided no nursing or medical services. Instead, the majority of physical health care was provided by the district nurse and the general practitioner, which placed an extra burden on the local primary care services.

This situation was primarily due to a policy undertaken by the social services, which selected residents with a higher level of functioning and those who needed less on-site medical care. The physical design of the social services facilities, which made no provision for wheelchair access, reinforced the pre-existing selection criteria and prohibited more disabled patients from entering those houses.

The inherent problem of such community facilities is that once the residents' health starts to decline with age, they need more physical and medical support. If these are not available on site, then the residents will be forced to move elsewhere (for the second time). This leads us to the conclusion that in planning a facility for elderly people, one must never underestimate the current as well as future physical needs, and must set the standards for the environment accordingly.

Observational Study of the Social Milieu

This method was pioneered by Godlove et al (1981). The observers record sequentially the precise times spent by particular individuals engaged in specified events, and whether or not these activities occur while interacting with others. The aggregated data provide a measure of the intensity and quality of activities and human contacts with others.

A group of 92 hospital patients based on six EMI wards and a comparable group of 82 community residents were each observed as described (Wills and Leff, 1996). For the majority of time, both in hospital and the community settings, residents were observed sitting without any contact whatsoever (on average 73 per cent of time in hospital and 64 per cent in the community). This is perhaps not surprising, considering the severity of social withdrawal of this type of patient. Residents in the community had almost double the amount of contact with people compared with the hospital patients (mean percentage of time: 12 per cent in hospital and 20 per cent in the community). The proportion of time spent in social contact (rather than contacts related to physical nursing care) was also considerably greater in the community settings, and the residents seemed to be more encouraged by the staff to talk. The same applies to the amount of time spent with relatives in the community. These observations, as we shall see, were compatible with the views expressed by the relatives themselves.

Differences between hospital and community settings were evident in many aspects of the daily routine. Residents in the community facilities enjoyed more freedom of choice and were cared for in a more flexible way. Thus, residents were not expected to eat their meals at a certain time, and if they wished to do so, they could eat within the privacy of their own rooms. Other daily routines such as watching television, going out for a stroll, receiving visits from relatives, or getting off to sleep, were not regulated. As one might anticipate, these opportunities remained theoretical for some of the residents due to their very severe disabilities.

The Resettlement from the Relatives' Point of View

How do relatives feel about the new form of care provided in the community? In a study by Wills and Leff (1996), two groups of family members were asked whether they were satisfied with the service provided for their relatives. One group was asked about relatives who were still in hospital, while the other group was asked about relatives who resided in four community facilities.

Overall, there seemed to be little difference in relatives' satisfaction with hospital care in comparison with care provided in the community. Both groups of relatives expressed appreciation of the skills, devotion and tolerance of the staff. Nevertheless, some differences of opinion did exist. Relatives of hospital patients tended to complain that the numbers of nursing staff were not sufficient. They reported being quite distressed whenever they came to visit their relatives in hospital. Forty per cent of them stated that they would not recommend hospital care for their friends or family members.

Relatives of the community residents said they had felt quite relaxed while visiting their relatives. They also felt encouraged by the staff to take their relatives for a walk or bring them home over the weekend. The relatives recognized the opportunity for privacy within the community facilities. Some mentioned the presence of personal items in the rooms, such as family pictures, an armchair or a decorative object brought from home.

Relatives had the impression that carers in community homes were more inclined to talk to the residents as part of their routine. All these points, as raised by the relatives, were to a large extent compatible with the direct observations of the living environment as described earlier.

The Transition to the Community—from the Point of View of Staff

A group of nurses in hospital and a group of carers in community-based facilities were asked for their attitudes regarding care practices and the impact of the changing conditions on their lives. Carers in both groups were dissatisfied with their current pay and chances for promotion. They often expressed some concerns about what the future might hold for them. Interestingly, the level of frustration among the community carers was somewhat higher than their colleagues in hospital. The community carers tended to complain about vaguely defined care policies, little use being made of their personal skills and a lack of supervision and authoritative guidance. They also reported some friction between care staff coming from different backgrounds.

While hospital staff tended to be more practice-oriented and prioritized reliable provision for the patients' basic needs, community staff were somewhat more aware of higher level needs such as promoting self sufficiency and facilitating social interactions. In spite of attitudes which were often characterized by role confusion and concerns about the future, the community staff did not seem to differ much from the hospital staff in the way they perceived certain aspects of care such as comfort, quality of support and consideration for the client's views. The majority of the hospital carers recognized the potential advantages of a homely environment for the patients. Only a few carers expressed some reservations with regard to the compulsory transfer of elderly patients, which they believed to be potentially harmful for such frail people.

Some carers in the community facilities highlighted particular conflicts they face in their daily practice. They were expected, for example, to give consideration to the families' views of whether they want their relatives to be resuscitated. The ethical dilemma was particularly difficult for carers with a medical background. Similarly, nurses in community settings run by social services were not allowed to inject any medication, a practice which was considered incompatible with a normal homely environment.

Such feelings among people currently working in NHS community facilities are understandable, considering that many of them have practised for years in the well-structured environment of a hospital. Their comments reveal how painful and difficult it was for them to give up aspects of their professional identity, and be detached from the familiar hierarchy and codes of practice of an institution.

COGNITIVE AND BEHAVIOURAL OUTCOMES FOLLOWING REPROVISION

Given the accumulating evidence of the organic origin of schizophrenia, doubts are cast on the extent to which the environment affects the clinical picture in terms of behavioural and cognitive disabilities. While Wing and Brown (1970) demonstrated the deleterious influence of the institutional environment on the functioning of schizophrenic subjects, Johnstone et al (1981) concluded that the deficits of chronic schizophrenia are an integral feature of the disease process and that any effects of institutionalism are negligible.

From a theoretical point of view, any way of isolating the "institutional effect" could illuminate this debate. Practically, the more impact the environment proves to have on the deficits of schizophrenia, the greater is the potential for change, and eventually that potential is bound to determine the limits of our expectations while planning alternative provisions for the chronically mentally ill.

The closure of psychiatric hospitals, with the resulting transfer of long-stay psychogeriatric patients to community-based facilities, provided a rare opportunity to assess the impact of institutional care on elderly inpatients, many of whom have lived for decades in a psychiatric hospital.

A precondition to any comparative study is that the alternative community provisions should differ substantially from the EMI hospital wards. As we have seen from the observational study (Wills and Leff, 1996), the community facilities for elderly patients indeed provided a better quality of life and a more socially active environment.

A comparative study (Trieman et al, 1995), examined the outcome for two groups of functionally ill, elderly, long-stay patients. One group consisted of 36 residual patients, who at a census date in 1992, three years after the baseline EMI survey in 1989 (Anderson and Trieman, 1995), were still at Claybury hospital. The other group consisted of 35 subjects who were discharged, mostly during the year 1990, to six, newly developed EMI care facilities in the community. All 71 patients were assessed for behavioural and cognitive functioning at baseline (1989) and three years later (in 1992).

The two groups were remarkably similar in their demographic composition, and in particular with respect to their baseline cognitive functioning and the level of their behavioural disability. The similarity in basic features was by and large the consequence of a unique mechanism of reprovision in which groups of elderly patients moved *en bloc* from a hospital ward to a community home. The selection process was thus based to a great extent on administrative rather than functional criteria. The only factor which seemed to play a role was physical health, so that the most feeble patients were left in hospital until last. That policy probably explains the higher proportion of patients who died in hospital over the three year follow-up period compared to those discharged to community facilities.

When outcomes of the community group were compared to the hospital group it was found that patients who were placed in the community showed stability in their behavioural functioning, in contrast to a marked deterioration among patients who remained in hospital. The latter subjects became increasingly more withdrawn and dependent over time.

It is concluded that behavioural deterioration, at least in part, is the consequence of the impoverished environment of a psychiatric hospital in the course of closing down. The accelerated decline within the hospital, which stands in contrast to the favourable behavioural outcome in the community, indicates a need to move elderly "functional" patients out of hospital as early as possible in the course of a reprovision programme.

Another intriguing outcome result, based on direct cognitive measurements, suggests that patients who remained in hospital had become markedly more cognitively disabled, while the community patients showed a more moderate decline in cognitive performance.

This finding is compatible with the observation made by Johnstone et al (1981) that ". . . impaired cognitive function has developed in the inpatients to a greater extent than in the outpatients."

One way to interpret this finding is that a behavioural-related component, which might be referred to as pseudodementia, is superimposed on the natural cognitive decline resulting from the ageing process. Arguably, this component (attributed to long-term hospitalization) is potentially reversible following a change in environment.

We conclude that new forms of milieu, which have proved to be more stimulating and interactive than hospital wards, seem to sustain a potential of slowing down the declining course of cognitive functioning among elderly schizophrenic patients.

SUMMARY

Two main operative recommendations arise from our study:

1. When planning new facilities, attempts must be made to avoid a mixture of elderly functionally ill patients (the so called "graduates") with patients suffering from senile dementia.

The rationale is that mixed composition, such as within EMI wards, may reduce the "graduates" to the lowest common level of functioning. Conversely, functionally ill patients retain some potential to communicate, and if encouraged, as indeed proved to have happened, by a milieu which facilitates social interactions, their cognitive and behavioural deterioration may be reduced to a minimum.

2. Psychogeriatric facilities in the community should be designed to provide for maximal levels of physical needs. A realistic balance between an aim to achieve normal life conditions and the need to provide daily nursing should be sought. In this respect, a policy of radical demedicalization is not advisable.

Overall, and with relatively few exceptions, we find plenty of evidence that the reprovision for elderly psychiatric patients from Friern and Claybury hospitals was highly successful. Notably this programme fulfilled two crucial conditions: continuity of care was preserved and the quality of life in the alternative facilities exceeded in some aspects that in the hospital. Perhaps more than any other sector of the former long stay population, ageing schizophrenic patients and those suffering from dementia proved capable of resettling successfully within the community.

REFERENCES

Anderson, J. (1990) The TAPS Project 1: Previous diagnosis and current disability of long-stay psychogeriatric patients: A pilot study, *British Journal of Psychiatry*, **156**, 661–666.

Anderson, J. and Trieman, N. (1995) The TAPS Project 21: Functional and organic comorbidity and the effect of cognitive and behavioural disability on the placement of elderly psychiatric inpatients—a whole hospital survey. *International Journal of Geriatric Psychiatry*, **10**, 959–966.

Andreasen, N., Ernhardt, J., Swayze, V., Alliger, R.J., Yuh, W.T., Cohen, G. and Ziebell, S. (1990) Magnetic resonance imaging of the brain in schizophrenia—the pathophysiologic significance of structural abnormalities, *Archives of General Psychiatry*, **47**, 35–44.

Bleuler, E. (1950) Dementia Praecox or the Group of Schizophrenias. International Universities Press, New York.

Ciompi, L. (1987) Ageing and the schizophrenic psychosis, *Acta Psychiatrica Scandinavica* (Suppl), **319**, 93–97.

Cutting, J. (1979) Memory in functional psychosis, *The Journal of Neurology, Neurosurgery and Psychiatry*, **42**, 1031–1037.

Folstein, M.F., Folstein, S.E. and McHugh, P.R. (1975) "Mini-Mental State"—a practical method for grading the cognitive state of patients for the clinician, *Journal of Psychiatric Research*, **12**, 189–198.

Godlove, C., Richard, L. and Rodwell, G. (1981) *Time for Action: An Observation Study of Elderly People in Four Different Care Environments.* University of Sheffield Joint Unit for Social Services Research. Social Services Monographs. Research in Practice, Sheffield.

Gold, J. and Harvey, P. (1993) Cognitive defects in schizophrenia, *Psychiatric Clinics of*

North America, **16**, 295–312.

Goldberg, T.E., Karson, C.N. and Leleszi, P.J. (1988) Intellectual impairment in adolescent psychosis. A controlled psychometric study, *Schizophrenia Research*, **1**, 261–266.

Goldstein, G. and Zubin, J. (1990) Neuropsychological differences between young and old schizophrenics with and without associated neurological dysfunction, *Schizophrenia Research*, **3**, 117–126.

Greb, J. and Cancro, R. (1989) Schizophrenia: clinical features. In H. Kaplan and B. Sadock (eds) *Comprehensive Textbook of Psychiatry*, Williams and Wilkins, Baltimore (765 pages).

Heaton, R.K. and Drexler, M. (1987) Clinical neuropsychological findings in schizophrenia and ageing. In N.E. Miller and G.D. Cohen (eds) *Schizophrenia and Ageing*, Guilford Press, New York, pp. 145–161.

Hyde, T.M., Nawroz, S., Goldberg, T.E., Bigelow, L.B., Strong, D., Ostrem, J.L., Weinberger, D.R. and Kleinman, J.E. (1994) Is there cognitive decline in schizophrenia? A cross-sectional study. *British Journal of Psychiatry*, **164**, 494–500.

Johnstone, E.C., Crow, T.J., Frith, C.D., and Owens, D.G. (1976) Cerebral ventricular size and cognitive impairment in chronic schizophrenia. *Lancet*, ii, 924–926.

Johnstone, E.C., Cunningham Owens, D.G., Gold, A., Crow, T.J. (1981) Institutionalization and the defects of schizophrenia. *British Journal of Psychiatry*, 139, 195–203.

Kraepelin, E. (1919) *Dementia praecox and paraphrenia*. E & S Livingstone, Edinburgh.

Moos, R.H. and Lemke, S. (1984) *Multiphasic Environmental Assessment Procedure Manual*. Palo Alto CA: Social Ecology Laboratory, Veterans Administration and Stanford University Medical Center.

Pearlson, G., Kim, W., Kubos, K., Moberg, P., Jayaram, G., Bascom, M., Chase, G., Goldfinger, A. and Tune, L. (1989) Ventricular-brain ratio, computed tomographic density and brain area in 50 schizophrenics. *Archives of General Psychiatry*, **46**, 690–697.

Prohovnik, I., Dwork, A., Kaufman, M. and Wilson, N. (1993) Alzheimer-type neuropathology in elderly schizophrenic patients. *Schizophrenia Bulletin*, **19**, 805–816.

Trieman, N., Wills, W., Leff, J. (1995) The TAPS Project 28: Does reprovision benefit elderly long-stay mental patients? *Schizophrenia Research*, **21**, 199–208.

Wilkin, D. and Jolley, D. (1979) *Behavioural problems among old people in geriatric wards, psychogeriatric wards and residential homes*. Department of Psychiatry and General Practice, University of Manchester.

Wills, W. and Leff, J. (1996) The TAPS Project 30: Quality of Life for elderly mentally ill patients—A comparison of hospital and community settings. *International Journal of Geriatric Psychiatry*, **11**, 953–963.

Wing, J. and Brown, G. (1970) *Institutionalism and schizophrenia*. Cambridge University Press.

Chapter 8

THE EFFECT OF REPROVISION ON THE ACUTE SERVICES

Robert Sammut* and Julian Leff[†‡]
*Ashford Mental Health Centre; [†]Team for the Assessment of
Psychiatric Services (TAPS); [‡]Institute of Psychiatry

At its peak in the mid-1950s, Friern hospital housed over 2000 beds for acutely ill, rehabilitation, long-stay and elderly mentally infirm patients from four areas of central London: Islington, the South Camden sector of Bloomsbury, North Camden (Hampstead), and West Haringey. In this chapter we consider the effects of reorganisation of the acute services for two of these districts, Bloomsbury and Islington, as part of the reprovision for Friern hospital.

BED CHANGES IN BLOOMSBURY AND ISLINGTON

In addition to the loss of admission and rehabilitation beds at Friern, changes in South Camden included closure of admission and rehabilitation wards at St Pancras hospital, and an admission ward at University College Hospital (UCH). In their place, three admission wards have opened at the newly refurbished former Royal Ear Hospital on the UCH site in central London. Beds serving the North East Westminster sector of Bloomsbury, at St Luke's hospital in Muswell Hill, have remained unchanged. Changes for Islington include closure of rehabilitation wards at Friern and Whittington hospitals, and transfer of the Friern admission ward to the psychiatric unit at Whittington. There are no grounds at either of the UCH or Whittington hospital sites.

Admission and rehabilitation beds are considered together here on account of the difficulty in distinguishing specific functions of some of these at any particular time. Between 1990 and 1993 there was an overall reduction in the number of these beds by around 50 for Bloomsbury and 70 for Islington. The figures take account of a new 21-bedded rehabilitation ward opened in 1993 to cope with the increased pressure for admission. A number of additional

Care in the Community: Illusion or Reality?
Edited by Julian Leff. © 1997 John Wiley & Sons Ltd.

residential facilities, with varying levels of support, have opened in the community, but it is not possible to give a figure for places available because that given after the changes includes beds for the elderly mentally ill, not included in the original numbers.

AIMS OF STUDY

In view of the reduction in the number of admission beds available in the two health districts, we considered it possible that there might be an increase in the number of patients referred for admission for whom a bed could not be found. To investigate this we decided to monitor the emergency referrals to on-call junior doctors outside the working day. Another possible effect of the increased pressure on the admission beds could be a change in the use of day care facilities. Therefore it would be informative to determine the diagnostic mix of and length of attendance of patients receiving day hospital care, before and after the closure of Friern hospital. Both patients and staff would be likely to have a different experience of the admission wards in Friern hospital compared with those in DGHs. Consequently, their views of the setting should be sought, recognising that due to the relatively brief stays on admission wards, there would be little overlap between the patient samples.

Aspects of the acute psychiatric service considered most likely to be affected by the changes under consideration and which were examined include:

1. numbers and types of referrals to on-call junior doctors, and their management;
2. utilisation of day care facilities;
3. patient views of the service they receive;
4. nursing staff views of the service provided.

Referrals Data

Data relating to *all* admissions in Bloomsbury during and out of hours were obtained from the hospitals' administration departments, allowing comparison of the first six months of 1990 (before the changes) with the first six months of 1992. Changes in data collection and storage in Islington between Times 1 and 2 mean that it is not possible to make such comparisons for this health district.

A pilot study highlighted poor compliance amongst junior doctors requested to complete forms detailing referrals over 24-hour periods. Data were therefore restricted to out-of-hours periods only. On-call junior doctors were telephoned at 9 a.m. each morning, and asked for information on all referrals for admission the previous night or over the weekend. This included: patients' gender, area of residence, source of referral, clinical diagnosis, need for admission, and outcome. The diagnostic categories used were: schizophrenia, non-specific psychosis, hypomania, clinical depression, confusional state, alcohol abuse, drug-related problems, neurosis, personality disorder, social difficulty, and no identifiable disorder. Details such as patients' names, ages, and previous contact with services could not be collected with any consistent reliability, and were therefore omitted.

Bloomsbury baseline data were collected for 70 days randomly spread between November 1990 and April 1991. Follow-up data were collected on 70 days over the equivalent months during the following year. Islington data were collected on 91 days in September 1990 to June 1991, and 182 days during September 1992 to June 1993. Each day of the week was equally represented in the data.

Comparisons were made between the two districts at baseline and across time. As the data were not uniformly distributed, the Kruskal–Wallis test was used. Statistical analysis of dichotomised data was carried out by chi-square tests. Results at Time 2 for Islington are halved where relevant, so as to make for easy comparison with Time 1.

Results

Administrative data

There was a 33 per cent increase in the number of admissions to acute psychiatric wards, and a 27 per cent decrease in the average length of hospital stay, with bed occupancy rising from 83 per cent at baseline to 91 per cent. (By 1993, bed occupancy was well over 100 per cent.) The proportion of male admissions rose from 35 to 47 per cent, while that of involuntary admissions was unchanged (though the numbers increased). Bed occupancy on the Islington psychiatric admission wards before and after the ward changes has been consistently over 100 per cent.

Referrals Data

There was a 19 per cent increase in the number of out-of-hours referrals for admission in Bloomsbury, compared with a 21 per cent increase in Islington. The diagnostic distribution was very similar for the two districts at both points in time, with around two thirds of patients suffering from psychotic illnesses.

At Time 1, significantly more referrals in Bloomsbury came from professionals, though the difference was smaller at Time 2. Significantly more referrals in Bloomsbury were of patients residing outside the area, probably due to the presence in Bloomsbury of three mainline railway termini and the close proximity of London's West End. The difference was particularly marked for patients of no fixed abode. There was no increase in patients with no settled address at Time 2, indicating that the changes under review largely affected

Table 8.1 Referrals in Bloomsbury and Islington

	BLOOMSBURY		ISLINGTON	
	Time 1	Time 2	Time 1	Time 2
No. weeks	10	10	13	26
No. referrals	288	342	278	674
% male	53	58	55	47
Average per day	4.11	4.89	3.05	3.70
Median per day	3.50	4.00	3.00	4.00
Source of referral	Time 1 (%)	Time 2 (%)	Time 1 (%)	Time 2 (%)
Self/family/ friends	76 (26)[1]	92 (27)	119 (43)[1]	271 (40)
Professional	170 (59)[1]	199 (58)	121 (43)[1]	305 (46)
Police	42 (15)	52 (15)	38 (14)	97 (14)
Area of residence	Time 1 (%)	Time 2 (%)	Time 1 (%)	Time 2 (%)
Bloomsbury, Islington	191 (67)[2]	241 (73)	240 (87)[2]	595 (90)
Other	58 (20)	63 (19)	33 (12)	43 (6)
NFA	37 (13)[3]	26 (8)	3 (1)[3]	25 (4)

[1] $df = 1$, chi sq $= 17.7$, $p = <0.001$
[2] $df = 1$, chi sq $= 30.3$, $p = <0.001$
[3] $df = 1$, chi sq $= 30.1$, $p = <0.001$

residents within the two areas. Very similar proportions of the referrals in the two areas were from the police, and this did not change over time.

At Time 1, 72 per cent of the referrals in Bloomsbury required admission, compared with 60 per cent in Islington, of whom 61 per cent and 46 per cent respectively were actually admitted. The total number of patients not admitted for a variety of reasons doubled in Bloomsbury following the changes, and increased by a third in Islington. These increases were not due to the number of patients who refused admission, but to other reasons listed in Table 8.2.

As we have seen, beds in Islington were filled beyond capacity at Time 1, and more patients in this district were turned away owing to the lack of a bed. There was an increase in the number of referrals from general medical wards in both districts, and more patients who had recovered from their physical illnesses were required to remain on these wards pending the availability of a more appropriate psychiatric bed. The pressure on beds in Bloomsbury at Time 2 led to use of private hospital beds for the first time. Additionally, a small number of patients were kept in police cells at least overnight while hospital beds were sought.

Some patients are too vulnerable to survive long outside hospital without adequate support, and need "asylum in the community" (Wing, 1990). Yet the provision of affordable, supported housing, (the "cornerstone of community care", Thornicroft and Bebbington, 1989) has not kept pace with bed closures

Table 8.2   Outcome of assessment

	BLOOMSBURY		ISLINGTON	
	Time 1	Time 2	Time 1	Time 2[3]
Admission required	204 (72)[1]	256 (76)	165 (60)[1]	423 (65)
Admitted	173 (61)[2]	202 (59)	128 (46)[2]	325 (49)
Admissions out of area	49 (29)	51 (25)	13 (10)	40 (12)
Formal admissions	58 (33)	52 (26)	26 (20)	74 (23)
Admissions required but not admitted				
Patient refusal	14	14	17	18
Medical reason	8	20	5	11
Other	2	1	2	0
No psychiatric beds				
Medical ward	1	2	0	5
Other NHS hospital	4	6	2	9.5
Private hospital	0	14	2	3
Police cell	0	1	1	1.5
Not admitted	4	9	14	11
TOTAL	33	67	43	59

[1] df = 1, chi sq = 9.1, p = <0.005
[2] df = 1, chi sq = 11.9, p = <0.005
[3] Numbers quoted for Islington at Time 2 have been halved, to allow direct comparison with Time 1.

(Shelter, 1989) so that only a small proportion of former patients are in such facilities (Shelter, 1989; Hirsch, 1992). Approximately 9 per cent of former long-stay patients discharged from psychiatric hospitals are now occupying an admission bed (Gooch, person communication), and with as many as one third of acutely ill patients needing admission to hospital at some time, even with the availability of an assertive community outreach programme (Dean and Gadd, 1990), bed losses mean that admission can only be offered to those in crisis (Emergency Bed Service, 1992; Patrick et al, 1989; Holloway et al, 1992). There is increasing difficulty caring for others in need, (Emergency Bed Service, 1992; Patrick et al, 1989; Holloway et al, 1992) and many require repeated short-term admissions, (NACRO, 1992) or are denied admission altogether. These patients may be at risk of self harm, self-neglect or harm to others (Morgan, 1992) and are liable to be lost to follow-up (Patrick and Holloway, 1990). Those who lose all contact with health or social services make up the bulk of the homeless mentally ill (Patrick and Holloway, 1990; Weller et al, 1989) and the mentally ill in gaol (Gunn et al, 1991).

The increase in patients referred from general hospital wards following self-injury may indicate a real increase in their numbers, or earlier referral from these wards, themselves under pressure from cuts in bed numbers. In any case, occupancy of general hospital beds by psychiatric patients adds to the hidden costs of the changes under review (Salmon et al, 1993). The difficulty finding beds locally for many patients, meanwhile, is resulting in many being placed in NHS beds outside their own area, or in expensive private hospital beds. The role of finding such beds "out of hours" often falls to the doctor on-call, and may take up to twelve hours or more. This factor undoubtedly helps to raise the threshold for *need* for admission in the (often tired) assessing doctor's mind.

DAY HOSPITAL STUDY

Day care, sometimes following brief hospitalisation, can have favourable results in terms of clinical outcome compared with traditional inpatient treatment, by reducing symptoms, (Herz et al, 1971; Dick et al, 1985) delaying relapse (Herz et al, 1971) reducing readmissions (Herz et al, 1971) and lessening total time spent in hospital (Herz et al, 1971). Despite evidence that over one third of acute psychiatric admissions could be avoided if a day hospital place were available (Creed et al, 1990, 1991), the reduction in hospital beds has not been accompanied by commensurate increases in day hospital places (Holloway, 1991; Hirsch, 1992; Vaughan, 1983, 1985).

The effects of reduction in psychiatric admission beds on the day hospital service in South Camden were examined by comparing referral rates and characteristics of patients referred, during nine month periods (September to June) before and after the closure of the South Camden admission ward at Friern hospital. Information gathered included: socio-demographic data, admission and discharge dates, ICD-9 and case-note diagnoses, treatments received, patient level of functioning according to the Global Assessment Scale (GAS) (Endicott et al, 1976) on admission and at discharge, and records of violent behaviour. Data were analysed using t-tests for continuous data and chi-square tests for categorical data.

Results

There was a 64 per cent increase in the number of day hospital referrals between Time 1 and Time 2, with a rise in admissions by 51 per cent. There were no significant differences in terms of source of referral, marital status, ethnicity, accommodation status, or the length of time between referral and assessment (just over 10 days). The number of patients with psychotic illness referred almost doubled, compared with an increase by nearly a quarter of neurotic patients referred. The numbers admitted at Time 2 increased by 56 per cent for psychotic patients and 37.5 per cent for neurotic patients. The number of patients exhibiting violent behaviour increased from 4 at Time 1 to 11 at Time

Table 8.3   Day hospital results

	All patients		Psychotic		Neurotic	
	Time 1	Time 2	Time 1	Time 2	Time 1	Time 2
Referrals	87	143	52	99	35	43
Attenders	55	83	39	61	16	22
Time attended (days)	150.8	99.8	162.9	102.3	121.2	92.4
GAS on admission	35.6	33.8	36.0	32.9	34.7	36.8
GAS on discharge	61.5	60.3	64.5	57.0[1]	53.7	66.8[2]
GAS difference	26.2	26.6	28.6	24.1	19.0	30.0

[1] $t = 2.26$, d.f. $= 43$, $p < 0.05$
[2] $t = 2.66$, d.f. $= 63$, $p < 0.05$

2. No serious incidents were recorded. There was a reduction of one-third in the duration of attendance for all patients.

All patient groups showed significant improvement between admission and discharge. However, the level of functioning of psychotic patients at the time of discharge was superior at Time 1, compared with Time 2. Neurotic patients at Time 2, however, had a higher level of functioning at discharge compared with their counterparts at Time 1.

There is a widespread view that in-patient treatment is more effective than day treatment for psychosis (Platt et al, 1980; Lancet, 1985; Vaughan, 1985) with day care more suitable for neurotic patients (Tyrer and Remington, 1979; Dich, 1985). Increasing pressure on hospital beds is, however, leading to many patients, including those with psychoses, being denied admission or facing early discharge into the community. The lack of more appropriate facilities (Hirsch, 1992; Wilkinson, 1984; Vaughan, 1983) results in their accumulation in day hospitals where they displace many of the neurotic patients for whom the day hospital was originally intended (Pryce, 1982; McGrath and Tantam, 1987).

Many clinicians are reluctant to advocate day care at all for many of their patients, (Herz et al, 1971; Bowman et al, 1983), probably reflecting an awareness of inherent clinical risks, including suicide (Platt et al, 1980). The lack of an adequate supportive network in the community is another common reason for choosing hospitalisation over day care (Bowman et al, 1983). It is questionable whether those exhibiting florid psychotic symptoms or disturbed behaviour are likely to derive any benefit at all from day care. Indeed, such behaviour from the increased number of these patients now attending the day hospital is probably disruptive to the treatment programmes of others (Vaughan, 1985).

A further factor identified as an important predictor of satisfactory outcome of day care is longer duration of stay (Carney et al, 1970). Yet there has been a marked reduction in average period of attendance following bed reductions. Our findings indicate, however, that while decreased length of treatment may negatively affect outcome for psychotic patients, there is perhaps room for increased efficiency of day hospital use by neurotic patients (Table 8.3).

PATIENT SATISFACTION

Patients satisfied with their treatment are generally more compliant with the treatment offered (Grob et al, 1978; Larsen, 1979), leading to increased treatment success (Edwards et al, 1978) and briefer hospitalisation (Eisen and Grob, 1992). It is therefore important to know their views of the type, quality and quantity of the service provided, and the physical environment in which it is given (Eisen and Grob, 1992; Dowds and Fontana, 1977; Skodol et al, 1980). Surveys by questionnaire are probably the best means of assessing patient views (Lebow, 1982), and have been shown to be reliable and valid (Raphael and Peers, 1972; Weinstein, 1979; Fontana and Dowds, 1975). Such studies consistently report psychiatric patients as satisfied with the services they receive (Weinstein, 1979), but they may only be meaningful if attention is given to those dissatisfied with the service, or to aspects of the service giving least satisfaction. Additionally, the relative satisfaction of similar clients in alternative service modalities can be examined, or changes can be monitored over time (Fontana and Dowds, 1975).

Methodology

A questionnaire was compiled following a survey of the literature (Sammut, unpublished a), focusing on aspects of the service most likely to be affected by the changes (see table 8.4). These included: physical environment (Kotin and Shur, 1969; Joint Commission on Accreditation of Hospitals, 1979) ward atmosphere (Moos et al, 1973) and crowding (Keith-Speigel et al, 1970), treatment received (Elzinga and Barlow, 1991) contact with doctors (Keith-Speigel et al, 1970) and nurses (Weinstein, 1981), activity levels (Raphael and Peers, 1972), noise and ward disturbance (Bouras et al, 1982), personal safety (Zusman et al, 1972) and privacy (Raphael and Peers, 1972; Kotin and Schur, 1969).

Visits were made to Bloomsbury and Islington acute and short-term rehabilitation psychiatric wards over several weeks before and after the ward changes (Times 1 and 2). All in-patients of at least 3 days standing at the time of the visits were asked to complete the questionnaire. Confidentiality was emphasised, as was the researcher's independence. No patient answered more than one questionnaire at any time, thus preserving independence of the groups.

A subsidiary study examining patient compliance with the study and consistency of their views was carried out by administering the questionnaire on two separate occasions, several days apart, to a group of in-patients at Friern hospital. This showed a high level of consistency in patients' views over time.

Results

Out of a cumulative total of 779 in-patients, 614 (78.8 per cent) agreed to participate in the main study, and 74.6 per cent (289 at Time 1 and 292 at Time 2) actually returned a questionnaire. This ranks as a very good return rate compared with similar studies elsewhere (Lebow, 1982). District, sex, and age had little effect on compliance, but formally detained patients and those with a greater length of stay were less likely to participate.

The majority of patients were happy with most aspects of their hospitalisation, with significantly more patients at the older hospitals satisfied with the hospital grounds (74.1 per cent and 57.1 per cent respectively), and the ward atmosphere (74.5 per cent and 63.1 per cent). A comparison over time of patients in DGH units revealed significant differences for hospital grounds (57.1 per cent at Time 1, compared with 43.4 per cent at Time 2) and fewer at Time 2 felt better as a result of treatment (down from 67.5 per cent to 56.7 per cent). Those aspects of the service causing least satisfaction failed to show any improvement over time.

Although most patients were satisfied, satisfaction is not universal, and those who refused to participate in the study were probably the least satisfied of all

Table 8.4 Patient satisfaction

	n	% pos
Nurses' support	(551)	77.3
Crowding	(554)	75.3
OT environment	(375)	75.2
Ward comfort	(560)	74.8
Nearby streets	(519)	71.9
Bathing facilities	(563)	71.2
Safety on ward	(543)	70.9
Ward atmosphere	(566)	68.9
Recommend service	(526)	65.2
Right treatment	(510)	65.1
Enough treatment	(510)	62.7
Feel better	(530)	62.6
Hospital grounds	(536)	60.1
Quick attention	(547)	60.1
Privacy	(567)	59.3
Discharge plans	(387)	58.1
Doctor availability	(558)	57.3
Noise level	(559)	54.9
Better service	(418)	53.6
Patients' behaviour	(567)	52.9
Enough activity	(571)	48.5
Level of theft	(545)	46.6
Boredom	(560)	36.4

All groups combined, $n = 581$

(Lebow, 1982). It is of particular concern that those areas of greatest dissatisfaction failed to improve, or worsened, over time.

A marked lack of activity was reported by patients in this study, made worse by the changes, despite the recognition that meaningful occupation is therapeutic for psychiatric patients (Wing and Brown, 1970). Although this problem was potentially remediable at the older hospitals by increases in staffing levels, this recourse cannot overcome design limitations of the newer units, particularly the lack of adequate space.

Attention to the physical environment may exert a beneficial effect on staff mood and reduce absenteeism, and can halve the amount of violent behaviour shown by patients (Christenfeld et al, 1989). Whereas the older psychiatric hospitals were generally set in ample grounds, and were a pleasure for patients to walk round or look out on, the newer units are mostly located in busy city centres, with little or no outside space available. This was reflected in the expressed views of respondents at Time 1. The deterioration in satisfaction with hospital grounds at the DGHs over time may be explained by the fact that many patients had previous experience of the older psychiatric hospitals, giving them a basis for comparison.

Reduced numbers of hospital beds results in an increased threshold for admission and increased rates of patient turnover (Holloway et al, 1992). This inevitably leads to a decrease in the amount of treatment received by in-patients, and a rise in the proportion of acutely disturbed patients on the wards. This in turn affects the levels of noise, violent incidents and sexual harassment (Burke, 1983). Not surprisingly, patients expressed increased concern over the behaviour of their fellow residents, and fear for their personal safety, and it is little wonder they are said to prefer extramural care (Muijen et al, 1992).

PSYCHIATRIC NURSES' SATISFACTION

Nurses play a central role in the management and administration of care for psychiatric hospital patients, and, of all staff, have the most direct one-to-one contact with them. Thus, they have important effects on patients' well-being and behaviour, and on their attitudes to, satisfaction with and outcome from, any treatment given (Brady et al, 1980). Patients view them as having at least as important a role in therapy as doctors (Caine and Smail, 1968).

Nursing staff working with seriously mentally ill patients are particularly vulnerable to job-related stress (Hiscott and Connop, 1990), and this may lead to job dissatisfaction and low morale (Frisch et al, 1991), increased staff conflict, absenteeism and high staff turnover (Brady et al, 1980). In order to attract and maintain the best trained and most effective mental health workers it is essential, therefore, to maintain favourable working conditions (Brady et al, 1980), and to pay attention to their views of the service provided. Important factors affecting job satisfaction and morale include congruence between nurses' attitudes and that of their supervisors and with hospital policy (Phillips and Hayes, 1978), the quality of their interpersonal relations with doctors, and the quality of care given (Frisch et al, 1991; Leatt and Schneck, 1980).

Sources of stress, on the other hand, include insufficient resources and work overload (Frisch et al, 1991), inadequate numbers of nursing staff (Frisch et al, 1991; Leatt and Schneck, 1980) and insufficient availability of doctors (Leatt and Schneck, 1980). Troublesome patients present a particular problem (Frisch et al, 1991), and as many as three quarters of staff members working with mentally ill patients expect to be physically assaulted at some time in their careers (Poster and Ryan, 1989). Anecdotal reports of those who have left the field of psychiatric nursing because of the risk of physical harm are not uncommon (Ryan and Poster, 1989).

A "nurses satisfaction" questionnaire was compiled following a search of the literature (Sammut, unpublished). Nursing staff on all 15 Bloomsbury and Islington psychiatric admission and short-term rehabilitation wards were approached before and after Friern hospital's closure and asked to complete the questionnaire, indicating their views of the ward environment and service provided.

Results

Nurses in psychiatric hospital admission wards expressed greater satisfaction with a number of aspects of the service provided than staff at the DGH units (Table 8.5). These included the level of doctors' support, ward crowding, the number of violent incidents, and the surrounding environment. Significantly fewer nurses at the DGHs would recommend the service to a friend or relative in need.

Following reorganisation, DGH staff views of the hospital grounds deteriorated greatly, and more were unhappy with the level of doctor availability, crowding, noise and violent behaviour on the wards. Not surprisingly, they expressed greater fear for their own safety. Also, more at Time 2 felt that patients had too little to do and were being discharged too soon. Staff morale plummeted from an already low level, and less than half felt able to recommend the service to others.

DISCUSSION

Changes to the acute psychiatric services in Bloomsbury and Islington are similar to those occurring throughout Britain, where the move towards community care has included large scale reduction in admission and rehabilitation bed numbers and the loss of supporting facilities. The findings of this study are therefore relevant to other areas of the UK.

Reduced numbers of hospital beds results in an increased threshold for admission and increased rates of patient turnover (Holloway et al, 1992). There is a considerable added burden on medical and nursing staff involved in

Table 8.5 Nursing staff satisfaction

Institutions vs DGHs (Time 1 only)	Inst.	DGHs			
	% pos	%pos	d.f.	chi sq	p
Crowding	78	42	1	17.0	<0.005
Grounds	74	6	1	53.2	<0.005
Streets	70	40	1	12.9	<0.005
Help available	81	63	1	5.0	<0.05
Violence	80	36	1	23.4	<0.005
Doc. available	68	49	1	4.2	<0.05
Doc.communic	92	52	1	25.5	<0.005
Doc. support	78	60	1	4.6	<0.05
Recommend	68	28	1	19.1	<0.005
Significant changes over time (DGHs only)	% pos	% pos	d.f.	chi sq	p
Crowding	64	41	1	12.3	<0.005
Noise	66	45	1	9.5	<0.005
Grounds	48	30	1	8.0	<0.05
Safety	75	56	1	9.1	<0.005
Violence	63	47	1	6.0	<0.05
Pt. Activity	24	9	1	8.9	<0.005
Doc. available	60	40	1	9.9	<0.005
Doc.communic	76	61	1	5.9	<0.05
Early discharge	77	62	1	6.4	<0.05
Better service	58	27	1	18.4	<0.005
Morale	37	15	1	11.5	<0.005

administrative duties relating to admission and discharge of patients, a decrease in the amount of treatment received by in-patients, and in one-to-one patient–staff contact. Concomitantly, increases in compulsory admissions reported by the hospitals' administration departments reflect anecdotal reports of greater numbers of disturbed patients in the community and on the wards, and result in increased custodial attitudes amongst staff (Schwartz and Taylor, 1989).

Patients and staff have expressed greater fear for their personal safety, and there has been a dramatic drop in nurses' morale. Along with other effects of the changes in the acute psychiatric services, these are likely to exert a deleterious influence on patient care (Francis and Smith, 1991). It is, therefore, to the nurses' credit that there has as yet been no diminution of the patients' appreciation of their support.

CONCLUSIONS

This multi-faceted investigation into the effects of the changes in admission facilities following the closure of Friern hospital has revealed the one area of service reprovision which failed to reach adequate standards, and which in fact deteriorated as a result of the changes. Patients needing admission were sent home or admitted to expensive private facilities, which cannot provide adequate after-care. Psychotic patients admitted to the day hospital attended for a shorter period and fared less well than previously. Patients and nursing staff were less satisfied with the new units in the DGH than with the admission wards in the psychiatric hospital.

The failure to address the needs of the new generation of long-term mentally ill people means that many patients with active symptoms, who would have previously remained in hospital, are being denied admission or are discharged early to a badly organised and underfunded system of "community care" (Thornicroft and Bebbington, 1989) without adequate assessment of the service they are receiving (Groves, 1990). The dearth of hospital beds has resulted in increased back-pressure on the day hospital service, with effects on referrals and admissions that mirror those on the in-patient service. There have been similar effects on the caseloads carried by the CPN, voluntary and social work services.

The right balance is required of admission, rehabilitation, long-stay and day care facilities, as well as supported accommodation in the community, tailored to suit the needs of individual districts (Jarman et al, 1992). In addition, regular and systematic clinical audit in the area of patient satisfaction is essential, as a valid and constructive means of monitoring the care available (Smith, 1990). This can lead to practical recommendations for improved treatment and patient welfare (Edwards et al, 1978). Meanwhile, the extent of the drop in morale amongst nursing staff is alarming, and should be a major cause for concern for those charged with providing a quality service.

REFERENCES

Bouras, N., Trauer, T., Watson, J.P. (1982) Ward environment and disturbed behaviour. *Psychological Medicine*, **12**, 309–319.

Bowman, E.P., Shelley, R.K., Sheehy-Skeffington, A., et al. (1983) Day patient versus inpatient: factors determining selection of acutely ill patients for hospital treatment. *British Journal of Psychiatry*, **142**, 584–587.

Brady, C.A., Kinnaird, K.I., Friedrich, W.N. (1980) Job satisfaction and perception of social climate in a mental health facility. *Perceptual and Motor Skills*, **51**, 559–564.

Burke, G.F. (1983) Caring for the medically ill psychiatric patient on a psychiatric unit. *Psychiatric Annals*, **13**, 627–634.

Caine, T.M., Smail, D.J. (1968) Attitudes of psychiatric patients to staff roles and treatment methods in mental hospitals. *British Journal of Medical Psychology*, **41**, 291–294.

Carney, M.W.P., Ferguson, R.S., Sheffield, B.F. (1970) Psychiatric day hospital and community. *Lancet*, June 6, 1218–1221.

Christenfeld, R., Wagner, J., Pastva, G., Acrish, W.P. (1989) How physical settings affect chronic mental patients. *Psychiatric Quarterly*, **60**, 253–264.

Creed, F.H, Black, D., Anthony, P. et al. (1990) Randomised controlled trial comparing day and inpatient psychiatric treatment. *British Medical Journal*, **300**, 1033–1037.

Creed, F.H, Black, D., Anthony, P. et al. (1991) Randomised controlled trial comparison of two hospitals. *British Medical Journal*, **158**, 183–189.

Dean, C., Gadd, E.M. (1990) Home treatment for acute psychiatric illness. *British Medical Journal*, **301**, 1021–1023.

Dick, P., Cameron, L., Cohen, D., Barlow, M., Ince, A. (1985) Day and full-time psychiatric treatment: a controlled comparison. *British Journal of Psychiatry*, **147**, 250–253.

Dowds, B.N., Fontana, A.F. (1977) Patients' and therapists' expectations and evaluations of hospital treatment: satisfactions and disappointments. *Comprehensive Psychiatry*, **18**, 295–300.

Edwards, D.W., Yarvis, R.M., Mueller, D.P., Langsley, D.G. (1978) Does patient satisfaction correlate with success? *Hospital and Community Psychiatry*, **29**, 188–190.

Eisen, S.V., Grob, M.C. (1992) Patient outcome after transfer within a psychiatric hospital. *Hospital and Community Psychiatry*, **43**, 803–806.

Elzinga, J., Barlow, J. (1991) Patient satisfaction among the residential population of a psychiatric hospital. *International Journal of Social Psychiatry*, **37**, 24–34.

Emergency Bed Service. (1992) Caseload Report. London: EBS.

Endicott, J., Spitzer, R.L., Fleiss, J., et al. (1976) The Global Assessment Scale: a procedure for measuring overall severity of psychiatric disturbance. *Archives of General Psychiatry*, **33**, 766–771.

Fontana, A.F., Dowds, B.N. (1975) Assessing treatment outcome. *Journal of Nervous and Mental Diseases*, **161**, 221–230.

Francis, V.M., Smith, A. (1991) The run-down and closure of a psychiatric hospital. Effects on patients' behaviour. *Social Psychiatry and Psychiatric Epidemiology*, **26** Part 2, 92–94.

Freddolino, P.P., Moxley, D.P., Fleishman, J.A. (1989) Advocacy model for people with long-term disabilities. *Hospital and Community Psychiatry*, **40**, 1169–1174.

Frisch, S.R., Dembeck, P., Shannon, V. (1991) The Head Nurse: perceptions of stress and ways of coping. *Canadian Journal of Nursing Administration*, **4**, 6–13.

Grob, M.C., Eisen, S.V., Berman, J.S. (1978) Three years follow-up monitoring: perspectives of formerly hospitalized patients and their families. *Comprehensive Psychiatry*, **19**, 491–499.

Groves, T. (1990a) The Future of Community Care. *British Medical Journal*, **300**, 923–924,

Groves, T. (1990b). After the asylums: who needs long-term psychiatric care? *British Medical Journal*, **300**, 999–1001.

Groves, T. (1990c). After the asylums: what does community care mean now? *British Medical Journal*, **300**, 1060–1062.

Groves, T. (1990d). After the asylums: the local picture. *British Medical Journal*, **300**, 1128–1130.

Gunn, J., Maden, A., Swinton, M. (1991) Treatment needs of prisoners with psychiatric disorders. *British Medical Journal*, **303**, 338–340.

Herz, M.I., Endicott, J., Spitzer, R.L., et al. (1971) Day versus inpatient hospitalisation: a controlled study *American Journal of Psychiatry*, **127**, 1371–1382.

Hirsch, S.R. (1992) Services for the severely mentally ill: a planning blight. *Psychiatric Bulletin*, **16**, 673–675.

Hiscott, R.D., Connop, P.J. (1990) The health and wellbeing of mental health professionals. *Canadian Journal of Public Health*, **81**, 422–426.

Holloway, F. (1991) Day care in an inner city. *British Journal of Psychiatry*, **158**, 805–816.

Holloway, F., Silverman, M., Wainwright, A. (1992) "Not waving but drowning": psychiatric services in East Lambeth in 1990. *International Journal of Social Psychiatry*, **38**, 131–137.

Jarman, B., Hirsch, S.R., White, P., Driscoll, R. (1992) Predicting psychiatric admission rates. *British Medical Journal*, **304**, 1146–1150.

Joint Commission on Accreditation of Hospitals. (1979) *Consolidated Standards for Client, Adolescent and Adult Psychiatry*, Alcoholism and Drug Abuse Programme. Chicago.

Keith-Spiegel, P., Grayson, M., Spiegel, D. (1970) Using the discharge interview to evaluate a psychiatric hospital. *Mental Hygiene*, **54**, 298–300.

Lancet (Editorial, 1985) Day hospitals for psychiatric care. *Lancet*, iv, 1106–1107.

Leatt, P., Schneck, R. (1980) Differences in stress perceived by head nurses across nursing specialities in hospitals. *Journal of Advanced Nursing*, **5**, 31–46.

Lebow, J. (1982) Consumer satisfaction with mental health treatment. *Psychological Bulletin*, **91**, 244–259.

McGrath, G. Tantam, D. (1987) Long-stay patients in a psychiatric day hospital. *British Journal of Psychiatry*, **150**, 836–840.

Moos, R.H., Shelton, R., Petty, C. (1973) Perceived ward climate and treatment outcome. *Journal of Abnormal Psychology*, **82**, 291–298.

Morgan, H.G. (1992) Suicide prevention. Hazards on the fast lane to community care. *British Medical Journal*, **160**, 149–153.

Muijen, M., Marks, I.M., Connolly, J., Audini, B., McNamee, G. (1992) The Daily Living Programme. Preliminary comparison of community versus hospital-based treatment for the seriously mentally ill facing emergency admission. *British Journal of Psychiatry*, **160**, 379–384.

NACRO (1992) Revolving Doors, London: NACRO Publications.

Patrick, M., Holloway, F. (1990) A two-year follow-up of new long stay patients in an inner city district general hospital. *International Journal of Social Psychiatry*, **36**, 207–215.

Phillips, E., Hays, J.R. (1978) Job satisfaction and perceived congruence of attitude between workers and supervisors in a mental health setting. *Perceptual and Motor Skills*, **47**, 55–59.

Platt, S., Knights, A.S., Hirsch, S.R. (1980) Caution and conservatism in the use of a psychiatric day hospital: evidence from a research project that failed. *Psychiatric Research*, **3**, 123–132.

Poster, E.C., Ryan, J.A. (1989) Nurses' attitudes toward physical assaults by patients. *Archives of Psychiatric Nursing*, **3**, 315–322.

Pryce, I.G. (1982) An expanding stage army of long-stay psychiatric day-patients, *British Journal of Psychiatry*, **141**, 595–601.

Raphael, W., Peers, V. (1972) *Psychiatric Hospitals Viewed by Their Patients*. King Edward's Hospital Fund for London.

Ryan, J.A., Poster, E.C. (1989) The assaulted nurse: short- and long-term responses. *Archives of Psychiatric Nursing*, **3**, 323–331.

Salmon, J.B., Armstrong, R.F., Cohen, S.L., Cobb, J.P. (1993) Schizophrenic patients requiring intensive care – a worrying and expensive trend (letter). *British Medical Journal*, **307**, 508.

Sammut, R.G. (Unpublished, a) Psychiatric patients satisfaction with services received: a literature review. In: The effects of changes to the acute psychiatric services in Bloomsbury and Islington (M.D. Thesis).

Sammut, R.G. (Unpublished, b) Psychiatric nursing staff views of the service they provide. A literature search. In: The Effects of Changes to the Acute Psychiatric Services in Bloomsbury and Islington (M.D. Thesis).

Schwartz, L.S., Taylor, J.R. (1989) Attitudes of mental health professionals towards alcoholism recognition and treatment. *American Journal of Drug and Alcohol Abuse*, **15**, 321–337.

Shelter. (1989) Raise the roof campaign. London: Shelter Publications.

Skodol, A.E., Plutchik, R., Karassu, T.B. (1980) Expectations of hospital treatment: conflicting views of patients and staff. *Journal of Nervous and Mental Diseases*, **168**, 70–74.

Smith, T. (1990) Medical Audit *British Medical Journal* **300**, 65.

Thornicroft, G., Bebbington, P. (1989) Deinstitutionalisation – from hospital closure to service development. *British Journal of Psychiatry*, **155**, 739–753.

Tyrer P. and Remington, M. (1979) Controlled comparison of day hospital and outpatient treatment for neurotic disorders. *Lancet*, ii, 1014–1016.

Vaughan, P.J. (1983) The disordered development of day care in psychiatry. *Health Trends*, **15**, 91–94.

Vaughan, P.J. (1985) Developments in psychiatric care, *British Journal of Psychiatry*, **147**, 1–4.

Weinstein, R.M. (1979) Patient attitudes toward mental hospitalization: a review of quantitative research. *Journal of Health and Social Behaviour*, **20**, 237–258.

Weinstein, R.M. (1981) Mental patients attitudes to hospital staff. A review of quantitative research. *Archives of General Psychiatry*, **38**, 483–489.

Weller, M.P.I., Tobiansky, R.I., Hollander, D., Ibrahimi, O.S. (1989) Psychosis and destitution at Christmas 1985–1988. *Lancet*, ii, 1509–1511.

Wing, J.K. (1990) The functions of asylum. *British Journal of Psychiatry*, **157**, 822–827.

Wing, J.K., Brown, G.W. (1970) *Institutionalism and Schizophrenia*. Cambridge University Press, 1970.

Zusman, J., Slawsan, M.R. (1972) Service quality profiles: development of a technique for measuring quality of mental health services. *Archives of General Psychiatry*, **27**, 692–698.

Chapter 9

TRAINING LEVEL AND TRAINING NEEDS OF STAFF

Vivien Senn[*], Rowena Kendal[†], Lucy Willetts[‡] and Noam
Trieman[*]
*Team for the Assessment of Psychiatric Services (TAPS); †Institute of
Psychiatry; ‡West Berkshire Priority Care Service

The shift to community provision of residential services for long-term mentally
ill patients poses interesting questions with regard to the qualifications and
training of care staff. It might be expected that in the current ideological
climate, with most community homes aiming to create as culturally normative
a domestic environment for residents as possible, there would be less demand
for nursing staff. This does seem to be the case in the few studies investigating
the professional characteristics of care staff in residential facilities for the
mentally ill. In a large-scale survey in the US, Randolph et al (1991) reported
that the majority of community staff had no professional training in a mental
health field. In the UK, a small scale survey of private community care in a
district of Bristol found a similar predominance of unqualified staff (Arnott,
1993).

The range of community homes provided for the long-stay Friern population
is described in Chapter 4. The profile of care staff and training opportunities
within the staffed group homes developed for the Friern Hospital reprovision
was examined approximately one year after closure (Senn et al, in press). The
managers of 48 staffed homes were interviewed to gather information about the
staff characteristics and qualifications, and the training opportunities available.
There were a total of 502 staff in post at the time, and this study similarly
revealed that the majority of care staff (53.8 per cent) were unqualified. The
homes surveyed were run by a number of different agencies (see Table 9.1) and
the highest percentage of unqualified staff was found in the private sector (see
Figure 9.1).

The finding that increasing numbers of unqualified staff are providing care
for people with mental illness raises important issues with regard to training and

Care in the Community: Illusion or Reality?
Edited by Julian Leff. © 1997 John Wiley & Sons Ltd.

Table 9.1 Number of homes and staff

Agency	Health Authority/ Local Authority	Consortium	Private	Voluntary
Number of homes	8	10	6	24
Number of staff	92	93	85	232

Potential posts = 554
Total no. of staff = 502
Vacancies = 52 (9.4%)

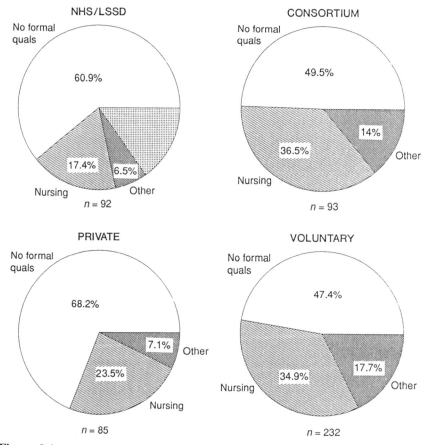

Figure 9.1

its availability. Whereas psychiatric nursing training was previously centrally located at Friern Hospital, the community facilities are now geographically and organisationally dispersed. Given that community staff may come from a variety of different backgrounds and that many may not have had previous contact with mentally ill people, it is important to consider how training should be organised in the community.

Although current guidelines recommend that individual training packages should be drawn up for community care staff (London Borough of Hackney, 1993), this is left up to the discretion of running agencies with the result that the standard of training varies considerably across organisations. Technically there is a wide variety of training on offer, provided by statutory, private and voluntary agencies. A minority of managing agencies run well-planned, structured induction programmes for new staff, but in many other facilities it appears that arbitrary decisions are made on who benefits from training opportunities and which of the multitude of available courses are used. It would be advantageous if all training budgets were allocated per staff member rather than per project, which can result in limited resources being allocated to certain staff members, or for supervision and support. Providing staff cover presented a problem in some of the homes. In practice the uptake of training courses depends on whether or not there are adequate resources.

We distributed questionnaires to the care staff in 16 representative homes in this North London region. We asked whether they felt they had received adequate training, or whether they had unmet needs, and what they thought about their career prospects. Almost 69 per cent stated a training need that was not being met within their current situation, so clearly there are shortcomings in many programmes. The needs stated were diverse, but the top three—management, community care and first aid—were general areas that might be considered part of basic training.

The picture becomes gloomier when staff reports of their career prospects are considered: one third of those questioned saw only limited opportunities and one third did not respond, suggesting morale may be low among community staff. This could be due to the typical two-tier hierarchy of group home organisation with the care staff accountable to managerial staff. In contrast to the structured hospital nursing hierarchy, this presents little opportunity for promotion.

The Friern experience, in line with other surveys, indicates that with the shift to community residential care there is an increase in the employment of unqualified staff. With the emphasis on providing as normal a home environment as possible, the lack of nursing qualifications among the staff may not be seen as a disadvantage. However, carers need to be capable of early recognition of a deterioration of mental state, and to manage residents who sometimes display disturbed behaviour. The role of care staff in residential settings requires a multiplicity of skills in order to fully benefit clients and ensure quality of service. It is therefore of the utmost importance that comprehensive training programmes are implemented, and disappointing that so many staff felt that their training was inadequate. The lack of formal regulation in this area with regard to minimum levels of basic training effectively leaves it to the discretion of the running agencies. Standards vary depending on resources allocated and the agencies' commitment to ensure that training is a priority.

Our findings from the survey of training needs prompted us to develop a pilot training programme which would attempt to fill the gap revealed. Our thinking about the content of the programme was strongly influenced by research that has been conducted over the past 30 years on family relationships and schizophrenia. The link between these two areas needs some explanation.

EXPRESSED EMOTION IN COMMUNITY CARE FACILITIES

Staff–client relationships within community care facilities for the mentally ill have been focused upon in recent years. These relationships may be crucial to the welfare of the mentally ill client, in particular for the prognosis of their mental health difficulties. This relatively new area of study, for the most part, stems from the comprehensive literature on family relationships in schizophrenia, in particular, the role of expressed emotion.

Expressed emotion is in essence a measure of the quality of interactions between two people, usually a carer and a dependent, and focuses on certain components of those interactions, namely criticism, hostility, positive remarks and warmth, and emotional overinvolvement. High levels of criticism, hostility or emotional overinvolvement within family settings lead to relapse in schizophrenic patients (e.g. Brown et al, 1972). The same may be true of relationships in community care settings, in which staff often spend much of their day in close proximity with patients. Certainly, high levels of expressed emotion have been found between carers and patients in group homes for the mentally ill (e.g. Ball et al, 1992; Moore and Kuipers, 1992; Snyder et al, 1994; Baxter and Leff, in preparation) (see Table 9.2). These are reflected by high levels of criticism, while less hostility and emotional overinvolvement have been noted. Some warmth and positive remarks have also been recorded, but it is unclear what role these factors play. It is possible that there is a link between high levels of criticism and poor outcome in the clients towards whom it is directed (Ball et al, 1992). In two hostels in Camberwell, where high and low levels of expressed emotion were recorded, distinctly different outcomes were reported for their clients. Where high levels of expressed emotion were present, "negative" discharges involving a move to more dependent accommodation were five time more likely to occur than in the "low expressed emotion" hostel. It is therefore possible that the presence of expressed emotion was detrimental to the well-being and progress of their mentally ill clients.

Few generalisations can be made at this stage, although as the authors concluded, it does seem likely that "the emotional climate of a hostel may dramatically influence the patients' capacity to be contained and to benefit from care and rehabilitation".

In exploring the concept of expressed emotion further, it has been reported that high levels are directly linked to patient characteristics. For example,

Table 9.2 Levels of expressed emotion in residential community care settings

		High EE (%)	Critical comments	Hostility	EOI	Warmth	Positive remarks
Ball et al (1992)	A	20	1.8	–	–	2.4	2.0
	B	57	8.9	–	–	1.7	1.4
Moore and Kuipers (1992)		62	4.95	37.5%*	–	2.6	2.8
Snyder et al (1994)		13	2.3	0.03	0.07	2.1	1.5
Baxter and Leff (in preparation)		33	1.0**	0.13	0.29	2.6	2.5
Vaughn et al (1984) (family study)		67	6.9	28.0%*	1.7	2.9	2.5

*   Scored 1, 2 or 3
** Logarithmic mean due to skewed distribution

increased criticism has been associated with perceived patient deficits in warmth, social interaction, and general activity levels as well as aggression and attention-seeking tendencies (Moore et al, 1992). Furthermore, resident's overall psychopathology has been found to correlate with high levels of expressed emotion exhibited by their carers. It seems therefore that high levels of criticism in these settings are a reaction to specific client characteristics rather than a rigid maladaptive response by a carer to all clients. These observations provide useful information which could inform interventions aimed at reducing levels of criticism and overall expressed emotion in community care settings. The content of family interventions with schizophrenic patients is also a useful resource, when contemplating such a task.

THE DEVELOPMENT OF A STAFF TRAINING PROGRAMME

A staff training programme has recently been developed with the aim of reducing levels of expressed emotion between staff and clients in residential units (Baxter and Leff, in preparation). It has drawn upon both the family intervention studies and the more recent expressed emotion research within the community, highlighted above, in addition to previous training programmes for staff working with the mentally ill. A pilot study of the course, involving ten participants, has been carried out with encouraging results.

The training programme is primarily based on the "Thorn Initiative" course for community psychiatric nurses which includes a module on working with families of patients with schizophrenia (Lam et al, 1993), one of the aims of which is to teach the participants how to aid the reduction of expressed emotion within the family setting. The course has a set structure for each session: formal teaching, a group exercise, a warm-up game, role play, and feedback and discussion, which appeared to work very well and was hence adopted for the staff programme. The topic coverage needed much adaptation and now includes the following areas: general epidemiological information including symptoms and treatment regimes; problem-solving skills; communication skills; negative symptoms; delusions and hallucinations; irritability and violence; and staff members' own coping strategies. During the ten sessions, attempts were made to identify and address critical and hostile attitudes of staff members towards clients, indicative of high levels of expressed emotion. Positive reframing was one technique used for this purpose. In addition, a general philosophy of viewing the client as the expert on their own illness was encouraged, along with discussions and consultation with them.

A number of questionnaires and interview measures were used to evaluate the efficacy of the course, including measures of expressed emotion levels at baseline and at three months follow-up (see Table 9.2). It was found that the training programme did serve to increase the use of appropriate strategies for dealing with client-related difficulties within the community care setting (see Table 9.3). In particular, staff members were more inclined to use strategies that involved the consideration of their client's perspective, for example, finding out more about the difficulty from the client or acknowledging how the client felt. Strategies that aimed at effecting change were also used more often following training. These included simple behavioural programmes or reassuring and encouraging the client. Finally, interventions that drew on staff members' own views about the situation were used less, for example, telling the client that they could not possibly be hearing a voice or telling them to get out of bed despite their feeling of tiredness. These responses are characteristic of highly critical family members. The shifts in management skills noted indicate that staff members were able to approach difficult situations in a more client-centred way and hence, often in a less critical or hostile fashion. Levels of expressed emotion in staff–client relationships did not change in relation to the training programme, but the highlighted shift in management strategies may in the long-term produce a lessening of expressed emotion, particularly in the form of reduced criticism.

Staff evaluation indicated that the course was extremely useful, particularly in its wide topic coverage. It was presumed that the staff members had a general knowledge of mental health and relevant management/intervention skills and therefore did not require provision of any generic mental health course. In fact, reflecting the findings of the survey reported above, most staff had no professional training or qualifications when taking up a post. The programme served as both an introduction to the field of residential mental health and also a refresher for more experienced staff.

The course did not, however, achieve its aim of reducing levels of expressed emotion between staff and clients. Perhaps it was not possible to alter maladaptive responses, in particular, criticism and hostility in such a short period of time while also aiming to impart more specific information and skills. We have made the following recommendations with regards to further

Table 9.3   Management of schizophrenic patients checklist (Berkowitz and Heinl, 1984). Effect of training programme on category use

Category	Mean difference in use	Significant or not?
A) Confirming patient's view of self:		
acknowledge patient's perspective		
reasons for patient's view	(+) 2.12	No
meaning for the patient		
allowing patient to express feelings		
B) Communicating nurses' own perspective:		
communication of nurses' perspective		
reasons for the view	(−) 1.50	No
expression of nurses' own feelings		
C) Change (attempt to bring A & B closer):		
understanding the illness		
nurturing	(+) 6.75	Yes*
unstructured programme		
structured programme		
D) Resources (use of):		
support group		
medical	(+) 3.75	Yes*
learning to cope with oneself		
flexibility		

*$p < 0.05$.

development of the course. A longer programme could be implemented to allow time to address and redress these maladaptive attitudes, perhaps with the use of supervision sessions in addition to more formal teaching, where real life client-related difficulties can be addressed in more detail and monitored on a weekly or fortnightly basis. In addition, the presence of a second trainer may increase the likelihood of critical attitudes being identified and addressed. Along with this, and in line with the family intervention studies, perhaps part of the teaching should be conducted in the form of more therapeutic sessions incorporating both behavioural and systemic techniques. For this to be successful, smaller groups of staff members would be required.

In conclusion, this staff programme has provided a useful base on which to build an effective staff training programme which increases knowledge and skills needed to work in the community care setting as well as altering unhelpful critical attitudes towards clients. It is recommended that such a course should be available to all mental health workers. We have argued elsewhere (Leff and Gamble, 1995) that it is unrealistic to expect family members to cope with schizophrenic patients without instruction and training. The same obviously applies to professional staff, particularly those working in small residential care facilities, in which the environment approximates to that in a family home.

REFERENCES

Arnott, S. (1993) The landladies of Fishponds: A study of private community care, *Psychiatric Bulletin*, **17**, 713–715.

Ball, R.A., Moore, E. and Kuipers, L. (1992) Expressed emotion in community care staff: a comparison of patient outcome in a nine month follow-up of two hostels, *Social Psychiatry and Psychiatric Epidemiology*, **27**, 35–39.

Baxter, L. and Leff, J. (in preparation) Expressed Emotion and community care facilities for the mentally ill: The development of a staff intervention programme.

Berkowitz, R. and Heinl, P. (1984) The management of schizophrenic patients: the nurses view. *Journal of Advanced Nursing*, **9**, 23–33.

Brown, G.W., Birley, J.L.T. and Wing, J.K. (1972) Influence of family life on the course of schizophrenic disorders: a replication, *British Journal of Psychiatry*, **121**, 241–258.

Lam, D.H., Kuipers, L. and Leff, J.P. (1993) Family work with patients suffering from schizophrenia—the impact of training on psychiatric nurses' attitude and knowledge. *Journal of Advanced Nursing* **18**, 233–237.

Leff, J. and Gamble, C. (1995) Training of community psychiatric nurses in family work for schizophrenia, *International Journal of Mental Health*, **24**, 76–88.

London Borough of Hackney Inspection and Quality Assurance Service (1993) *The Registered Homes Act 1984 Guidance for Registration: a code of practice for people in London who run residential care homes (March 1993 edition)*, endorsed by London Boroughs' Association and Association of London Authorities.

Moore, E. and Kuipers, L. (1992) Behavioural correlates of expressed emotion in staff-patient interactions, *Social Psychiatry and Psychiatric Epidemiology*, **27**, 298–303.

Moore, E., Ball, R.A. and Kuipers, L. (1992) Staff–patient relationships in the care of the long-term adult mentally ill: a content analysis of expressed emotion interviews, *Social Psychiatry and Psychiatric Epidemiology*, **27**, 28–34.

Randolph, F.L., Ridgway, M.S.W. and Carling, P.J. (1991) Residential programs for persons with severe mental illness: a nationwide survey of state-affiliated agencies, *Hospital and Community Psychiatry*, **42**, 1111–1115.

Senn, V., Kendal R. and Trieman, N. (1996) The TAPS Project 38: Level of training and its availability to carers within group homes in a London district, *Social Psychiatry and Psychiatric Epidemiology* (in press).

Snyder, K.S., Wallace, C.J., Moe, K. and Lieberman, R.P. (1994). Expressed emotion by residential care operators and residents' symptoms and quality of life, *Hospital and Community Psychiatry*, **45**, 1141–1143.

Vaughn, C., Snyder, K.S., Jones, S., Freeman, W.B. and Falloon, I.R.H. (1984). Family factors in schizophrenic relapse: replication in California of British research on expressed emotion, *Archives of General Psychiatry*, **41**, 1169–1177.

Chapter 10

ATTITUDES OF THE MEDIA AND THE PUBLIC

Geoffrey Wolff
Institute of Psychiatry

INTRODUCTION

Throughout the Middle Ages and well beyond, there was very little institutional provision for the mentally ill. They were looked after (or neglected) within the family and watched over by the community. With the Enlightenment of the eighteenth century came the beginnings of the era of *institutionalisation* or *the great confinement* (Foucault, 1991). This trend persisted into the middle of this century when institutionalisation gave way to *de-institutionalisation* and the move toward *community care*. This move has been facilitated by new drug treatments in conjunction with advances in social psychiatry and has led to an increase in the number of severely mentally ill people being looked after in the community. Patients discharged from long-stay hospital care often have major psychological and social functioning deficits precluding independent living (O'Driscoll et al, 1993). Many of these patients have been resettled in small group homes in residential neighbourhoods (Dayson, 1993) but need considerable support from health and social services staff.

Attitudes are all important in this swing of the pendulum away from hospital care towards community care although it has been postulated that if public attitudes lag behind, there may be a backlash against the trend (Bhugra, 1989) and this may well affect patients' rehabilitation and social integration. There is some evidence to support the suggestion of a hardening of attitudes in areas with greater community-based care (Brockington et al, 1993) and there has recently been much debate in the media about the dangers of community care (e.g. *Newsnight*, 1993).

This chapter examines attitudes and stigma toward the mentally ill expressed in the media and by the public and describes a new approach to the

Care in the Community: Illusion or Reality?
Edited by Julian Leff. © 1997 John Wiley & Sons Ltd.

reintegration of long-stay psychiatric patients into the community using a public education strategy.

ATTITUDES AND STIGMA

The cultural and psychological underpinnings of attitudes and stigma toward the mentally ill are diverse. Perceptions of madness can be traced from a common cultural heritage rooted in the powerful traditions of Ancient Greece and Christianity (Porter, 1987a, b). The stigma of schizophrenia, for example, may be related to notions of mental illness as a form of demonic possession and punishment for sin (Dain, 1994). The consequences of these perceptions have persisted through the Middle Ages, the Restoration and beyond.

More recently, the notion of *degeneration theory* and belief in the incurability of schizophrenia has contributed to this stigma (Zubin et al, 1985). There is also evidence from research that people with physical illness are more likely to be rejected or stigmatised if the illness is perceived as either severe or as having a behavioural causation (Crandall and Moriarty, 1995). It is likely that similar mechanisms contribute to attitudes to mental illness.

It has been postulated that stigma is also a function of a fear of that which normal people dread or fear becoming themselves (Stein, 1979). Stigma may also be related to the excessive value given to independence, self-reliance, beauty and health (Hahn, 1988) or the fact that disabled people violate normal people's belief in a just world (Rubin and Peplau, 1975).

Stigma was thought to have a profound effect on patients' symptomatology. Adherents to the now unfashionable *labelling theory* (Scheff, 1963, 1966) argued that much psychiatric symptomatology was secondary to stigmatisation. It is clear now, however, that the lion's share of deviance is primary. Indeed, although stigma has adverse social, economic, political and psychological consequences, its effects on self-esteem, for example, are not as negative as was once thought and there may actually be benefits for members of a stigmatised group, such as protection of one's self-esteem by: attributing negative feedback to prejudice against their group; selectively comparing their outcomes with those of members of their own group; and by selectively devaluing those attributes on which their own group fares poorly and valuing those attributes on which their group excels (Crocker and Major, 1989). However, whether or not they are successful in managing stigma, labelled deviants are still confronted with problems not faced by the "straight" world.

ATTITUDES SHOWN BY THE MEDIA

Studies of Media Attitudes

One of the main sources of information about mental illness is through the media, especially newspapers and television. In a recent review of the reporting of mental illness in British news, Barnes (1993) found that the mentally ill were portrayed almost exclusively in a negative light. The mentally ill were reported as conforming to obvious stereotypes. Patients suffering from psychotic illness were presented as violent criminals, committing murder or rape. Those suffering from non-psychotic illnesses were figures of fun, more to be pitied or laughed at than understood.

Another study of media representations of mental illness found that the number of reports involving violence to others outweighed sympathetic reports by four to one. Reports of violence tended to be headline news, whereas sympathetic reports were "back-page" in their profile (Philo, 1994). In a workshop on the subject, Philo found links between media representations of mental illness and attitudes to policies such as community care. One woman, for example who related her own beliefs about violence and mental illness to "Hollywood film and television drama" went on to say that she felt that government policies in Britain of care in the community were dangerous. Philo also found that many people (21 per cent of his sample) who had experience of the mentally ill which was non-violent had their opinion "overlaid" by violent portrayals in the media which resulted in their thinking of the mentally ill as violent.

Recent Media Coverage

During Christmas 1992, Ben Silcock was severely mauled after climbing into the lions' den at London Zoo (*The Daily Telegraph*, 5 August 1993). Concern for the lack of care for the mentally ill grew with reports such as: "Community care may increase suicide risk" (*The Independent*, 30 July 1993). An editorial in the *Evening Standard*, "A lack of real care" (12 August 1993) accused the then Secretary of State for Health, Virginia Bottomley, of having *contrived to vandalise* London's hospitals. It described care in the community policy as *discredited*. It quoted Mrs Bottomley as stating that *the pendulum had swung too far in one direction*.

There have been many reports recently of people with psychiatric problems and severe mental illness harming others. These cases, especially that of Christopher Clunis, were widely reported in the media (e.g. *Newsnight*, 1993; *The Daily Telegraph*, 5 August 1993) and led to new guidelines from the Government which included supervision registers. Headlines reported: "Controls on mentally ill promised" (*The Daily Telegraph*, 8 July 1993); "Tighter controls for dangerous patients" (*The Daily Telegraph*, 5 August 1993); "Mentally ill to be better supervised" (*The Independent*, 12 August 1993) and "Dangerous patients face new curbs" (*The Daily Telegraph*, 13 August 1993).

However, the new guidelines were also treated with some scepticism and were lampooned in the press (see Figure 10.1—cartoon by Martin Rowson, 1993).

Sympathy for the plight of the mentally ill continued to be expressed with headlines such as: "Patients 'left isolated and destitute'" (*The Independent*,

Figure 10.1　What's Up? By Martin Rowson (Reproduced by permission of Martin Rowson)

20 April 1994) and "Death of a 'dumped' schizophrenic" (*The Independent*, 20 April 1994).

Despite the introduction of supervision registers, there has been continued criticism of psychiatric care in the press with headlines such as: "Doctor had cleared attacker" (*The Times*, 3 February 1996); and it was reported that one judge even refused to send a schizophrenic offender to Broadmoor on the grounds that he was too dangerous: "Disturbed killer 'too dangerous for hospital'" (*The Independent*, 2 February 1996) despite the fact that psychiatrists argued that he should undergo treatment in a secure hospital and that discharge procedures from secure hospitals are stricter than for prisoners serving life sentences. Predictably, attacks in the tabloid press were even more scathing and sensational with headlines such as: "Hospital bungle released beast for sex spree" (*South London Press*, 9 February 1996); "The fools who let out the madmen" (*Evening Standard*, 20 February 1996). Funds have recently been promised for areas with a high incidence of violence by psychiatric patients: "Action on care in community: Hit list to target health areas setting patients free to kill and rape" (*Evening Standard*, 20 February 1996).

Even the term "care in the community" itself has come under fire and is described as "much criticised" and replaced by the term "spectrum of care" by the Secretary of State for Health to acknowledge the importance of hospital care ("Dorrell drops the term 'care in the community'", *The Times*, 21 February 1996).

Reports thus expressed both fear of and sympathy for the mentally ill. The perception of dangerousness of the mentally ill is symbolised by sensational cases such as that of Christopher Clunis. The perception of the neglect of and sympathy for the mentally ill is symbolised by the case of Ben Silcock in the lions' den. Although the failures and shortcomings of the implementation of community care policy are clearly expressed, the remedy is seen as a slowing down of hospital closure until community care can be delivered effectively (with tighter control and increased funding) rather than a swing of the pendulum back to institutional care. However, the community's attitude has a major bearing on the long-term success of the policy.

ATTITUDES SHOWN BY THE PUBLIC

Previous Studies of Public Attitudes

Attitudes toward the mentally ill are highly complex and difficult to evaluate. Research is beset by methodological problems and has produced markedly divergent results (Brockman et al, 1979). Work in this field has been criticised for being atheoretical, cross sectional and failing to examine the behavioural correlates of attitudes (Taylor, 1988).

Sociodemographic correlates of attitudes

Research has consistently shown that the main demographic determinants of tolerance of the mentally ill are age, education, occupation and acquaintance with the mentally ill. Older respondents have consistently been shown to be more intolerant (Rabkin, 1974; Ojanen, 1992; Brockington et al, 1993; Murphy et al, 1993). Ojanen interpreted this as a generational effect due to a higher educational level in younger people. Higher educational level has consistently been shown to be associated with tolerance (Maclean, 1969; Brockington et al, 1993; Murphy et al, 1993), as has higher occupational level (Taylor and Dear, 1981; Brockington et al, 1993). Some authors have found an association with sex, females being more tolerant (Maclean, 1969; Taylor and Dear, 1981), but some others have not (Brockington et al, 1993).

Attitudes to mental illness and mentally ill people

About half of respondents in studies of public attitudes towards mental illness have personal experience of the mentally ill (Maclean, 1969; Richards, 1982); around a third have relatives with mental illness (Maclean, 1969) and one in seventeen admit that they have suffered with a mental illness themselves (Maclean, 1969). Being acquainted with somebody with mental illness has been found to be associated both with tolerance (Taylor and Dear, 1981; Brockington et al, 1993) and with intolerance (Willcocks, 1968).

Between a fifth and a third of people perceive the mentally ill as dangerous (Maclean, 1969; Bhugra and Scott, 1989): however, many express sympathy and concern.

Attitudes to psychiatric services and community care policy

Around a third of respondents know somebody who has been in a psychiatric hospital (Reda, 1992). The majority agree that mental hospitals are necessary for the treatment of mentally ill, but a substantial minority think they are like prisons (Bhugra and Scott, 1989).

Almost three quarters of people have heard of hospital closure (Loam and Egan, 1990) but only about a quarter to a third know of local facilities (Rabkin et al, 1984; Huxley, 1993b). They do not therefore constitute a great burden to the community.

Most people object to hospital closure (Reda, 1992; Loam and Egan, 1990) but only a few object to mentally ill in the community (Richards, 1982) and about three quarters are in favour of caring for mentally ill in the community (*Independent*, 12 August 1993).

Surveys in North and South London

North London

Reda (1992, 1995) conducted an attitude survey of local residents around a newly opened supported house for the mentally ill in North London. The study group consisted of 100 of the immediate neighbours of the house. The control group comprised 100 residents of a road parallel to that of the study group.

Respondents were interviewed using a semi-structured interview before patients were discharged into the house and 6 months later.

Reda found that residents' attitudes showed little change over the period of the study. She postulated that this may have been because the patients were protected from contact with members of the public by the staff. Demographic variables exerted no effect on their attitudes. This is not in keeping with other studies and is probably an artefact of the lack of a suitably sensitive attitude variable. Although local residents strongly objected to hospital closure, they welcomed the opening of mental health facilities in their area. There was an untapped pool of goodwill in the community around a staffed group home. Of the neighbours interviewed, 68 per cent expressed a willingness to offer their help to the local facility. There was considerable ignorance about mental illness and 35 per cent of respondents were unable to distinguish between mental illness and mental handicap. They labelled the mentally ill as strange with poor communication and potentially hostile toward children and the public. Social factors were considered the most important cause of mental illness. Local residents expressed the desire to learn about mental illness.

One third knew somebody in a psychiatric hospital. An overwhelming majority of the local residents showed positive attitudes toward the opening of a mental health facility in their neighbourhood. They also showed an interest in offering help to the facility. They indicated that there are too few facilities for the promotion of mental health and that the government should remedy this. The study group said that the supported house caused no disturbances in the neighbourhood and that patients were accompanied by members of staff most of the time. There was little direct interaction between the local residents and the patients.

Half the residents knew about the decision to replace psychiatric hospitals through talking to friends. Community care was seen as isolating patients, lacking professional support, facilities and expertise. It was considered to be in the politicians' interests rather than the public interest in order to save money and achieve privatisation of the hospitals. This was inferred from the practice of ignoring public opinion and neglecting to inform them about the decision to close psychiatric hospitals. Local residents who preferred community care considered it more normal than hospital treatment and less stigmatising.

Local residents requested information on the background of the patients; the type of supervision they received; the facilities; and practical advice on how to approach patients and who to contact in case of trouble due to the presence of the facility.

Residents living with others showed a more positive reaction than those living alone. Females with children showed more interest in learning about mental illness than those without children.

A surprising finding of this study was the high proportion of respondents expressing willingness to help with local facilities (68 per cent) and a considerable desire for more information.

South London

West Lambeth Community Care (NHS) Trust has been responsible for implementing the closure of Tooting Bec Hospital. As a part of resettlement of patients from the hospital, around fifteen supported group homes have been opened. Prior to the opening of two of these houses, one in Herne Hill (in April 1993) and another in Streatham Hill (in July 1993), we conducted a study of public attitudes toward mental illness in the neighbours of these houses (Wolff et al, 1996a–c).

Respondents were asked about their knowledge of and attitudes towards mentally ill people and community care policy, and they were administered the "Community Attitudes to the Mentally Ill" (CAMI) inventory (Taylor and Dear, 1981). This is a forty statement inventory, subjects being required to rate each statement on a five-point scale (strongly agree, agree, neutral, disagree and strongly disagree). Subjects were also asked to complete a self-report inventory of questions about fear of and behavioural intentions toward the mentally ill constructed especially for this study. This was a ten item questionnaire with a five point response scale.

Most respondents had heard of community care policy but few knew about the imminent opening of local facilities. The majority agreed with long-stay patients being discharged into the community although a substantial minority thought it would have a bad effect. An overwhelming majority thought it was important for residents to be given information about new facilities, echoing the finding of the north London survey. Respondents were worried about inadequate support and dangerousness. If community care policy is to succeed, attention needs to be paid to the community's opinions.

Statistical analysis of underlying factors in the Community Attitudes toward the Mentally Ill (CAMI) inventory revealed three components: *fear and exclusion, social control* and *goodwill* (see Figure 10.2). Within each component, some items are phrased in a positive way and some in a negative way to avoid response bias.

A significant minority of respondents endorsed items indicating fearful and exclusive attitudes. Fifteen percent agreed, for example, that: "It is frightening to think of people with mental problems living in residential neighbourhoods" and 15 percent agreed that: "Residents have good reason to resist the location of mental health services in their neighbourhood."

A significant minority of respondents endorsed items indicating socially controlling attitudes. Fifteen percent agreed, for example, that: "As soon as a person shows signs of mental disturbance, he should be hospitalised."

The vast majority of respondents endorsed items indicating goodwill toward the mentally ill. Ninety five per cent agreed for example that: "We have a responsibility to provide the best possible care for the mentally ill."

An analysis of underlying factors was carried out on the CAMI scale and the relationship between these attitude components and sociodemographic factors

(a) Components of *fear and exclusion*
- Locating mental health facilities in residential neighbourhoods does not endanger local residents
- Residents have good reason to resist the location of mental health services in their neighbourhood.
- It is frightening to think of people with mental problems living in residential neighbourhoods.
- Residents have nothing to fear from people coming into their neighbourhood to obtain mental health services.
- Having mental patients living within residential neighbourhoods might be good therapy but the risks to residents are too great.
- Locating mental health facilities in a residential area downgrades the neighbourhood.
- I would not want to live next door to someone who has been mentally ill.
- Mental health facilities should be kept out of residential neighbourhoods.
- Residents should accept the location of mental health facilites in their neighbourhood to serve the needs of the local community.
- No one has the right to exclude the mentally ill from their neighbourhood.
- The mentally ill should be isolated from the rest of the community.

(b) Components of *social control*
- Mental patients need the same kind of control and discipline as a young child.
- One of the main causes of mental illness is lack of self-discipline and willpower.
- As soon as a person shows signs of mental disturbance, he should be hospitalised.
- Anyone with a history of mental problems should be excluded from public office.
- There is something about the mentally ill that makes it easy to tell them from normal people.
- The best way to handle the mentally ill is to keep them behind locked doors.

(c) Components of *goodwill*
- We have a responsibility to provide the best possible care for the mentally ill.
- We need to adopt a far more tolerant attitude toward the mentally ill.
- The mentally ill don't deserve our sympathy.

Figure 10.2 Components of fear and exclusion

was examined. The only determinant of *fear and exclusion* was having children. The main determinants of *social control* were: social class, ethnic origin, age, having suffered mental illness and having children. The main determinant of *goodwill* was educational level. The attitude factors were predictive of respondents' behavioural intentions toward the mentally ill. Respondents with children and non-whites were more likely to object to the mentally ill living in their neighbourhood.

It is important to understand that these factors are not mutually exclusive and people may hold a conflicting range of attitudes, including socially controlling, fearful and benevolent at the same time. This kind of paradox was observed by Somerset Maugham (1938) who wrote: "What has chiefly struck me in human beings is their lack of consistency. I have never seen people all of a piece. It has amazed me that the most incongruous traits should exist in the same person and for all that yield a plausible harmony.''

Although our three factors accounted for only 37.3 per cent of the variance, this is in keeping with Taylor and Dear's finding that only 42 per cent of the variance could be accounted for in their data by four factors.

Our *fear and exclusion, social control* and *goodwill* account for 79 per cent, 13 per cent and 9 per cent of the shared variance respectively compared with 39 per cent, 37 per cent and 23 per cent for the equivalent factors in Brockington and Hall's data. This suggests that fear of the mentally ill and their exclusion from residential areas may have been relatively more important in shaping attitudes in our sample compared with theirs.

The recent wave of media publicity concerning community care and dangerousness in psychiatric patients (especially in areas of London) may also have crystallised attitudes and bonded opinions more closely to underlying emotive issues such as personal safety (Brockington's data were collected in 1989 in the Midlands before these issues had come to the fore in the media).

Our data also differed in other important ways from those of Brockington and Hall (see below) and around a third of our respondents were aware of the facility about to open up on their doorstep. This may have accentuated the "NIMBY" (Not In My Back Yard) phenomenon. In addition, our population has been exposed to many people, whom they believe to be mentally ill, behaving oddly in the street, shouting or approaching them for money.

Most respondents (80 per cent) knew of somebody who had had a mental illness, but a substantial proportion of respondents had little knowledge about mental illness. *Social control* showed an association with knowledge of mental illness. Groups who showed more socially controlling attitudes (especially those over 50 years old, those of lower social class, and those of non-white ethnic origin) had less knowledge about mental illness. Regression analysis revealed that when knowledge was taken into account, age had no effect on *social control,* and the effect of social class and ethnic origin was diminished. Respondents with children, who showed more *fear and exclusion,* were not less knowledgeable about mental illness. Therefore, it would be expected that increasing knowledge should alter attitudes, except for those with children.

MALLEABILITY OF ATTITUDES

Introduction

There have been many studies of attitudes toward mental illness but little is known about the malleability of public attitudes or their effect on patients' general wellbeing or social integration. Only Cumming and Cumming (1957) in Canada and Gatherer and Reid (1963) in Northamptonshire have evaluated a public education campaign in local communities. Neither study was linked to a specific facility and both studies found education to be ineffective. Indeed, in

Cumming and Cumming's study, the community "closed ranks" against them and rejected the whole educational package. These attempts may have failed because they were unfocused and the public did not feel the *need to know*.

There is little evidence that any effort is currently made to inform or educate the public about specific local facilities and there have been no controlled studies of the effect of education linked to specific facilities. Indeed, new facilities tend to be established as unobtrusively as possible and with little, if any, public consultation, mainly due to the fear of provoking hostile attitudes from the community.

We conducted a study to investigate the malleability of public attitudes in the light of an educational campaign focused on a specific facility for the long term mentally ill, and the effect of the intervention on patients' social networks.

Educating People About Mental Illness: Information and Attitude Change

An integral part of psychosocial interventions for relatives of patients with schizophrenia has been an educational component including information on diagnosis, symptomatology, aetiology, treatment and course (e.g. Leff et al, 1982; Falloon et al, 1982; Anderson et al, 1982). However, even small changes in knowledge following an educational program for relatives of patients with schizophrenia were associated with important changes in attitude and behaviour toward patients (Berkowitz et al, 1984, 1990; Tarrier et al, 1988). Tarrier and Barrowclough (1986) suggest some tentative guidelines from their experience of providing information to relatives of patients with schizophrenia, namely: information should be *interactive, specific, selective, concise, reassessed,* and should be given *sooner rather than later*. However, a different strategy may be necessary in order to combat stigma in people who may well have had little or no contact with people with schizophrenia. Here, direct contact may well be essential. Penn et al (1994) suggest that the most important factor in reducing stigma is direct contact. They suggest that visits to ex-psychiatric patients in group homes may free individuals of negative perceptions. Indeed, in terms of reducing prejudice in general, Allport (1954) suggests what is most important is *acquaintance with* the field rather than *knowledge about* the field.

The purpose of educational campaigns is not merely to impart information but to effect an attitudinal change. It is unlikely that a campaign will succeed purely by the delivery of information. Indeed, in his influential work on the nature of prejudice, Allport (1954) asserted that *information seldom sticks unless mixed with attitudinal glue*. In order to structure a persuasive intervention, it is important to understand the factors, such as credibility and power of the source, and sociodemographic and personality variables of the receiver, which influence the effectiveness of persuasion. A good review of this field is provided by Burgoon et al (1994).

A Public Education Campaign to Alter Attitudes

Method

We conducted and evaluated a controlled study of a focused public education campaign for around 150 immediate neighbours of supported houses for the mentally ill (Wolff et al, 1996d).

The educational campaign comprised a primarily didactic component (an information pack containing a video and information sheets), a primarily social component (social events and social overtures from staff) and a mixed component (a formal reception and informal discussion sessions).

The reception, which took place about nine months after the facility opened, will be described below. Over the next nine months, the manager of the supported houses gradually contacted neighbours and offered them the information pack and the opportunity to discuss the material, ask any questions and to visit one of the houses.

This intervention utilised an important and under-utilised resource; the clinical teams involved in the day to day care of the mentally ill. The intervention may also address the problem of low morale and lack of training in carers in group homes identified by TAPS (see Chapter 9) and overcome staff reservations, identified during this study, about actively involving the neighbours in the process of patients' rehabilitation (Wolff et al, 1996d).

The video lasts about 20 minutes and includes the following: an introduction about the local services explaining where the patients came from and how many there are; the history and rationale of community care; what it is like for patients in a long-stay hospital and the difficulties of institutionalisation and readjusting to day-to-day living in the community and re-learning to make decisions; how people are chosen and prepared for care in the community (including screening out of patients with violent and sexually problematic behaviour) and how patients are treated and supported (including the role of the community support team and of medication); acknowledgement of neighbours' concerns about dangerousness and the safety of their children; experience of a local resident from north London who has befriended patients in a supported house in her area; local tradespeople from another area describing their experiences with patients; a former resident of a supported house in another area describing his experience of being transferred from hospital into supported accommodation. At the end of the video, neighbours are invited to make contact with the manager of the supported houses and with patients to give them a sense of belonging in the community.

The information sheets covered four topics: community care policy; mental illness; schizophrenia; and supported houses in West Lambeth. Names and contact numbers were provided for staff responsible for the running of the houses.

The reception was held in the local church hall. About twenty people attended. Drinks were served and neighbours were given the information sheets. Staff from the supported houses and the research team were present.

The video was introduced and shown. Questions were invited afterwards in a formal question-and-answer session with staff from the supported houses. Questions asked were as follows: How many residents are there in the houses? Who are they? Would residents resent neighbours going to visit? What staff are there in the homes? What carers have they got? How much independence do they have? What are they able to do for themselves? What are the houses like inside? What sort of layout do they have? Are the residents of the houses happier being out of hospital? Do some of them want to go back? Has there been any resentment or hostility about the houses in the street? Why couldn't there have been a meeting like this closer to the opening of the houses? Are they dangerous? What are the day-care opportunities, things they can do outside the houses? Why were these houses chosen? How much did they cost? Can the residents claim income support?

After the question-and-answer session, a buffet was served and staff mingled with neighbours giving a chance for informal discussion and the opportunity to meet other staff from the houses. This provided the manager of the houses with the opportunity to meet neighbours on a one-to-one basis, and to invite them to one of the houses, to encourage them to get to know patients and to speak to staff if they had any concerns or if they wished to get involved.

Neighbours commented that they appreciated the open and honest discussion. They thought the most useful things about the reception were meeting the staff, finding out about staffing arrangements and meeting other neighbours. Some commented that they would like to have met some of the patients or seen them on the video and seen the inside of the houses.

The discussion sessions following the reception were held in neighbours' homes. Neighbours were invited to watch the video and read the information sheets with a member of staff who provided an opportunity for discussion. The main issues they asked about were level of support and possibility of aggression. Neighbours were invited to visit the houses and were asked if they wished to befriend one of the patients. Most expressed interest in the houses and some expressed interest in befriending a patient.

Neighbours were invited to a barbecue and two other social events in the houses to meet staff and patients. Around fifteen people attended the social events.

Results

Respondents exposed to the didactic component of the campaign showed only a small increase in knowledge about mental illness. However, there was a significant lessening of fearful and rejecting attitudes (but not of socially controlling attitudes and goodwill) toward the mentally ill in the experimental area and not in the control area (see Table 10.1). The campaign was thus successful in reducing fear.

Neighbours in the experimental area were more likely to make social contact with both staff and patients. In the experimental area, 13 per cent of neighbours

Table 10.1 FEAR and EXCLUSION, SOCIAL CONTROL and GOODWILL at
baseline and follow-up in the two areas

	Baseline		Follow-up	
	Mean	SD	Mean	SD
Fear and exclusion				
Control area (*n* = 55)	2.13	0.73	2.11	0.74
Experimental area (*n* = 43)	2.25	0.75	1.97	0.60
RMANOVA[1] Area by *fear and exclusion; P*<0.05				
Social control				
Control area (*n* = 55)	2.17	0.71	2.20	0.74
Experimental area (*n* = 45)	2.16	0.65	2.08	0.57
RMANOVA Area by *social control;* not significant				
Goodwill				
Control area (*n* = 55)	4.34	0.49	4.35	0.53
Experimental area (*n* = 44)	4.32	0.45	4.27	0.56
RMANOVA Area by *goodwill;* not significant				

[1] Repeated measures analysis of variance (This statistical test examines the significance of
differences between areas over time controlling for baseline differences).
Reproduced from Wolff et al (1996b) by permission of the Royal College of Psychiatrists.

had made friends with patients or invited them into their homes, whereas none
of the control neighbours had done so. Furthermore, 28 per cent of the
neighbours in the experimental area but only 8 per cent of the control
neighbours had visited patients. The remaining 60 per cent of the neighbours in
the experimental area and 92 per cent of the neighbours in the control area had
lesser contact [chi^2 = 17.72; 2 d.f.; *p* <0.001]. It was social contact with
patients which was directly associated with improved attitudes rather education
per se.

More than half the patients in the experimental area (5/8) but none in the
control area (0/6) made regular social contacts with neighbours including
friendships (chi^2 = 5.8; 1 d.f.; *p* <0.05. Fisher's exact test).

DISCUSSION

Difficulties in mounting the campaign

The educational campaign was planned in consultation with staff from the
supported houses in Streatham Hill. However, various problems arose. Some
staff objected to the educational campaign in principle on the grounds of
normalisation ideology; they were concerned that it might draw attention to the
patients and that there was no reason to encourage their integration into the
community as they were just the same as anybody else and they should not be

labelled as mentally ill. These issues are not peculiar to this study. Marks (1994) commented on the re-emergence of anti-psychiatry in the non-medical professions that make up the major part of our community mental health services.

Others didn't believe that neighbours were interested and didn't feel it would have any beneficial effects for the patients. Practical considerations such as staffing levels often made it difficult for staff to find time to put into the project. These problems needed addressing at various stages as the project progressed. Thus time needed to be spent with staff providing explanation of the rationale of the study and on feedback about the very positive response from the neighbours.

At baseline, an overwhelming number of respondents (91 per cent) had expressed a desire for information (Wolff et al, 1996a). However, only around a third (34/102) of the sample in the experimental area took up the offer of educational material.

Possible confounding factors. This was an opportunistic study with the experimenters having no control over the siting or structure of the services or number or level of disability of the residents in the houses. It may be, therefore, that there were confounding characteristics in the facilities themselves or in the neighbours in the two areas. However, it seems unlikely that these confounding variables significantly influenced the results.

Outcome of the attitude survey. The results of the follow-up survey suggest that although the public education intervention may have had, at best, only a modest effect on knowledge, it is associated with an improvement in overall attitudes and behaviour toward the mentally ill (with a decrease in fear and exclusion and increased levels of social contact) in the experimental area. This is consistent with the finding of Berkowitz et al (1990) who found that even small changes in knowledge following an educational program for relatives of patients with schizophrenia were associated with important changes in attitude and behaviour toward patients.

However, the education campaign did not, in itself lead directly to less fearful attitudes, whereas contact with patients did. It is likely, therefore, that the campaign exerted its effect on overall attitudes indirectly by encouraging contact with patients. Such contact may well exert its effect on attitudes, in part, by the reassurance such contact gives about the two main concerns of neighbours about new facilities in their area. These concerns are to do with wanting to know whether the patients are adequately supported and whether or not they are likely to be dangerous (see Wolff et al, 1996a).

Patients' assessments. The findings from the attitude survey are clearly supported by the patients' accounts, with several of the patients in the experimental area but none in the control area reporting having made contact with and even friendships with neighbours. Indeed, two out of eight of the patients in the experimental area interviewed at follow-up had made friendships with neighbours. To put this in context, about a third of all neighbours had reported at baseline interview that they had made friendships with other neighbours. Sadly, when asked about whether he had any contact with neighbours, one ex-patient in the control area replied: "Of course not, how can I see the neighbours, this is a psychiatric unit, not a private home." Perhaps patients also need to be involved in discussion regarding their perception of their position in the community.

Suggestions

The intervention is fairly time consuming but it can be taken at a slow pace and any effort expended has a knock-on effect as there is an indirect dissemination of information from neighbour to neighbour. This is important given that a significant number of neighbours were not directly reached by the campaign.

In order to make the maximum continuing impact with the minimum outlay in time and effort the following suggestions may be helpful. Firstly, it may be useful to target groups with the most negative attitudes. People with children in the household and Africans and Caribbeans, for example, are the groups which are more likely to object to the mentally ill in the community (Wolff et al, 1996b).

Secondly, repeating the reception for people who could not attend the first time and seeing neighbours together rather than individually may well allow the campaign to reach a greater proportion of the local population without taking up excessive time.

Thirdly, it may be better to see neighbours in small groups, as research has shown that it is easier to change attitudes in individuals formed in a group (Lewin, 1952) and the changes are more permanent (Olmsted, 1959).

Fourthly, momentum in campaigns is of vital importance. The effect on attitudes of several interventions is greater than the sum of the effect of each (Allport, 1954). In order to keep up momentum it is important to have an enthusiastic staff member who will continue the campaign and it may be useful to organise interested neighbours to become befrienders and to help with continuing liaison with neighbours both new and established. Only then is it likely that long-stay patients leaving the institutions will achieve some degree of social integration into the neighbourhoods in which they live.

SUMMARY AND CONCLUSIONS

There is clearly a great deal of goodwill toward the mentally ill in the community, but a significant minority hold fearful, exclusive and socially controlling attitudes. These attitudes clearly have a bearing on community care policy, which has come under intense criticism in the aftermath of several high-profile cases involving the failure of community care in individual cases. These cases were extensively reported in the media and there is a danger of the pendulum of public attitudes swinging back too far towards institutional control if they are not given a balanced view.

Fear of a backlash as experienced by Cumming and Cumming (1957) or a hardening of attitudes by an educational intervention are clearly not borne out by our experience of conducting a public education campaign. Moreover, it improved attitudes even against the background of largely negative portrayal by the media.

The campaign probably exerted an effect because the intervention was focused on an area around a specific facility. We hope this may well pave the way to greater openness and involvement of local residents around new or existing facilities in the future and encourage others to explore similar ways of improving patients' social integration.

REFERENCES

Allport, G.W. (1954) *The Nature of Prejudice*. Addison-Wesley, New York.

Anderson, C., Hogarty, G.E. and Reiss, D. (1982) The psychoeducational family treatment of schizophrenia. In M.J. Goldstein (ed.) *New Developments in Interventions with Families of Schizophrenics*, Jossey Bass, San Francisco.

Barnes, R.C. (1993) Mental illness in British newspapers (or My girlfriend is a Rover Metro). *Psychiatric Bulletin*, 17, 673–674.

Belson, W.A. (1957) The Hurt Mind. Audience research report, BBC.

Berkowitz, R., Eberlein-Fries, R., Kuipers, L. and Leff, J. (1984) Educating relatives about schizophrenia. *Schizophrenia Bulletin*, 10(3), 418–428.

Berkowitz, R., Shavit, N. and Leff, J.P. (1990) Educating relatives of schizophrenic patients. *Social Psychiatry and Psychiatric Epidemiology*, 25, 216–220.

Bhugra, D. (1989) Attitudes towards mental illness. A review of the literature. *Acta Psychiatrica Scandinavica*, 80, 1–12.

Bhugra, D. and Scott, J. (1989) The public image of psychiatry—a pilot study. *Bulletin of the Royal College of Psychiatrists*, 13, 330–333.

Brockington, I.F., Hall, P.H., Levings, J. and Murray, C. (1993) The community's tolerance of the Mentally Ill. *British Journal of Psychiatry*, 162, 93–99.

Brockman, J., D'Arcy, C. and Edmonds, L. (1979) Facts or artifacts? Changing public attitudes towards the mentally ill. *Social Science and Medicine*, 13A, 673–682.

Burgoon, M., Hunsaker, F.G. and Dawson, E.J. (1994) *Human Communication*. Sage, London.

Crandall, C.S. and Moriarty, D. (1995) Physical illness, stigma and social rejection. *British Journal of Social Psychology*, 34(1), 67–83.

Crocker, J. and Major B. (1989) Social stigma and self esteem: The self-protective properties of stigma. *Psychological Review*, 96(4), 608–630.

Cumming, E. and Cumming, J. (1957) *Closed Ranks—An Experiment in Mental Health Education*. Harvard University Press.

Dain, N. (1994) Reflections on antipsychiatry and stigma in the history of American Psychiatry. *Hospital and Community Psychiatry*, 45(10), 1010–1014.

Dayson, D. (1993) The TAPS Project. 12: Crime, vagrancy, death and readmission of the long-term mentally ill during their first year of local reprovision. *British Journal of Psychiatry*, 162 (suppl. 19), 40–44.

Falloon, I.R.H., Boyd, J.L., McGill, C.W., Razani, J., Moss, H. and Gilderman, A.M. (1982) Family therapy of schizophrenics with high risk of relapse. *New England Journal of Medicine*, 306, 1437–1440.

Foucault, M. (1991) *Madness and Civilisation. A history of insanity in the age of reason.* (trans. Richard Howard) Routledge, London.

Gatherer, A. and Reid, J.J.A. (1963) Public attitudes and mental health education. *Northamptonshire Mental Health Project.*

Hahn, H. (1988) The politics of physical differences: disability and discrimination. Journal of *Social Issues,* **44,** 39–48.

Huxley, P. (1993a) Location and Stigma: A survey of community attitudes to mental illness Part I. Enlightenment and stigma. *Journal of Mental Health,* **2,** 73–80.

Huxley, P. (1993b) Location and Stigma: A survey of community attitudes to mental illness Part II: Community mental health facilities—anonymity or invisibility. *Journal of Mental Health,* **2,** 157–164.

Leff, J.P., Kuipers, L., Berkowitz, R., Eberlein-Vries, R. and Sturgeon, D. (1982) A controlled trial of social intervention in the families of schizophrenic patients. *British Journal of Psychiatry,* **141,** 121–134.

Lewin, K. (1952) Group decision and social change. In G. Swanston, T. Newcomb and E. Hartley (eds) *Readings in Social Psychology.* Henry Holt & Co., New York.

Loam, O. and Egan, M. (1990) Public perceptions of psychiatric services, *Nursing Times,* **86**(28), 56.

Maclean, U. (1969) Community attitudes to mental illness in Edinburgh. *British Journal of Preventive and Social Medicine,* **23,** 45–52

Marks, J. (1994) The re-emergence of antipsychiatry. *Hospital Update,* **20**(4), 187–190.

Murphy, B., Black, P., Duffy, M., Kieran, J. and Mallon, J. (1993) Attitudes towards the mentally ill in Ireland, *Irish Journal of Psychological Medicine,* **10**(2), 75–79.

Newsnight (1993) with Jeremy Paxman. 30 June, BBC2.

O'Driscoll, C., Wills, W., Leff, J. and Margolius, O. (1993) The TAPS Project 10: The long stay populations of Friern and Claybury Hospitals, *British Journal of Psychiatry,* **162** (supp. 19), 30–55.

Ojanen, M. (1992) Attitudes towards mental patients. *The International Journal of Social Psychiatry,* **38**(2), 120–130.

Olmsted, M.S. (1959) *The Small Group.* Random House, New York.

Penn, D.L., Guynan, K., Daily, T., Spaulding, W.D., Garbin, C.P. and Sullivan, M. (1994) Dispelling the stigma of schizophrenia: What sort of information is best? *Schizophrenia Bulletin,* **20**(3), 567–578.

Philo, G. (1994) Media images and popular beliefs, *Psychiatric Bulletin,* **18,** 173–174.

Porter, R. (1987a) *Mind Forg'd Manacles.* Athlone, London.

Porter, R. (1987b) *A Social History of Madness.* Weidenfeld and Nicolson, London.

Rabkin, J. (1974) Public attitudes toward mental illness: a review of the literature. *Schizophrenia Bulletin,* **10,** 9–33.

Rabkin, J.G., Muhlin, G. and Cohen, P.W. (1984) What the neighbours think: community attitudes towards local psychiatric facilities, *Community Mental Health Journal,* **20**(4), 304–312.

Reda, S. (1992) *The Discharge of Long Stay Psychiatric Patients into the Community: A Study of the Patients, the Staff and the Public,* PhD thesis, Institute of Psychiatry, University of London.

Reda, S. (1995) Attitudes towards community mental health care of residents in North London. *Psychiatric Bulletin,* **19,** 731–733.

Richards, K. (1982) A mind disordered: The Public View. *Nursing Mirror,* Oct 13, 55–56.

Rubin, Z. and Peplau, L. (1975) Who believes in a just world? *Journal of Social Issues,* **31,** 65–89.

Scheff, T.J. (1963) The role of the mentally ill and the dynamics of mental disorder: a research framework. *Sociometry,* **26,** 436–453.

Scheff, T.J. (1966) *Being Mentally Ill. A Sociological Theory.* Aldine, Chicago.

Somerset Maugham, W. (1938) *The Summing Up.* Pan, London.

Stein, H.F. (1979) Rehabilitation and chronic illness in American culture. *Journal of*

Psychological Anthropology, **2**, 153–176.

Tarrier, N. and Barrowclough, C. (1986) Providing Information to Relatives About Schizophrenia: Some Comments. *British Journal of Psychiatry*, **149**, 458–463.

Tarrier N., Barrowclough C., Vaughn C., Bamrah J.S., Porceddu K., Watts S. and Freeman H. (1988) The Community Management of Schizophrenia: A Controlled Trial of a Behavioural Intervention with Families to Reduce Relapse. *British Journal of Psychiatry*, **153**, 532–542.

Taylor, S.M. (1988) Community reactions to deinstitutionalisation. In C.J. Smith and J.A. Giggs (eds). *Location and Stigma: Contemporary Perspectives on Mental Health Care.* Unwin Hyman, London.

Taylor, M.S. and Dear, M.J. (1981) Scaling community attitudes toward the mentally ill. *Schizophrenia Bulletin*, 7(2), 225–240.

Willcocks, A. (1968) Cited by: Anon (1968) Public attitudes to mental health education. Editorial. *British Medical Journal*, 5584, 69–70.

Wolff, G., Pathare, S., Craig, T. and Leff, J. (1996a) Who's in the lions' den? The community's perception of community care for the mentally ill. *Psychiatric Bulletin*, 20(2), 68–71.

Wolff, G., Pathare, S., Craig, T. and Leff, J. (1996b) Community attitudes to mental illness. *British Journal of Psychiatry*, **168**, 183–190.

Wolff, G., Pathare, S., Craig, T. and Leff, J. (1996c) Community knowledge of mental illness and reaction to mentally ill people. *British Journal of Psychiatry*, **168**, 191–198.

Wolff, G., Pathare, S., Craig, T. and Leff, J. (1996d) Public education for community care: a new approach. *British Journal of Psychiatry*, **168**, 441–447.

Zubin, J., Oppenheimer, G. and Neugebauer, R. (1985) Degeneration theory and the stigma of schizophrenia. *Biological Psychiatry*, **20**, 1145–1148.

Part III

The Pitfalls
and
How to Avoid Them

Chapter 11

THE DOWNSIDE OF REPROVISION

Julian Leff
Team for the Assessment of Psychiatric Services (TAPS); Institute of Psychiatry

INADEQUATE ACCOMMODATION

In the process of observing programmes for reprovision, we have often noticed that expedient solutions to problems take precedence over optimal ones, even when the latter have initially been incorporated in the plans. For example, one response to economic pressure is to abandon plans for new buildings and instead to adapt existing structures. In one of the health districts responsible for the Friern reprovision, plans to build a new admission facility to replace the old admission wards in the hospital and elsewhere were jettisoned, and a former ear hospital was utilised to create psychiatric admission wards. As we described in Chapter 8, patients much preferred the equivalent wards in Friern hospital both on account of the noise level and the availability of external grounds.

During the 1970s and 1980s an opportunity was seen to provide cheap accommodation for long-stay patients by utilising seaside boarding houses. These are usually empty during the winter and many of them close down until the summer season. Hence the offer of permanent residents all the year round, albeit suffering from psychiatric illnesses, was understandably attractive to their owners. The economic advantage of this strategy was, however, greatly outweighed by the failure to provide for many of the basic needs of the patients (Barnes and Thornicroft, 1993). There is a paucity of suitable work opportunities for patients during the summer season and none in the winter. In terms of leisure activities, there are few places as desolate as an English seaside resort out of season. Television documentaries dealing with this situation presented unforgettable images of psychiatric patients in raincoats wandering along deserted rainswept promenades. Patients discharged to these seaside locations were even further from their districts of origin than they had been in the psychiatric hospitals.

Care in the Community: Illusion or Reality?
Edited by Julian Leff. © 1997 John Wiley & Sons Ltd.

TRAINING OF CARE STAFF

Perhaps the most disastrous deficiency in the service provided was the failure to give any training to the people who ran the boarding houses. They were managing a commercial venture, the main motive for which was to make a profit. They were contracted to provide accommodation and meals, and their responsibilities extended no further than this. Patients' needs for occupational and recreational facilities were unfulfilled.

A parallel situation developed in the US around the provision of board and care, but on a vaster scale. Whereas only a small proportion of British patients were discharged to seaside boarding houses, in America, board and care was the mainstay of deinstitutionalisation programmes. This form of providing care for profit developed into a major industry with a turnover of $16 billion per year (Brown, 1985). As in Britain, no training in the care of the mentally ill was offered the purveyors of board and care, and very little or nothing was provided for patients' occupational and recreational needs. Furthermore, some instances came to light in which greed for profit led to patients being housed in inhumane conditions and fed inadequately.

The failures of these policies in the US and Britain became public scandals, but we need to record one development that met with limited success.

When the "dowry" arrangement for Friern and Claybury patients was instituted, it attracted the interest of some psychiatric nurses working in the two hospitals. They established houses for up to four patients which they ran themselves. The upper limit was four because above that a home would have to be registered and be subject to various regulations. The nurses usually kept their jobs in the hospitals and ran the homes as an extra responsibility. This meant that they could only spend a limited amount of time with the patients. However, they could usually arrange for the patients to attend a day centre during the weekdays. Obviously they had appropriate training and experience to look after the patients, and an additional advantage was that they often knew the patients very well. This came about because they themselves selected patients they knew to live in their homes. These entrepreneurial activities flourished in the early phase of the reprovision programme and then petered out as the more disabled patients began to be discharged. These patients required more daily supervision than could be provided by the nurses, who were still doing jobs in the hospitals.

These examples highlight the issue of training for carers of patients with severe mental illness. It is unreasonable to expect family members to look after such patients without giving them information about the nature of the illnesses concerned and training in how to handle the problems that arise daily (Kuipers et al, 1992). It is equally irrational to expect unrelated carers to cope without training, whether they are running a home for profit or employed in sheltered accommodation managed by an organisation (see Chapter 9). The contents of training programmes need to be focused on the common problems encountered in sheltered accommodation, particularly coping with negative symptoms. We have found that professional staff can be just as critical of these behaviours as family members.

Private care in itself is not necessarily to be decried as failing to provide a therapeutic environment. The observations made by the Commissioners in Lunacy in their Report of 1847 are as relevant today as they were 150 years ago: "We are fully convinced that the Lunatic Poor of England will never be altogether properly provided for, until Public Asylums for the benefit of every County shall have been erected. At the same time we must observe that there are some private Asylums in which the pauper patient is exceedingly well taken care of, and is as judiciously treated as in County Asylums; whilst on the other hand, there are a few County Asylums which are inferior to many licensed houses." Nevertheless, when the motive for providing care is profit, there is a temptation to cut corners, and adequate training of staff is readily omitted. In the board and care programme in the US this sometimes led to disastrous consequences, but this can be equally true in non-profit organisations, as the Jonathan Newby Inquiry of 1995 found. An expert witness giving evidence to this inquiry into the homicide of a volunteer worker by a psychotic patient commented that there had been "a total absence of nationally agreed programmes and qualifications for the majority of the workforce" in the residential care field (p. 133). The Inquiry considered that the position in the voluntary sector was particularly bad as a result of cost constraints, the difficulty in releasing staff for training, and the *ad hoc* nature of many of the courses on offer. The important message is that no body setting up sheltered accommodation for the severely mentally ill can afford to neglect the provision of appropriate training for its staff.

HOMELESSNESS

One of the most poignant sights of the western city today is the large number of homeless people of all ages sleeping on the streets throughout the year. Wrapped in newspapers, layers of old clothes, blankets, plastic bags, constructing cardboard cities, they cannot fail to raise our compassion and to prompt questions about the origins of this public scandal. Some of them are obviously abusing alcohol, some are young people with no evident mental health problem, while others, garbed strangely, talking or shouting to the air, or pushing supermarket trolleys containing their worldly possessions, are "mad" by the standards of the public. The media have repeatedly blamed the closure of mental hospitals for the alarming increase in the visibility of the mentally ill on the streets. In investigating this allegation we first need to ask whether there has indeed been an increase in the homeless mentally ill.

It is very difficult to obtain an accurate figure for the number of homeless people in a city, because it is not possible to cover in a census all the places in which they could be sleeping; derelict houses, cars, doorways. However, using its restrictive definition of homelessness, the Department of the Environment estimated that the number of homeless families in England more than doubled over the decade to 1992, reaching 146 000. Shelter, a voluntary housing organisation, has estimated that this represents at least 420 000 people. Among western European countries, Great Britain has the largest and most visible homeless population (Toro and Rojansky, 1990). The salience of this problem in the UK is partly attributable to a major reduction in the availability of low-rent accommodation. The number of new council homes built fell from 160 000 in 1975 to 15 000 in 1990 (Greve, 1991), and there was a 60 per cent reduction in the amount of accommodation available for renting (Mariasy, 1987). Losses also occurred from the existing stock through the policy of selling council properties to tenants. The right-to-buy policy led to 1.5 million homes being sold during the 1980s (Gay, 1989). The rise in interest rates resulted in some new owners being unable to meet the mortgage repayments and subsequently having their homes repossessed. In 1987, evictions due to mortgage default or rent arrears accounted for approximately 13 per cent of homelessness (Central Statistics Office, 1989). These trends have been compounded by a reduction in direct access (i.e. self-referral) hostel beds in recent years. Resettlement units run by the Department of Health have all been closed, but the plan to replace them with smaller hostels provided by local authorities and voluntary organisations has not been achieved (Her Majesty's Stationery Office, 1991). Direct access beds have also disappeared from the voluntary sector by the conversion of charitable housing to commercial ventures, for example the metamorphosis of Rowton Houses to hotels, and the closure of some Salvation Army hostels. In all, there has been a 75 per cent reduction in direct access hostel beds over the last decade (Craig and Timms, 1992).

The next question is whether the rise in the number of homeless has been accompanied by a disproportionate increase in the number of mentally ill in their ranks. A number of surveys of the homeless have been conducted in recent years to determine the proportion of the mentally ill. An early study of the Camberwell Reception Centre, a direct access hostel now closed, found that 29 per cent of the residents were suffering from a severe psychiatric disorder, excluding those with alcohol abuse (Tidmarsh and Wood, 1972). Twenty years later, Timms and Fry (1989) surveyed the men arriving at a Salvation Army hostel and found that a quarter were suffering from schizophrenia. In a report published in the same year, Stark et al (1989) interviewed users of a resettlement unit with structured instruments. They found that the prevalence of psychosis ranged between 20 per cent and 30 per cent. Since the 1970s, surveys of homeless people in residential settings have estimated the prevalence of severe mental illness at between 25 per cent and 45 per cent. Hence there is no suggestion that the proportion of severely mentally ill among the homeless has increased over the past 20 years. Therefore the increased presence of the mentally ill on the streets must be a direct consequence of the increased number of homeless people. The mentally ill have few financial resources and so suffer the fate of others at the lowest socio-economic levels when low-rent accommodation becomes scarce.

This interpretation is supported by our own study of long-stay patients discharged from psychiatric hospitals (see Chapter 5). We found that only seven out of nearly 700 became homeless in the first year, and of the 340 followed up for five years, no further patients were lost. In a similar study of the closure of Cane Hill hospital in south London, of 103 long-stay patients followed up one year after discharge, none had become homeless (Pickard et al, 1991), and in a comparable study of Tooting Bec hospital, only one of 150 patients adopted anything resembling a vagrant life-style (Craig and Timms, 1992). These findings suggest that patients discharged after long stays in psychiatric hospitals are making only a small contribution to the homeless population.

Confirmation of this is provided by some studies of the homeless mentally ill which have enquired about their psychiatric history. A study of people using a shelter in Boston found that of the 30 users suffering from a psychosis, only five had spent longer than five years in total in a psychiatric hospital (Bassuk et al, 1984). A survey of 124 homeless men using a Salvation Army shelter found that over half were suffering from psychiatric disorders but only seven had spent more than a year in hospital (Timms and Fry, 1989). In an experimental study of a case management service for homeless mentally ill people, only two out of 94 clients referred in a year reported an admission to a psychiatric hospital of longer than one year (Brent-Smith and Dean, 1990). During the first year of the London homeless mentally ill initiative 544 homeless people were identified as suffering from severe mental illness. Of these, only three had experienced a continuous hospital admission lasting five years or more (Craig and Timms, 1992). All these studies show that the great majority of the homeless mentally ill have spent only short periods of time as psychiatric inpatients.

If the discharge of thousands of long-stay patients from psychiatric institutions is not the cause of the rise in the number of mentally ill living on the streets, what is their origin? The answer must lie in the inadequacy of after-care for patients passing through the admission wards. The difficulty of finding appropriate accommodation to discharge patients to, and the pressure of patients waiting to be admitted (see Chapter 8), inevitably lead to insufficient planning for after-care. A study of single homeless people with psychiatric histories by the Policy Studies Institute found that two-thirds of psychiatric patients had left admission wards without discussing with staff where they would go on discharge (Medical Campaign Project, 1990). Patients were often discharged to "bed and breakfast" or emergency accommodation, and were not pursued vigorously if they failed to attend outpatient appointments. The introduction in 1993 of the Care Programme Approach (CPA) for vulnerable patients was meant to lower the chance of their falling out of care. The CPA requires staff responsible for a patient's care to ensure that he/she has appropriate accommodation to go to, a psychiatrist who will monitor his/her medication, and a named key worker, often a community psychiatric nurse, who will endeavour to keep in touch with him/her. Time will tell whether this enforced discharge planning will have the desired effect of preventing patients from drifting into homelessness. Another development which may help is the introduction of sectorisation by many health authorities, and now NHS trusts. Patients living in a sector, however resistant they may be to engagement by the sector mental health teams, remain their responsibility, and cannot be passed on to someone else.

PREVENTION OF THE DRIFT INTO HOMELESSNESS

We saw in Chapter 5 that of the small number of long-stay patients who became homeless in the first year after discharge, the majority had a prior history of vagrancy. It seems that a vagrant life has its attractions for patients who have once experienced it. Alternatively, it may be that such patients have become intolerant of social contact and prefer not to live with other people. It is noteworthy, however, that no patient in our sample drifted away from staffed housing and fell out of contact. There is a clear lesson from this that patients with a previous history of vagrancy require supervised accommodation, which may well prevent further episodes of homelessness.

Another approach to prevention is to intervene at the very beginning of the process. The problem with this notion is that we remain ignorant of the factors which lead the mentally ill to sever contact with their social networks and drift into a vagrant existence. This gap needs to be filled by reconstructing the life histories of the homeless mentally ill, but in the absence of these data we can at least make some educated guesses.

Studies of the childhood histories of homeless people indicate a high prevalence of institutional care (Bassuk, 1984). This is often the result of parental neglect and/or physical and sexual abuse leading the authorities to remove the child from their home. In a study of homeless psychiatric patients, Herzberg (1987) found a history of separation from parents of over three years in half the sample. These findings suggest that disruption of parent–child relationships has the long-lasting effect in some individuals of attenuating the formation of bonds and facilitating the drift into vagrancy.

In the case of patients with an established schizophrenic illness the nature of family relationships has been illuminated by the use of the Expressed Emotion (EE) measure (Leff and Vaughn, 1985). When relatives in the household are highly critical of the patient, relapse of schizophrenia is more likely (Vaughn and Leff, 1976). Patients tend to respond to criticism from a relative either with social withdrawal or with anger. If the latter, then conflict usually escalates to the point of verbal or physical aggression, since high EE relatives are unable to defuse arguments.

In a study of 100 consecutive referrals to Resettlement Units, Scott (personal communication) found that the main reason given for homelessness was family disputes. The same finding has emerged from a study of young homeless persons in London (Craig, personal communication). It is likely, therefore, that for some schizophrenic sufferers, the path to homelessness begins when family conflicts lead to ejection from the home or voluntary departure. Whereas it is difficult to conceive of ways of ameliorating the effects of early separation from parents and of institutional care, work with high EE families has proved to be efficacious (Leff et al, 1985, 1990). Intervention is particularly effective in modifying criticism. Hence there is good reason to work with families as soon as feasible once a diagnosis of schizophrenia has been made in one of the members. The aim is not necessarily to maintain the patient in the family home indefinitely. Indeed one of the prime aims is to assist the patient to achieve independence from her/his parents. However, work on this issue is directed at accomplishing a separation in which the relationship between patient and parents alters but remains intact, so that the patient retains her/his natural support network. Thus we would argue that work with families in the early stages of a schizophrenic illness may prevent some patients from taking the path that leads to social isolation and homelessness.

REFERENCES

Barnes, J. and Thornicroft, G. (1993) The last resort? Bed and breakfast accommodation for mentally ill people in a seaside town. *Health Trends*, 25(3), 87–90.

Bassuk, E.L. (1984) The homeless problem. *Scientific American*, 6, 40–45.

Bassuk, E.L., Rubin, L. and Lauriat, A.S. (1984) Is homelessness a mental health problem? *American Journal of Psychiatry*, 141, 1546–1550.

Brent-Smith, H. and Dean, R. (1990) *Plugging the Gaps*. Lewisham and North Southwark Health Authority, Lewisham.

Brown, P. (1985) *The Transfer of Care: Psychiatric Deinstitutionalisation and its Aftermath*. Routledge and Kegan Paul, Henley-on-Thames.

Central Statistics Office (1989) *Social Trends*, 19. HMSO, London.

Craig, T. and Timms, P.W. (1992) Out of the wards and onto the streets? Deinstitutionalization and homelessness in Britain. *Journal of Mental Health*, 1, 265–275.

Gay, O. (1989) *Homeless*. Background Paper No.229. House of Commons Research Division, London.

Greve, J. (1991) *Homelessness in Britain*. Joseph Rowntree Foundation, York.

Her Majesty's Stationery Office (1991) The Resettlement Units Executive Agency. *Annual report and financial statement 1990/91*. HMSO, London.

Herzberg, J. (1987) No fixed abode: a comparison of men and women admitted to an East London psychiatric hospital. *British Journal of Psychiatry*, 150, 621–627.

Kuipers, L., Leff, J. and Lam, D. (1992) *Family Work for Schizophrenia: A Practical Guide*. Gaskell, London.

Leff, J.P. and Vaughn, C.E. (1985) *Expressed Emotion in Families: Its Significance for Mental Illness*. Guilford, London.

Leff, J., Kuipers, L., Berkowitz, R. and Sturgeon, D. (1985) A controlled trial of social intervention in the families of schizophrenic patients: two year follow-up. *British Journal of Psychiatry*, 146, 594–600.

Leff, J., Berkowitz, R., Shavit, N., Strachan, A., Glass, I. and Vaughn, C. (1990) A trial of family therapy versus a relatives' group for schizophrenia, two year follow-up. *British Journal of Psychiatry*, **157**, 571–577.

Mariasy, J. (1987) Young people and homelessness. *Everywoman*, November, p. 12.

Medical Campaign Project (1990) *A Paper Outlining Good Practice on Discharge of Single Homeless People with Particular Reference to Mental Health Units*. Policy Studies Institute, London.

Pickard, L., Proudfoot, R. and Wolfson, P. (1991) *The Closure of Cane Hill Hospital: Report of the Cane Hill Evaluation Team*. Research and Development in Psychiatry, London.

Stark, C., Scott, J., Hill, M. and Morgan, W. (1989) *A Survey of the "Long-stay" Users of DSS Resettlement Units. A Research Report*. Department of Social Security, London.

Tidmarsh, D. and Wood, S. (1972) Psychiatric aspects of destitution: the Camberwell Reception Centre. In J.K. Wing and A.M. Hailey (eds) *Evaluating a Community Psychiatric Service*. Oxford University Press, London.

Timms, P.W. and Fry A. H. (1989) Homelessness and mental illness, *Health Trends*, **21**, 70–71.

Toro, P. and Rojansky, A. (1990) Homelessness: Some thoughts from an international perspective. *The Community Psychologist*, **24**, 8–11.

Vaughn, C. and Leff, J.P. (1976) The measurement of expressed emotion in families of psychiatric patients. *British Journal of Psychiatry*, **129**, 428–42.

Chapter 12

PATIENTS WHO ARE TOO DIFFICULT TO MANAGE IN THE COMMUNITY

Noam Trieman
Team for the Assessment of Psychiatric Services (TAPS)

A few horrific incidents, in which mentally ill persons were involved, have shaken the British public over the last few years. A notorious incident involved Christopher Clunis, a paranoid schizophrenic who unprovokedly killed a man by stabbing him in the eye on a London underground platform in 1993. The victim's widow, Jayne Zito, has formed a trust to campaign for a national support network for seriously mentally ill people. Another incident was that of Ben Silcock, a schizophrenic patient who climbed into the lions' enclosure at London Zoo in 1992 and was badly mauled. A third incident was the murder of Jonathan Newby, aged 22, an inexperienced voluntary worker who was left in charge of a hostel and was stabbed to death by one of the residents.

The three tragedies bear in common the demonic quality of acts beyond control. They echo the public's deepest fears of the "madman" and reconfirm the stigma in their mind. Metaphorically, it is the lion, incompetently guarded, who gets out of his cage, free to attack his innocent victim. In seeking some sense in these senseless events people tend to direct all the blame on "care in the community". The messages delivered by the media are often swift, over-simplistic and unequivocal, much like the front page headlines in the *Daily Express* (17 August 1994), following the publication of a report on this matter: "34 PATIENTS WHO WERE FREED TO KILL."

ARE THE MENTALLY ILL MORE LIABLE TO COMMIT HOMICIDES THAN OTHERS?

In 1989–90, there were 235 100 admissions to inpatient psychiatric facilities in England and Wales, of which 16 890 were formally detained under the Mental Health Act 1983. During this period there were 525 homicides (Home Office,

Care in the Community: Illusion or Reality?
Edited by Julian Leff. © 1997 John Wiley & Sons Ltd.

1993), somewhat less than the average 600–700 cases of homicide which are committed each year in this country. Preliminary findings of an inquiry into homicides by mentally ill people (Department of Health, 1994) showed that of 100 perpetrators with a psychiatric background, identified over 18 months, nearly two thirds had a psychotic illness. Thirty four cases were in some contact with the psychiatric service during the 12 months before homicide. Only one case was an inpatient at the time he committed the offence, the remainder were outpatients. Most perpetrators were males, the majority of victims were family members or otherwise acquainted with the offender. Among the female perpetrators, all but one were mothers who killed their children.

There are different ways to interpret these figures; The committee's report asserts that: "Homicide committed by psychiatrically ill people is very rare indeed in relation to the numbers of such persons who are admitted to hospital." This perspective highlights the fact that while hundreds of thousands of people are in contact with the psychiatric services each year, only a very small minority are involved in major crimes. However, the figures given above seem to indicate that the chance of a person diagnosed with schizophrenia committing a homicide is higher than for a non-schizophrenic person. This realisation may particularly stigmatise people with schizophrenia. In absolute terms, however, most serious assaults are committed by people considered by legal standards to be sane. Moreover, some other subtle mental pathologies, notably personality disorders, are associated to a greater extent than schizophrenia with serious tendency towards assault. We may cautiously conclude that people with severe mental illness indeed constitute a risk group, yet the absolute number of patients who have a propensity to extreme acts of violence is small, certainly smaller than it appears to be in the eyes of the public.

THE IMPACT OF SERIOUS OFFENCES ON PUBLIC OPINION

Whatever rationale is given, the accumulating effect of murders and rapes committed by mentally ill people shapes the public opinion of "care in the community". These events are perceived as scandals and signs of neglect on behalf of the authorities (see Chapter 10).

Let us remember that two centuries ago a series of public scandals regarding the appalling conditions in private lunatic asylums and in the houses of correction gave rise to the ideology of moral treatment (Jones, 1972). Public protest initiated the sweeping reform that brought about the massive Victorian asylums. These institutions, in turn, became a target of public criticism and stigma, as the optimism regarding cure ebbed away and scandals came to light. The once high expectations of community care led to similar disillusionment, not entirely justified. The media, which are far more influential now than they were in Charles Dickens' times, serve as a forceful incentive for the correction of the obvious defects in the care system. Yet the sensational nature of the reports has a damaging potential of turning public opinion against the whole idea of community care and throwing a shadow over the many achievements which proved to be obtainable, as clearly illustrated by studies such as the TAPS research project (see Chapter 5).

HOW REAL IS THE RISK TO SOCIETY FROM THE MENTALLY ILL?

In reality, despite all the advances of modern psychiatry, there are still no ideal solutions for people with severe mental illness, and so the old dilemma for society still prevails. Massive confinement of the mentally ill may certainly protect the public, yet is inconceivable nowadays. Integration in the community is desirable yet is bound to expose the public to some of the unpleasant aspects of mental illness.

The image of the mentally ill as dangerous is exaggerated, yet not utterly unfounded, as we have seen from the above data. It should be realized though, that most offences committed by people with a background of mental illness are of a minor nature such as pestering, indecent exposure in public or petty shop lifting. Moreover, we tend to concentrate on the criminal potential of the mentally ill, often ignoring the fact that these people are themselves vulnerable to abuse and exploitation. Indeed the TAPS follow-up study (Leff et al, 1996) revealed a higher number of victimized patients compared with mentally ill offenders.

Behaviours perceived as socially unacceptable are basically manifestations of mental illness, which are less concealed now than a few decades ago when patients were kept behind the walls of the asylums. Certain behaviours, such as drug abuse or wandering are the by-products of the demanding nature of modern life, with which patients find it difficult to cope. If we accept that integration of the mentally ill in the community inevitably leads to higher friction, then the next question is what level of tolerance can we expect from the public, and where to draw the line for the "unacceptable"?

Forensic definitions provide us with some guidelines, and to a limited extent reflect the level of tolerance of society. Nevertheless there is no precise index for criminal behaviour which applies to mentally ill people and consequently it is a dubious matter to establish their rate of criminality. Methodologically we need first to define criteria for mental illness and then to establish the norm of criminality in a control sample of the population. The rate of arrest, although frequently used, may not be an appropriate index since the mentally ill have higher arrest rates than non-mentally ill persons (Teplin, 1984), being more liable to detection and arrest after their offence. On the other hand, some trivial charges, even those due to violence, may be dropped in the case of a mentally ill person. This leaves convictions by the court as a crude index of criminality.

In an appraisal of criminal behaviour of discharged mental patients, Rabkin (1979) concluded that the rates of arrests and criminal convictions of violent offenders among people diagnosed as mentally ill are generally higher than the average for the general population. However, evidence of a clear causal link between mental illness and criminality has never been fully established. It is widely recognized that psychotic illness is not independently associated with criminality. Other factors such as youth, male sex, alcohol and drugs may often be much more relevant than mental illness *per se*.

Substance abuse is the most powerful cause of criminal activity today, and the new generation of mentally ill are no exception in this respect. Modestin and Ammann (1995) examined the criminal behaviour of a sample of 1265 inpatients and found that alcoholism and drug abuse contributed most significantly to criminal behaviour, independent of any sociodemographic factors. In the survey conducted by Gunn et al (1991) in a sample of 16 British prisons, nearly two thirds of prisoners with psychiatric disorders were diagnosed with substance abuse (some with comorbid personality or neurotic disorders). This change in the profile of morbidity among the mentally ill is probably associated with the increase in the criminality rate among psychiatric patients, reported to have occurred over the past two decades (Davis, 1992).

Criminality in the context of closing hospitals

Some sceptics in regard to the prospect of closing psychiatric hospitals (Levene et al, 1985; Weller, 1989; Lamb and Shaner, 1993), have argued that a considerable number of chronic inpatients would not be manageable in the community, either due to high dependency level or the potential risk they pose to the public or themselves.

Two basic assumptions of the "closure sceptics" have proved to be unfounded. Firstly, it became evident that even the highly dependent patients could be managed successfully outside the hospital setting (see Chapters 4, 5, 7). Secondly, only a minority of the hospital population turned out to be difficult to place in the community (due to inherent features of their illness). Moreover, most of these patients could reasonably be managed in specialized alternative facilities (see Chapter 13).

Concerns that systematic resettlement of mentally ill people in the community might intensify criminal activity were not supported by evidence. The TAPS study (Leff et al, 1996) has followed up 737 long-stay patients a year after they were discharged from hospital. Two patients were imprisoned, one for over a year for attempted rape, the other briefly before being transferred to a psychiatric hospital. Five other patients were admitted to psychiatric hospital on police orders under the Mental Health Act, three for assaults and two for abusive behaviour. Nine patients were the victims of crime: three were mugged, three were involved in road traffic accidents, two were victimized at work, and one was stolen from. These data indicate that a majority of the former long-stay patients can live safely in the community without posing a significant risk to the public.

However, there is a small yet important sector of the long-stay patients which bears a potential risk if special care is not provided. A Royal College of Psychiatrists Working Party (1993) has asserted that: "The majority of residential care homes are not designed to manage patients with multiple disabilities or challenging behaviours. Furthermore in most hospital closure programmes the most difficult cases tend to be the last to be resettled."

This sector of the hospital population is of major concern, both to clinicians and administrators faced with the closure of psychiatric institutions. The so called "difficult to place" (DTP) patients are of particular relevance to the issues of violence and criminality. In fact, these people are commonly designated by staff as "DTP" on the grounds of being offensive to the public and potentially dangerous. Understanding the special needs of DTP patients is highly relevant in the context of this chapter and therefore will be addressed here in some detail.

THE "DIFFICULT TO PLACE" PATIENTS

TAPS has launched a series of research projects to study the characteristics and outcomes of the DTP patients. On the basis our findings (Trieman and Leff, 1996), around 15% of the original Friern hospital long-stay population (in 1985), were eventually designated as DTP and moved to specialized facilities instead of ordinary community homes. This proportion is equivalent to a prevalence of 10–11 persons per 100 000 general population in the region of north London.

Seventy two DTP patients were transferred by early 1993 from Friern hospital to four inpatient care facilities. Among those were eight ex-Friern patients who were until that time provisionally treated at high cost in other hospitals. Each one of those identified as "difficult to place" (DTP) underwent a comprehensive psychiatric and social assessment shortly before leaving Friern hospital. The whole group of DTP patients was then compared with the former long-stay patients who settled over the years in community-based accommodation.

The DTP group consisted of younger patients with shorter duration of stay in comparison with the rest of the Friern former patients. While not being excessively disabled functionally or physically, DTP patients were slightly more disturbed in mental state. The distinctive features, however, were noted in social behaviour.

A range of 13 problem behaviours were designated by staff as a direct impediment to placing a patient in a community setting. The most common problem area was aggressiveness, exhibited by more than half of all patients. It took the form of persistent verbal hostility, destructiveness or assaults. Other modes of unacceptable behaviours were inappropriate sexual behaviour, non-compliance with treatment, fire risk, substance abuse, and stealing (see Table 12.1).

Table 12.1 Patients most liable to become "difficult to place"

1. Relatively young, male, new long-stay patients (the number of these depends on whether admissions continue over the final years of the hospital closure programme).
2. Those consistently aggressive, showing either verbal hostility or assaultiveness, or patients perceived as dangerous, mostly those with a history of unpredictable assaults.
3. Those with a single or multiplicity of intractable problem behaviours, such as inappropriate sexuality, stealing, smearing, disrobing, careless smoking/arson, wandering, substance abuse,
4. Patients non-compliant with medication, or drug resistant who are prone to frequent exacerbations of their illness (e.g. bipolar affective disorder).
5. Those with psychotic illness, presenting a range of symptoms stemming from extreme anxiety, such as agitation, ritualistic behaviour, somatic preoccupation etc.
6. Those stigmatized as troublesome either by the hospital or community staff, e.g. patients who made sexual advances to personnel in the past.
7. Those with physically related problems such as incontinence (mainly in younger patients who would not fit into nursing homes), convulsive disorder, polydipsia etc.
8. Persons with learning difficulty or those who suffered brain damage, exhibiting concomitant severe behavioural problems.
9. Those who are at risk to themselves, such as suicidal tendencies, self-mutilation, extreme carelessness (e.g. in crossing roads).

With few variations, (e.g. a focus on cognitive disability (Wykes et al, 1990), the symptom profiles of DTP patients, described in the literature, are quite consistent. However, the TAPS study has placed more emphasis on particular problematic behaviours rather than functional disabilities. This is based on a realization that patients with poor social and living skills are still manageable within maximum support facilities in the community, while certain modes of extreme behaviour may constitute an insurmountable impediment to community placement.

In the US, Bigelow et al (1988), provided a profile of "hard to place" patients at a state hospital in Oregon. The typical patient was described as a schizophrenic male in his 30s who had lost most social and self-care skills, had a tendency towards assault, had a drug abuse problem, and did not cooperate with treatment. The main risk behaviours were: tendency to assault, drug abuse, starting fires, wandering and self harm. Other problem behaviours listed were loud outbursts, isolation, ritualistic behaviour, impaired communication and excessive fluid intake. Notably, half of the patients had some form of cognitive deficit.

Gudeman et al (1984) from a study in Massachusetts, defined five categories of patients who cannot be cared for in community programmes:

1. elderly, demented and behaviourally disturbed;
2. mentally retarded and psychotic;

3. brain-damaged and assaultive;
4. chronically schizophrenic, disruptive and vulnerable;
5. psychotic and assaultive.

They estimated a prevalence of 15 "special needs" patients per 100 000 population. Two thirds of these patients were characterized by a combination of problem behaviours, including: unremittingly given to committing assault, suicidal, obstreperous, oppositional, threatening, eating garbage, inappropriate sexuality, disrobing, stealing, wandering and fire setting.

The high frequency of aggressive behaviour among the DTP patients features them as a major risk population. Some disruptive modes of behaviour exhibited by these patients may jeopardize their opportunity to live outside hospital. In many group homes aggressive behaviour is in fact a non-negotiable criterion for exclusion (Lewis and Trieman, 1995). A one year follow-up of DTP patients relocated in four different types of settings, mostly within other hospitals, indicate that some degree of friction with the public is unavoidable, particularly where the setting is non-restrictive and allows full access to the neighbourhood (see Chapter 13). A diary of disruptive incidents showed that most incidents occurred indoors. Most incidents outdoors were nuisance to the neighbourhood: swearing at people, shop lifting, begging, obstructing the traffic, exposing themselves. No major assault was recorded over the follow-up period. Most contacts with the police were associated with patients who absconded.

THE "NEW LONG STAY" (NLS) PATIENTS

Patients with severe persisting illness who are difficult to manage within the community are not going to vanish along with the psychiatric hospitals. In fact all the evidence shows that regardless of how good community services might be, patients continue to accumulate in psychiatric wards and have protracted stays. Socially deprived catchment areas were associated with higher prevalence rates of these patients (Thornicroft et al, 1992; Lelliott et al, 1994). It is anticipated that if access to long-term inpatient care is denied in the future, these, so called "new long stay" (NLS) patients, are the most likely people to drift into homelessness and be criminalized (see below).

The phenomenon of patients continuing to accumulate in hospitals (with a length of stay of more than one but less than five years) was observed early in the course of running down psychiatric hospitals in the United Kingdom (Wing, 1971; Mann and Cree, 1976). A recent national audit (Lelliott et al, 1994) revealed that NLS patients form a rather heterogeneous population. Predominantly these were younger men (aged 18–34), single, with a diagnosis of schizophrenia, 43 per cent of these had a history of serious violence, or admission to a special hospital, and over one third were formally detained. Another identifiable group was composed of older women with a diagnosis of affective disorder or dementia, being at high risk of self-harm.

While the terminology "NLS" indicates to some extent the difficulty of placing these patients in the community, it is not to say that all of the NLS patients are non-manageable out of hospital. In fact, in certain areas, the insufficiency of alternative facilities in the community simply means that more newly admitted patients are retained in hospital. Moreover, a considerable proportion of the NLS patients are capable of improving over time to the extent that resettlement becomes feasible (Leff et al, 1966). Hence, a large proportion, but not all NLS patients, should be considered DTP. Too often, these two distinctive terms are used interchangeably by service planners and researchers, ignoring the important notion that DTP is a more inclusive term, applying to some of the "old" as well as the "new" long-stay patients.

IS THE CLOSURE OF HOSPITALS ASSOCIATED DIRECTLY WITH HIGHER CRIMINALITY?

We conclude that well-planned reprovision of long-stay hospital populations is not associated with higher levels of crime (or vagrancy), regardless of how difficult placement might be for certain sectors of the long-stay population. Generally speaking, the problem is not associated with patients who receive continuing care, but rather from those "slipping through the net". In this respect the closure of psychiatric hospitals is just one factor in a complex systematic change in delivering care to consumers, particularly since the majority of people suffering from mental illness have no justifiable need to stay in hospital for long periods of time. Criminality and homelessness are to a certain extent the adverse effects of an incompetent system of care. The linkage frequently made between these phenomena and closing mental hospitals is rather concrete and over-simplistic. Only if as a result of closing down a psychiatric hospital, its catchment area is deprived of essential services, such as supported housing, admission beds or secure units, may one rightly expect grave consequences.

The reassuring evidence that former long-stay patients at Friern hospital have contributed very little to criminality following their reprovision, should be taken with some caution when generalized to other reprovision programmes. Reviews of studies comparable to the TAPS project (O'Driscoll, 1993; Braun et al, 1981), indicate that similar outcomes are expected, provided that a comprehensive range of alternative facilities are made available. We consider the real challenge to the future mental health services to stem from a new generation of patients, generally portrayed as young, mostly unemployed, less passive and frequently rejecting treatment or placement, and having a multiplicity of behavioural problems—notably drugs and alcohol abuse. Judging from the American experience of deinstitutionalization (Lamb and Shaner, 1993), if these people are not provided with reliable care in the community, and will not gain good access to inpatient care when necessary, they are most vulnerable to becoming homeless or to getting involved in crime. One indicator of these grave consequences is the phenomenon called transinstitutionalization.

CRIMINALITY AND TRANSINSTITUTIONALIZATION

The alarming concept known as transinstitutionalism (alternately termed criminalization of the mentally ill) (Teplin, 1990; Torrey et al, 1992, Lamb and Shaner, 1993), suggests that blocking the access to psychiatric hospitals without providing adequate community psychiatric resources will inevitably result in the shifting of responsibility for mentally ill people to other systems. The most devastating example is a shunting of mentally ill people in need of treatment from the mental health system into the criminal justice system.

Several studies conducted in the USA in the 1970s (Minkoff, 1978; Rabkin, 1979) and 1980s (Steadman et al, 1982, 1984; Lamb and Grant, 1982) indicated that this adverse consequence of running down state hospitals has indeed become a gloomy reality, as the proportion of mentally ill people arrested and kept in prisons keeps rising over the years.

Concerns have been expressed that a similar process might have been occurring in the UK, so that people who would have been admitted to psychiatric hospitals in the past, are becoming incarcerated in prisons because of the reduction in psychiatric beds (Rollin, 1977; Bluglass, 1988; Scannell, 1989; Weller, 1989).

In a survey conducted in 1989, 37 per cent of the male prison population in Britain were diagnosed as suffering from a psychiatric disorder, of whom only 2% (around 730 people) had a psychotic illness (Gunn et al, 1991). These figures were almost identical to a previous survey in 1972 (Gunn et al, 1978), which might suggest that the closure of hospitals has not resulted in the incarceration of patients in prisons, at least not yet.

While the predominantly practised "front door" policy in the USA (see Chapter 2) was prone to result in transinstitutionalism, the steady reduction of psychiatric beds in the UK was usually accompanied by a large scale reprovision of alternative facilities. Nevertheless, the profound changes in the administrative–economic culture of the mental health services, and the resultant imbalance across the range of psychiatric services has created conditions for this phenomenon to occur. Current evidence unequivocally indicates a shortage of acute admission beds (see Chapter 8), along with a shortage of medium-term rehabilitation facilities (Bridges et al, 1994), and of specialized care units designed for the new long-stay population (Lelliott et al, 1994). A scant 600 medium security beds were available nationwide in 1989—considerably less than the 2000 recommended by the Butler committee over 20 years ago (Interim report, 1974). An unpublished survey by Coid in 1994 found that the number of patients awaiting a bed in medium security institutions is growing.

In a system already overstretched by the needs for inpatient services, there are financial disincentives for health authorities to take on long-term difficult patients (bluntly speaking—an incentive for purchasers to leave mentally ill offenders on the doorstep of the Home Office). Under these circumstances hospitals are likely to reject convicted criminals with chronic psychiatric conditions who have little prospect of recovery. This is particularly relevant where no access to a regional secure unit is available (Coid, 1984). Some patients may even be labelled inappropriately as "psychopathic" in order to divert the responsibility away from the psychiatric services (Coid, 1988).

Alarming signs are already apparent. Delays in transferring patients from prison to medical custody have often been noted, even in cases where a medical recommendation existed (Joseph and Potter, 1993; James and Hamilton, 1991; Blumenthal and Wessely, 1992). In accordance with that, a relatively high number of psychiatric patients, mainly males (Maden et al, 1994), are found in remand prisons (Taylor and Gunn, 1984). Coid (1988) concluded that: "By finding their way into prison many (mentally ill people) are obtaining the only care and treatment anyone is prepared to offer them." This situation has been critically tackled by the media. Based on figures indicating a growing presence of mentally ill people in police cells, the *Guardian* (1 June, 1994) published a statement, typical of those being heard nowadays: "WHAT SORT OF SOCIETY OFFERS A CELL, NOT ASYLUM?"

WHAT IS TO BE DONE TO PROTECT THE PUBLIC?

In a context of growing public, professional and political concern over the incompetence of community services to maintain the continuity of care, notably the case of Christopher Clunis (Ritchie et al, 1994), there was a pressing need to enforce measures to cut the chain of horrendous events of murders and sexual assaults, which undermine the credibility of community care.

In principle, mentally disordered offenders should be cared for by health and social services, not in the criminal justice system. These agencies should accept full accountability for the offenders, as well as for patients who are at risk of committing crimes.

An effective system of care has two elements: dynamic and structural. The first is achievable by close coordination of the relevant agencies, active outreach policy, and the assignment of an accountable key worker for each patient. The introduction of the Care Programme Approach in Britain is certainly a step in the right direction. It is yet to be seen how effectively the policy is going to be implemented.

Another measure specifically designed to minimize the risk to the public from mentally ill offenders is supervision registers (Holloway, 1994). These were formally introduced into the NHS from April 1994. Guidelines issued by the NHS Executive, [HSG(94)5], state that all mental health provider units should "set up registers which identify and provide information on patients who are, or are liable to be, at risk of committing serious violence or suicide, or of serious self-neglect . . .". Taking this unusual step, which erodes civil rights and will inevitably stigmatise some of the users, reflects the accumulating impact of the "scandals" on the policy makers. They correctly sense that unless they do something, the public will hold them responsible for neglect and incompetence.

The structural element of care, namely a balanced continuum of facilities, from group homes to inpatient services, is equally important. In inner city locations, where psychiatric services are often seriously underfunded, a shortage of beds is almost universal. Availability of sufficient admission beds is a precondition in our view for a sound system of psychiatric services. This will alleviate the current risky situation in which patients with exacerbation of their illness are often denied access, or prematurely discharged from overcrowded hospitals.

The availability and accessibility of longer term inpatient care facilities are also mandatory. Specialized units should be established in which active rehabilitation is provided for patients with persistent challenging behaviours (see Chapter 13). A small, yet critical group of dangerous patients is manageable only within secure hospitals. Provision of sufficient secure beds must be planned on a regional and national levels.

In conclusion, not all violence by psychiatrically ill people is predictable and therefore avoidable. There will inevitably be a price to pay for a system of care which gives patients the degree of autonomy and freedom they seek and appreciate. The alternative is to lock up large numbers of people to secure a very small minority who cannot be identified with any certainty. The choice between these alternatives is a societal one.

REFERENCES

Bigelow, D.A., Cutler, D., Moore L., McComb, P. and Leung, P. (1988) Characteristics of state hospital patients who are hard to place, *Hospital and Community Psychiatry*, **39**(2), 181–185.

Bluglass, R. (1988) Mentally disordered prisoners; reports but no improvements. *British Medical Journal*, **296**, 1757.

Blumenthal, S. and Wessely, S. (1992) National survey of current arrangements for diversion from custody in England and Wales, *British Medical Journal*, **305**, 1322–1325.

Braun, P., Kochansky, G., Shapiro, R., Greenberg, S., Gudeman, J.E., Johnson, S. and Shore, M.F. (1981) Overview: deinstitutionalization of psychiatric patients, a critical review of outcome studies, *American Journal of Psychiatry*, **138**, 736–749.

Bridges, K., Davenport, S. and Goldberg, D. (1994) The need for hospital-based rehabilitation services, *Journal of Mental Health*, **3**, 205–212.

Coid, J. (1984) How many psychiatric patients in prison? *British Journal of Psychiatry*, **145**, 78–86.

Coid, J. (1988) Mentally abnormal prisoners on remand; I- Rejected or accepted by the NHS? *British Medical Journal*, **296**, 1779–1782.

Davis, S. (1992) Assessing the "criminalization" of the mentally ill in Canada, *Canadian Journal of Psychiatry*, **37**, 532–538.

Department of Health (1994) Confidential inquiry into homicides and suicides by mentally ill people (director: W.D. Boyd). ISBN 0 902241 75 3.

Gudeman, J.E. and Shore, M.F. (1984) Beyond Deinstitutionalization—a new class of facilities for the mentally ill, *The New England Journal of Medicine*, 311(13), 832–836.

Gunn, J., Robertson, G., Dell, S. and Way, C. (1978) *Psychiatric aspects of imprisonment*, London: Academic Press.

Gunn, J., Maden, A., Swinton, M. (1991) Treatment needs of prisoners with psychiatric disorders, *British Medical Journal*, 303, 338–341.

Holloway, F. (1994) Supervision registers, recent government policy and legislation, *Psychiatric Bulletin*, 18, 593–596.

Interim report of the committee on mentally abnormal offenders (1974) Her Majesty's Stationery Office, London (Cmnd 5698).

James, D. and Hamilton, L. (1991) The Clerkenwell scheme: assessing efficacy and cost of a psychiatric liaison service to a magistrates' court, *British Medical Journal*, 303, 282–285.

Jones, K. (1972) *A History of the Mental Health Services*, Routledge and Kegan Paul, London.

Joseph, L.A. and Potter, M. (1993) Diversion from custody. II: Effect on hospital and prison resources, *British Journal of Psychiatry*, 162, 330–334.

Lamb, H.R. and Grant, R.W. (1982) The mentally ill in an urban county jail. *Archives of General Psychiatry*, 39, 17–22.

Lamb, H.R. and Shaner, R. (1993) When there are almost no state hospital beds left, *Hospital and Community Psychiatry*, 44(10), 973–976.

Leff, J., Trieman, N. and Gooch, C. (1996) The TAPS Project 33: A prospective follow-up study of long-stay patients discharged from two psychiatric hospitals. *The American Journal of Psychiatry* 153(10), 1318–1323.

Lelliott, P., Wing, J. and Clifford, P. (1994) A national audit of new long-stay psychiatric patients. II: Impact on services, *British Journal of Psychiatry*, 165, 170–178.

Levene L.S., Donaldson L.J. and Brandon S. (1985) How likely is it that a District Health Authority can close its large mental hospitals? *British Journal of Psychiatry*, 147, 150–155.

Lewis, A. and Trieman, N. (1995) The TAPS Project 29: Residential care provision in North London: a representative sample of ten facilities for mentally ill people, *The International Journal of Social Psychiatry*, 41(4), 257–267.

Maden, T., Swinton, M. and Gunn, J. (1994) Psychiatric disorder in women serving a prison sentence, *British Journal of Psychiatry*, 164, 44–54.

Mann, S.A. and Cree, W. (1976) "New long-stay" psychiatric patients: a national sample survey of fifteen mental hospitals in England and Wales, *Psychological Medicine*, 6, 603–616.

Minkoff, K. (1978) A map of chronic mental patients. In: (ed. J. Talbott) *The chronic mental patient*. A.P.A., Washington D.C.

Modestin, J. and Ammann, R. (1995) Mental disorders and criminal behaviour. *British Journal of Psychiatry*, 166, 667–675.

O'Driscoll, C. (1993) Mental hospital closure—a literature review of outcome studies and evaluative techniques, *British Journal of Psychiatry*, 162 (suppl 19), 7–17.

Rabkin J.G. (1979) Criminal behaviour of discharged mental patients: a critical appraisal of research, *Psychological Bulletin*, 86, 1–27.

Ritchie J., Dick D. and Lingham R. (1994) *The inquiry into the care and treatment of Christopher Clunis*, Her Majesty's Stationery Office, London.

Rollin, H.R. (1977) "Deinstitutionalisation" and the community: fact and theory, *Psychological Medicine*, 7, 181–184.

Royal College of Psychiatrists Working Party (1993) Facilities and services for patients who have chronic persisting severe disabilities resulting from mental illness (Summary by T. Craig) *Psychiatric Bulletin*, 17, 567–568.

Scannel, T.D. (1989) Community care and the difficult and offender patient, *British Journal of Psychiatry*, **154**, 615–619.

Steadman, H.J., Monahan. J., Davis, F.K. and Robins, P.C. (1982) Mentally disordered offenders. A national survey of patients and facilities, *Journal of Law and Human Behaviour*, **6**, 31–38.

Steadman, H.J., Monahan, J., Duffee, B., Hartstone, E. and Robins, P.C. (1984) The impact of State hospital deinstitutionalisation on United States prison population 1968–78, *Journal of Criminal Law & Criminology*, **75**, 474–490.

Taylor, P.J. and Gunn J. (1984) Violence and psychosis. I. Risk of violence among psychotic men, *British Medical Journal*, **288**, 1945–1949.

Teplin, L.A. (1990) The prevalence of severe mental disorder among male urban jail detainees: comparison with the Epidemiologic Catchment Area program. *American Journal of Public Health*, **80**, 663–669.

Thornicroft, G., Margolius, O. and Jones, D. (1992) The TAPS Project 6: New long-stay psychiatric patients and social deprivation, *British Journal of Psychiatry*, **161**, 621–624.

Torrey, E.F. et al. (1992) *Criminalizing the Seriously Ill: the Abuse of Jails as Mental Hospitals*, Public Citizens Health Research, Washington DC.

Trieman, N. and Leff, J. (1996) The TAPS Project 24: Difficult to place patients in a psychiatric hospital closure programme, *Psychological Medicine*, **26**, 765–774.

Weller, M.P. (1989) Mental illness—who cares? *Nature*, **339**, 249–252.

Wing J.K. (1971) How many psychiatric beds? *Psychological Medicine*, **1**, 188–190.

Wykes, T., Sturt, E. and Katz, R. (1990) The prediction of rehabilitative success after three years. The use of social, symptom and cognitive variables, *British Journal of Psychiatry*, **157**, 865–870.

Chapter 13

PROVIDING A COMPREHENSIVE COMMUNITY PSYCHIATRIC SERVICE

Julian Leff*[†], Noam Trieman*

Team for the Assessment of Psychiatric Services (TAPS); [†]Institute of Psychiatry

When the National Health Service was introduced in the UK in 1948, almost all psychiatric services were provided from the psychiatric hospitals. Over subsequent decades, admission wards and outpatient clinics were established in district general hospitals (DGHs). In addition, posts for community psychiatric nurses were created, and their number expanded rapidly. The Marlborough Day Hospital, the first in the world, was opened in 1946, and many more followed. Psychiatrists began to run clinics in general practices, and by 1984 one in five were providing this service (Strathdee and Williams, 1984). In recent years, multidisciplinary teams have been operating from bases in the community, and include staff with novel job descriptions, such as community occupational therapists, and community psychiatrists who have no responsibility for beds.

These developments have occurred unevenly across the country, so that individual psychiatric hospitals vary in the degree to which they have retained their original functions. In no instance, however, has a psychiatric hospital simply withered away because all its functions were replaced by a network of community services. Instead, as in the reprovision for Friern and Claybury hospitals, a wide range of community services has to be created as a supplement to existing facilities, in order to replace the hospital functions. To what extent are they satisfactorily replaced? This is the question that TAPS was set up to answer, and which required the many diverse studies reported in this book. An overview of the findings of these studies is useful in identifying the areas in which reprovision was successful, and the gaps which were not filled, even by this generously funded programme.

Care in the Community: Illusion or Reality?
Edited by Julian Leff. © 1997 John Wiley & Sons Ltd.

LONG-STAY, NON-DEMENTED PATIENTS

With the exception of the difficult-to-place patients, who will be discussed below, the long-stay, non-demented patients were generally well served by the community facilities provided. The houses were domestic in scale and residents usually had their own bedroom, while they might have been sharing a dormitory with ten or more patients in the hospital. A freedom from restrictions prevailed in all the homes. However, their location in residential streets did not ensure the social integration of the patients into the neighbourhood. We would suggest that this problem can be tackled by education programmes which target the neighbours living close to the patients' homes.

PSYCHOGERIATRIC PATIENTS

Patients with dementia were better cared for in the community homes than in hospital (see Chapter 7) and we could detect no disadvantages to the former. We found that elderly patients with functional psychoses were often being cared for on the same wards as dementia patients, and were viewed by staff as having developed a form of dementia. However, when they were transferred to community homes, the deterioration that was occurring in their behaviour and cognitive function was halted. This suggests that much of this deterioration was attributable to the understimulating environment of the hospital psychogeriatric wards. Our study showed that although elderly patients with functional psychoses may be as dependent as dementia patients in terms of physical care, they function at a higher cognitive level (Trieman and Leff, 1995a). This has been confirmed by a comparable study in New York (Harvey et al, submitted). We recommend that these patients should not be mixed indiscriminately with dementia patients, but should be provided with separate facilities, in which care is provided that takes account of their greater cognitive capacity.

ADMISSION FACILITIES

The area of reprovision for Friern hospital which was least satisfactory was undoubtedly the admission facilities. The closure programme was used as an opportunity to reduce the total number of admission beds for the catchment population, for no logically argued reason. Consequently there was a strong suspicion that this decision was driven by financial pressures. Following the closure of Friern hospital, the occupancy of admission beds in the two health districts studied, those of Camden and of Bloomsbury and Islington, regularly exceeded 100 per cent (see Chapter 8).

It is not easy to determine how much of this was due to local circumstances and how much to a national problem, since an admission beds crisis has been building up in the UK over the past five years (Powell and Hollander, 1994). The Greater London Association of Community Health Councils (1995) issued a report on London's health services in 1995, in which they highlighted the insufficiency of psychiatric admission beds, and reported bed occupancy rates as high as 120–130 per cent. The report expressed concern at the fact that the overflow was dealt with by placing patients in hospitals outside London, far from family and friends, or in private hospitals leading to greater costs in the long run, and lack of accountability to the community. A national survey by the Research Unit of the Royal College of Psychiatrists indicated that the problem was widespread, affecting services in rural areas as well as cities (Lelliot and Wing, 1994).

The problem has complex origins in a number of factors emerging roughly contemporaneously, not all of which stem from psychiatric hospital closure. One of these is the loss of low-rent accommodation already referred to in discussing the roots of homelessness (see Chapter 11). As a result, some patients remain on admission wards long after they are well enough to be discharged, waiting for suitable accommodation to become available. Other patients stay for six months or more because their symptoms do not respond well to antipsychotic medication. In the psychiatric hospitals, these "treatment resistant" patients could be moved from the admission wards to rehabilitation wards, where their long-term symptoms and disabilities became the focus of therapy. The absence of rehabilitation facilities from community services disadvantages these patients in three ways (Bridges et al, 1994). An admission ward is a very stressful place because of the constant turnover of patients and the high level of disturbance of many of them. The environment is busy, crowded and noisy, with little opportunity for privacy. Patients on the admission wards of DGHs in the TAPS study complained of the level of noise compared to the psychiatric hospital, and the lack of grounds (see Chapter 8). Secondly, staff on admission wards pay more attention to recent admissions and have less time for those who have been in the ward for over six months (Hyde et al, 1987). Thirdly, it is difficult to carry out rehabilitation on an admission ward. Patients need a domestic environment in which to acquire and practise skills. In our view, each health district needs an intermediate stay rehabilitation unit for patients who require admissions of more than a few months. The unit should provide a domestic environment and is best located in the community to foster as non-institutional an ambience as possible. Input will be needed from occupational therapists and psychologists, both of whom have expertise in assessment of disabilities and remedial programmes. Units of this kind have been established in a few districts in the UK, for example Hahnemann House in East Dorset, UK. This unit is housed in an attractive building standing in its own grounds near the centre of Bournemouth. It was opened after the closure of the local psychiatric hospital. It offers places for 27 residents and 20 day patients, and includes three independent flatlets for residents preparing to move on. The average length of stay is ten months. The staff team includes a clinical psychologist, occupational therapists and a woodwork instructor. There is a horticultural centre on site, in which some of the patients work (Leung, 1993).

Another contributory factor to the bed crisis is a direct consequence of reprovision, namely the need of discharged long-stay patients for readmission. In the TAPS study of these patients, an average of 15 per cent were readmitted at least once during the first follow-up year. Readmission was associated with the following characteristics at baseline assessment: young age, new long-stay status, a diagnosis of mania, a high number of previous admissions, and observed signs of psychiatric illness on the PSE (Gooch and Leff, 1996). Other than the last, these characteristics are not modifiable. They point to psychotic illnesses in an early unstable phase of their natural history. Up to the point of closure of Friern hospital, these patients were readmitted to the acute wards there, but afterwards they had to be taken into the admission wards in the DGHs. We have calculated that at any time, nine beds are needed per 100 discharged long-stay patients to cater for their need for readmission. The number of beds required varies with the characteristics of the former long-stay population, being higher for younger patients, the new long-stay, those with more previous admissions than the average, and patients discharged into non-staffed accommodation.

In calculating the number of admission beds required for a catchment area without a psychiatric hospital, provision must be made for the readmission needs of discharged long-stay patients, taking into account the characteristics of that population.

"DIFFICULT-TO-PLACE" (DTP) PATIENTS

A review of the American experience of deinstitutionalization over the past 40 years (Bachrach, see Chapter 2), makes us realize that regardless of locality, structure or quality of community psychiatric services, a relatively small proportion of the chronic mentally ill population will always need some sort of long-term inpatient care. The current perspective we have on the process of closing psychiatric hospitals in Britain, confirms this conclusion (Mann and Cree, 1976; Hirsch et al, 1992; Thornicroft and Bebbington, 1989; Lelliot et al, 1994).

It became evident that any reprovision programme for a psychiatric hospital is bound to face a serious challenge of how to reprovide for a residual group of severely disabled patients for whom adequate care in community facilities is not possible (see Chapter 12).

In the UK, where the local health authorities are committed to providing a comprehensive range of community services to replace the psychiatric hospital, a pressing dilemma arises for the planners on deciding which type of settings would optimally meet the heterogenous needs of patients identified as "difficult-to-place".

Should the solution be in the form of a specialized, domestic type rehabilitation unit? This type of setting, although providing a better quality of life, might not suit the needs of all DTP patients, thus compelling the purchasers to buy expensive hospital services from providers elsewhere. Alternatively, should the solution be a replication of the traditional continuing care ward? This is certainly a less expensive solution with no pretence of active rehabilitation, but still capable of containing most of the DTP patients.

The dilemma is complex, involving political, therapeutic and moral considerations (hopefully, not in that order). Furthermore, in planning alternative facilities for the residual group of DTP patients, one must also envisage the future needs of the new chronic patients in an era when psychiatric hospitals no longer exist. These needs might not be quite the same as for those currently designated "difficult-to-place".

If we put aside the economic considerations and first explore what optimal therapeutic environment might suit DTP patients, we shall find a growing amount of evidence which indicates that hostel wards provide an effective form of care for highly disabled patients (Allen et al, 1993; Garety and Morris, 1984; Gibbons, 1986, 1988; Hyde et al, 1987; Shepherd et al, 1994; Shepherd, 1995). The model of a "ward in a house", originally formulated by Bennet (1980) was designed to combine the best features of hospital care (good staffing levels and well-trained professionals), with the best features of community based residential care (small, domestic type and accessible to the community) (Shepherd et al, 1994; Goldberg et al, 1985; Wykes and Wing, 1982). Curiously, as pointed by Shepherd (1995), this model is reminiscent of one of the very first institutions for the mentally ill, the York Retreat, founded in 1796. Progressive it might well be, yet the "ward in a house" model is certainly less innovative than one might tend to believe . . ..

The target population for a ward in a house is primarily the new long stay (NLS) patients (Wykes and Wing, 1982; Young, 1991). In this respect this setting seems to be of particular relevance to the needs of people designated as "difficult-to-place". Some questions are bound to arise: Can a hostel ward meet the heterogenous needs of the DTP patients? Is it capable of promoting the function skills of these patients? Can it modify the patients' challenging modes of behaviour? Is it a cost effective option?

Currently, the number of beds in hostel wards within the UK is 3.7 per 100 000 population, less than 6 percent of the total inpatient beds (Lelliot and Wing, 1994). There are quite a few variations among those settings in regard to the administration, principles of care, and target populations, thus making comparisons of outcomes a somewhat problematic task. In general, though, most of these setting are hospital-based, providing medium-term accommodation and employing a basic rehabilitation programme. Shepherd (1995) who summarised outcome data from "ward in a house" facilities, reached the conclusion that these units were more effective in improving social functioning and maintaining activity levels than traditional mental hospital wards. While there is substantial evidence that most such facilities are indeed successful in engaging their patients in constructive activity and in utilizing community amenities, reports are less consistent with regard to social functioning and performance of living skills. An outcome study of Douglas House in Manchester, one of the well-known hostel wards (Goldberg et al, 1985; Hyde et al, 1987), shows that the residents did not improve their social and self-care performance, yet gained better domestic skills.

The TAPS study (Trieman and Leff, 1996b) evaluated the outcomes of DTP patients in three types of hostel wards. We found that regardless of the different milieux and rehabilitation input, overall there had not been any significant change in the level of social and self-care functioning. We therefore believe that one should not expect substantial gains in this field. A key issue is whether specialized units for DTP have the potential to modify some of the most disruptive behaviours which impede the patients' progress. This aspect of care effectiveness is bound to determine the patients' future more than anything else.

We could demonstrate (Trieman and Leff, 1996b) that the profile of serious behaviour problems among DTP patients is not static. Aggressive behaviour—undoubtedly the most serious problem—proved to be potentially reversible. This was particularly apparent in one of the facilities, a fine example of a "ward in a house", employing non-restrictive and flexible non-intrusive attitudes. It succeeded in lessening the overall frequency of problem behaviours and most notably managed to reduce the levels of aggression (both verbal and physical). These findings should serve as an incentive for care planners to explore ways of modifying challenging behaviours, instead of directing all the rehabilitation efforts at the acquisition of living skills, which do not seem to be rewarding with regard to DTP patients.

One needs to bear in mind that malfunctioning is usually not the main impediment to placing a patient in the community. Instead, some intractable behaviours like aggression are the key factors, so they should be the prime goal of treatment.

With only a few exceptions (Allen et al, 1993), a ward in a house is heavily staffed and thus very expensive (Beecham et al, 1995). The cost of this facility is estimated to be the same as that of an acute admission ward in a general hospital and nearly double the costs of the "back" wards in psychiatric hospitals (Young, 1991). The next inevitable question is therefore: are these facilities cost effective? Two of the settings assessed by TAPS (Trieman, 1994; Trieman and Leff, 1996b) were highly resourced, with a nursing staff : patient ratio as high as 1.7 : 1. Comparison with less resourced facilities, based on parameters of containment and rehabilitation, reveals that costly facilities for DTP patients are no guarantee of better outcomes. Why should we then invest in expensive settings and not go for the cheaper options? This is a matter of judgement rather than solely a scrutiny of cost-effectiveness. We believe that the absence of restrictive and formal care practices promotes resident-oriented care, provides a good quality of life and fosters integration into the community. These qualities are difficult to measure, yet are the essence of progressive care. Moreover, in view of the practices employed over the past fifteen years in hostel wards, there is still room to develop more effective care programmes. The evident reduction in the level of aggressive behaviour, as described, is an important indicator of that. Another argument in favour of the hostel-ward model is that it is likely to fit better into the future community services and has the potential to adapt to the changing needs (such as growing proportions of drug abusers) if and when they occur. This prospect can hardly be attributed to the traditional "back" ward.

Although the hostel wards are capable of containing the majority of referrals, there is a sizable minority who are too difficult to manage in the physical space of such a domestic environment, and are too disruptive to gain free access to the neighbourhood. These individuals usually exhibit the highest levels of assaultiveness and extreme acting-out behaviour which pose a degree of danger. Most reports show that up to one third of patients referred to hostel wards are eventually transferred to a more secure setting (Shepherd, 1995). Based on the TAPS evaluation of similar settings, special units seem to sustain a higher ability to contain very difficult patients. Notably the least restrictive facility has managed to contain all but two of 28 patients, of whom half were consistently aggressive. Nevertheless, taking into account a number of patients who are not containable in either hospital hostels or rehabilitation wards, and adding them to those currently detained under section within existing secure wards, we come to realise that there is an "ultra" group of DTP people for whom a conventional secure ward is probably the only option. From an administrative point of view, the local NHS trusts often prefer to purchase medium secure beds for a limited number of their "ultra" difficult patients, either from private providers (hospitals such as Kneesworth in Hertfordshire) or from other districts which already have these facilities. Based on our experience, it appears that effective specialised units are capable of reducing the need for secure facilities, but under no circumstances can they abolish that need.

PRACTICAL SOLUTIONS FOR DIFFICULT-TO-PLACE PATIENTS

We regard a non-restrictive hostel ward as probably the best environment for the majority of patients with challenging behaviours, and potentially effective in diminishing aggression. It is not, however, the optimal environment for all DTP patients. Some of them might react adversely to growing levels of freedom and increasing expectations, and thus might fare better with stricter boundaries. The variety of care environments needed for DTP patients was discussed by Gudeman and Shore (1984), who suggested that a cluster of specialised units would be located in the grounds of a large campus, and provide for the entire DTP population within a region or even a whole state. We do not favour this option, since it practically means a revival of the old institutional model.

Instead, we recommend that every reprovision programme should set up one or more hostel wards in the locality, depending on the prevalence of DTP patients (Trieman and Leff, 1996b). From a managerial point of view, it seems more practical to situate such units in the grounds of a general hospital or next to an existing psychiatric hospital. It is perfectly viable, though, to place special care units in the community, provided they maintain close links with a nearby hospital. In order to accommodate the heterogenous needs, it is advisable to establish two to three specialised units (or divide one unit into sub-units) which will differ in the degree of structuring, social contact and rehabilitative endeavour. The units should be highly staffed, as we regard this a precondition for the feasibility of an "open door" policy, and for the delivery of good practice.

While we strongly recommend a non-restrictive environment for DTP patients, the interaction of patients with the public should be carefully monitored, and risks should not be taken with the security of the public. Accordingly, patients who are notoriously dangerous should not be placed in hostel wards and should be treated in secure wards.

Since the total cost of reprovision for the whole hospital population is significantly affected by the expensive provision needed for DTP patients, any rehabilitation endeavour which might reduce the numbers of DTP patients could potentially reduce the overall costs.

This can be done as part of a reprovision programme, two to four years before the hospital is due to close. It may take the form of an interim rehabilitation unit, which later evolves to become a permanent hostel ward.

We propose the following guidelines for a special care programme:

1. A non-restrictive, domestic type milieu;
2. A low expressed emotion (EE) environment (Leff and Vaughn, 1985);
3. Individualised care programmes, in which the intensity of contact/input is adjusted for each subject;
4. Revision of current medication, with the aim of introducing atypical antipsychotic drugs for every treatment-resistant patient;
5. Targeting one major disruptive behaviour in each patient at a time (Liberman et al, 1989).

As an integral part of the care programme, we suggest that staff members should acquire training in handling crisis situations and in reducing expression of critical attitudes towards the patients. This has been tried successfully by TAPS with residential community care workers in a sample of group homes (see Chapter 9).

WORK-LIKE ACTIVITIES

Whereas accommodation in the community was a distinct improvement over that provided in hospital, the area of work-like activities presented a very different picture. Friern hospital had particularly well-developed facilities for occupational and industrial therapies. The art therapy department was large with a well-equipped pottery, in which patients produced creative work of a very high standard. The industrial therapy department offered a wide variety of jobs, from repetitive assembly and packing tasks to the production of a range of wooden toys and furniture, designed in the department. The most skilled worker had been an engineer, and did precision drilling of steel blocks using industrial machinery. There was also a horticultural section, which was ideal for patients who worked at a slow pace and disliked repetitive tasks. The industrial therapy workshops employed 120 people daily, some of whom commuted from their homes, since nothing comparable was available in the community.

Friern hospital was not unique in the number and variety of jobs it offered. Netherne hospital, which has now closed, was designated as a national demonstration centre for rehabilitation. It provided a graded sequence of jobs, starting at the least demanding level with the folding of cardboard sleeves for light bulbs, and working up to the winding of armatures for rocket motors (Ekdawi, 1972).

There are major obstacles in the way of reproviding such sophisticated work schemes in the community. Much of the work depended on contracts from businesses and factories. To fulfil these, it is necessary to have quite a large work force. This was feasible in the centralised psychiatric hospital, but ceased to be so once the work force was scattered in small groups throughout a wide geographical area. As part of the planning of the Friern reprovision, possible solutions to this problem were discussed, such as setting up small work centres in a number of localities which would be linked by a transport service to enable the contract work to be distributed, and collected when completed. It was decided that this was not viable economically: the loss of the "economy of scale" of the psychiatric hospital was crucial to this decision.

It was not only the dispersal of the work force that hindered the development of community work schemes. Another potent factor was that the capital put up by NETRHA for the Friern reprovision, although a generous £20 million, was virtually all spent on providing homes for the patients, understandably the top priority. Some innovative projects were planned, such as a patient-run cafe with its own vegetable garden, but not many came to fruition. A small number of patients joined the few existing work schemes, such as a shop engaged in desktop publishing and the production of prints. Otherwise patients were offered attendance at day centres or drop-in centres, the latter often run by voluntary agencies. It was not surprising, therefore, that at the one year follow-up, 41 per cent of patients had no structured activities to attend, compared with 29 per cent in hospital. This trend becomes even more evident when we examine the 215 patients with relevant data at baseline, one year, and five year follow-up. The proportion with no structured activities increased progressively from 22 per cent, through 36 per cent, to 46 per cent, a highly significant change ($p < 0.001$) over the five years in the community.

In considering how this obvious deficiency in the services might be remedied, it is necessary to be realistic about the employment prospects of chronically ill patients in the context of high national unemployment in most western countries. Firstly we need to question whether it is equitable to expect patients over 60 to undertake work-like activities, when the majority of healthy people are now retiring at this age. This issue is germane to the TAPS long-stay sample, whose mean age was 55. For long-stay patients under 60 the prospects of working in open employment are slim, given the difficulty of accounting for long interruptions in their job record and the competitive demands of interviews. Creegan (1995) gives an account of a variety of schemes in North America which tackle this problem. In Ottawa the Community Work Project was established in a federal government office. A group of patients works together in the office under supervision of an occupational therapist. They work alongside regular employees for a maximum of five 3-hour periods per week. If successful, they graduate to individual positions with more autonomy. This scheme has been remarkably successful in enabling patients to progress to placements in employment, college and community vocational programmes, 59 per cent having achieved this (Vanier and Rivard, 1991). This is an example of transitional employment, which embodies the expectation that a proportion of clients will eventually be able to work in competitive employment. By contrast, supported employment, a more recent development, is predicated on continuous monitoring of the employees by a trained supervisor. This inevitably places considerable demands on the mobile job support worker (Cook and Razzano, 1992).

Another approach to providing patients with realistic work experience is the "clubhouse model". This was first developed at Fountain House in New York (Beard et al, 1982), and forms the nucleus of the COSTAR programme in Baltimore (Thornicroft and Breakey, 1991). Staff negotiate with potential employers on the basis that the job will get done regardless of the unpredictable absenteeism of patients. This guarantee is effected by ensuring that if a patient fails to turn up for work s/he is replaced by another clubhouse member, or a staff member if necessary. The clubhouse provides its members with the opportunity to socialise and with affordable meals, in addition to entry-level part-time employment. After being established for 30 years, this model has only recently crossed the Atlantic and is beginning to be taken up in the UK.

An alternative to competition in the job market is to create cooperatives run by and for patients. For this to be successful, the cooperative has to provide a service or produce goods which are needed by the public. A number of good examples exist in different countries. These include a courier service in Toronto, which began as a workers' cooperative owned and operated by former psychiatric patients (Creegan, 1995), a wooden toy factory in Arezzo, Italy, linked to a retail shop in the high street, and a horticultural project supplying a cafe with organic foods in Kent, England (Blackthorn Trust).

These enterprises have a number of advantages over both contract work and competitive employment. Patients are sheltered from the effects of occasional lateness or absence, although they do need to respond to the demands of a working environment. They have the companionship and understanding of colleagues with similar problems. In addition, each project offers a variety of positions with differing levels of responsibility, and varying demands for initiative. This is a major benefit for patients from a middle class background and/or higher education who may be able to take on managerial roles, or at least undertake tasks which are more varied and stimulating than the standard contract work.

It is evident that there exists a variety of interesting and creative alternatives to the repetitive work that characterised many hospital vocational rehabilitation programmes. Community reprovision for the psychiatric hospitals provides a golden opportunity to break free from the old custodial orientation towards industrial therapy. The Friern reprovision failed to take advantage of this opportunity. It is to be hoped that ongoing programmes will be more imaginative and that planners will assign as high a priority to facilities for occupation as to accommodation. The Richmond Fellowship, a British voluntary organisation which provides sheltered housing and work schemes, has recently enunciated a policy that each sheltered house should be closely linked with a facility providing opportunities for work. This is an ideal that all mental health providers should aim at. A practical arrangement to ensure this is the core and cluster model. Patients' homes are located within walking distance of a core facility that provides work opportunities. The proximity of the homes combats staff isolation, ensures staff support in case of crises, and offers patients the chance to move between more and less highly staffed settings as appropriate. A possible disadvantage of this arrangement is the creation of a psychiatric ghetto in the community. For this reason, no more than one home should be established in any one street.

REFERENCES

Allen, H., Baigent, B., Kent, A. and Bolton, J. (1993) Rehabilitation and staffing levels in a "new look" hospital-hostel, *Psychological Medicine*, **23**, 203–211.

Beard, J.H., Propst, R.N. and Malamud, T.J. (1982) The Fountain House model of psychiatric rehabilitation, *Psychosocial Rehabilitation Journal*, **5**, 47–53.

Beecham, J., Hallam, A., Knapp, M., Baines, B., Fenyo, A. and Asbury, M. (1995) *The Economic Evaluation of Community Psychiatric Reprovision: Final Report to North Thames Regional Health Authority.*

Bennet, D.H. (1980) The chronic psychiatric patient today, *Journal of the Royal Society of Medicine*, **73**, 301–303.

Bridges, K., Davenport, S. and Goldberg, G. (1994) The need for hospital-based rehabilitation services, *Journal of Mental Health*, **3**, 205–212.

Cook, J.A. and Razzano, L. (1992) Natural vocational supports for persons with severe mental illness: Thresholds Supported Competitive Employment Programme, *New Directions for Mental Health Services*, **56**, 23–41.

Creegan, S. (1995) An investigation of vocational programmes and services in North America, *British Journal of Occupational Therapy*, **58**, 9–13.

Ekdawi, M.Y. (1972) The Netherne Resettlement Unit: results of ten years, *British Journal of Psychiatry*, **121**, 417–424.

Garety, P.A. and Morris, I. (1984) A new unit for long-stay psychiatric patients: organization, attitudes and quality of care, *Psychological Medicine*, **14**, 183–192.

Gibbons, J.S. (1986) Care of "new" long-stay patients in a district general hospital psychiatric unit, *Acta Psychiatrica Scandinavica*, **73**, 582–588.

Gibbons, J. (1988) *Residential care for mentally ill adults*. In I. Sinclair (ed.), *Residential Care: The Research Reviewed*. National Institute of Social Work, Her Majesty's Stationery Office, London.

Goldberg, D.P., Bridges, K., Cooper, W., Hyde, C. and Wyatt, R. (1985) Douglas House: a new type of hostel ward for chronic psychotic patients, *British Journal of Psychiatry*, **147**, 383–388.

Gooch. C. and Leff, J. (1996) Factors affecting the success of community placement: The TAPS Project. 26, *Psychological Medicine*, **26**, 511–520.

Greater London Association of Community Health Councils (1995) *Diagnosis: Crisis—A report on the state of London's health services in 1995*. GLACHC, 356 Holloway Road, London N7 6PA.

Gudeman, J.E. and Shore, M.F. (1984) Beyond deinstitutionalization—a new class of facilities for the mentally ill, *The New England Journal of Medicine*, **311**(13), 832–836.

Harvey, P., Leff, J., Trieman, N., Anderson, J., Halm, S. and Davidson, M. Cognitive impairment and adaptive deficit in geriatric chronic schizophrenic patients: a cross national study in New York and London. *International Journal of Geriatric Psychiatry* (submitted).

Hirsch, S.R. et al. (1992) *Facilities and services for the mentally ill with persisting severe disabilities. Working party report on behalf of the Executive Committee of the General Psychiatry Section of the Royal College of Psychiatrists*, Royal College of Psychiatrists, London.

Hyde, C., Bridges, K., Goldberg, D., Lowson, K., Sterling C. and Faragher, B. (1987) The evaluation of a hostel ward: a controlled study using modified cost-benefit analysis, *British Journal of Psychiatry*, **151**, 805–812.

Leff, J. and Vaughn, C.E. (1985) *Expressed Emotion in Families: its Significance for Mental Illness*, Guilford, London.

Lelliot, P. and Wing, J.K. (1994) A national audit of new long-stay psychiatric patients. I: Method and description of the cohort, *British Journal of Psychiatry*, **165**, 160–169.

Lelliot, P., Wing J.K. and Clifford, P. (1994) A national audit of new long-stay psychiatric patients. II: Impact on services, *British Journal of Psychiatry*, **165**, 170–178.

Leung, G. (1993) *The ten year evaluation study of Hahnemann House*, Dorset Healthcare NHS Trust, Poole.

Liberman, R.P., DeRisi, W.J. and Mueser, K.T. (1989) *Social skills training for psychiatric patients*, Pergamon, Oxford.

Mann, S.A. and Cree, W. (1976) "New long-stay" psychiatric patients: a national sample survey of fifteen mental hospitals in England and Wales, *Psychological Medicine*, **6**, 603–616.

Powell, R. and Hollander, D. (1994) Heading for a breakdown: Crisis in admission beds, *Journal of Mental Health*, **3**, 430–432.

Shepherd, G. (1995) The "ward in a house": residential care for the severely disabled, *Community Mental Health Journal*, **31**, 53–68.

Shepherd, G., King, C. and Fowler, D. (1994) Outcomes in hospital hostels. *Psychiatric Bulletin*, **18**, 609–612.

Strathdee, G. and Williams, P. (1984) A survey of psychiatrists in primary care: the silent growth of a new service, *Journal of the Royal College of General Practitioners*, **34**, 615–618.

Thornicroft, G. and Bebbington, P. (1989) Deinstitutionalisation: from hospital closure to service development, *British Journal of Psychiatry*, **155**, 739–753.

Thornicroft, G. and Breakey, W.R. (1991) The COSTAR Programme 1: Improving social networks of the long-term mentally ill, *British Journal of Psychiatry*, **159**, 245–249.

Trieman, N. (1994) The concept and practice of a "Special Needs" unit. Presented at the 9th Annual TAPS Conference.

Trieman. N. and Leff, J. (1996a) The TAPS Project 24: Difficult to place patients in a psychiatric hospital closure programme, *Psychological Medicine*, **26**, 765–774.

Trieman, N. and Leff, J. (1996b) The TAPS Project 36: The most difficult to place long-stay psychiatric inpatients: outcome one year after relocation, *British Journal of Psychiatry*, **169**, 289–292.

Vanier, G. and Rivard, R. (1991) The community work project: an occupational therapy programme, *Canadian Journal of Occupational Therapy*, **58**, 123–128.

Wykes, T. and Wing, J. (1982) A ward in a house: accommodation for "new" long-stay patients, *Acta Psychiatrica Scandinavica*, **65**, 315–330.

Young, R. (ed) (1991) *Residential Needs for Severely Disabled Psychiatric Patients—the Case for Hospital Hostels*, Her Majesty's Stationery Office, London.

Chapter 14

THE FUTURE OF COMMUNITY CARE

Julian Leff
Team for the Assessment of Psychiatric Services (TAPS) Institute of Psychiatry

We have seen that, with the exception of the acute services, reprovision for Friern and Claybury hospitals achieved considerable success. We need to consider whether this is a unique programme on account of the length of time allotted to complete it (ten years), the careful planning, and the generous capital and revenue funding provided by the regional health authority. Is it replicable elsewhere in the UK, and would it have any relevance for other European countries, or even the USA? While 45 psychiatric hospitals in the UK have been closed over the past 20 years, no evaluative study of the breadth and duration of the TAPS Project has been initiated. It is difficult, therefore, to make comparisons across reprovision programmes. At least one, smaller scale, study has been completed which allows comparison with some of our data—the evaluation of the closure of Cane Hill hospital (Pickard et al, 1992).

THE CANE HILL EVALUATION

Whereas Friern and Claybury hospitals are situated in north London, Cane Hill hospital is located south of the city in a rural setting. Like the other two, it contained over 2000 patients at its peak in the early 1950s. When the research team was set up to evaluate the programme in 1988, there were only about 400 patients remaining, less than half the number in Friern and in Claybury hospitals when TAPS conducted its survey. In view of the process of selective discharge of the most able first, noted by Jones (1993), one would expect the remaining patients surveyed at Cane Hill hospital to be more disabled than the TAPS sample. The 246 long-stay patients at Cane Hill hospital were older than the TAPS group, with a mean age of 67, instead of 55. Their average length of stay was longer too, being 26 years. This contrast with the TAPS sample is

Care in the Community: Illusion or Reality?
Edited by Julian Leff. © 1997 John Wiley & Sons Ltd.

explained by the fact that the Cane Hill admission wards were almost all closed before the 1988 survey. Hence, very few new long-stay patients had accumulated in the hospital. The proportion of the Cane Hill sample who were married, 6 per cent, was very similar to that of the TAPS sample, 4 per cent. The measures of function were not easy to compare with the TAPS sample, since different instruments were used. However, 45 per cent of the Cane Hill patients were rated as poor or very poor in performance of basic living skills, suggesting a higher degree of disability than the whole TAPS sample. Another indication of this was the number of Cane Hill patients who went to staffed homes, all but five of the 222 resettled. This contrasts with the 22 per cent of the TAPS sample who were discharged to unstaffed accommodation.

The proportion of Cane Hill patients receiving visits from friends or relatives at least monthly was 20 per cent, comparable with the 25 per cent of TAPS patients who were in monthly contact with relatives. The main criteria for "hard-to-place" patients in Cane Hill hospital were socially unacceptable behaviour, a history of violence, dangerousness, physical disability, and involuntary detention. These closely resemble the characteristics of the equivalent patients in Friern hospital (see Chapter 12). Notably, half of the residual population in Cane Hill hospital in 1991, a year before its closure, was aged above 70. This is also a consequence of restricting new admissions to the hospital. The residual population in Friern hospital at a comparable stage of reprovision, comprised patients with a shorter duration of stay. This is one reason for the difference in the proportion of DTP patients among the residual populations: 25 per cent in Cane Hill compared with 54 per cent in Friern hospital.

In summary, the greater disability of the Cane Hill patients compared with the TAPS sample is attributable to the later stage in the run-down of the hospital at which the baseline survey was conducted. We need to take account of this when comparing the outcome for the Cane Hill and TAPS samples. As before, comparisons are limited by the use of different outcome measures in the two studies. However, some approximations can be made.

Administrative outcomes were similar in the two samples, the one year death rate being 5 per cent for Cane Hill and 3 per cent for TAPS patients. Readmissions in the first year were recorded for 10 per cent of Cane Hill patients compared with 15 per cent of TAPS patients. The younger age of the TAPS patients and the higher proportion of new long-stay would explain this modest difference (Gooch and Leff, 1996).

Clinical follow-up was available for only 48 of the Cane Hill sample. A moderate improvement in social functioning occurred for these patients. This varied according to setting, but significant gains were achieved in individual settings in self-care, domestic skills, community skills, social skills and responsibility. These outcomes are comparable with the TAPS findings for the Social Behaviour Schedule and the Basic Everyday Living Skills schedule.

The environment in the community homes for the Cane Hill patients was compared with that in the hospital wards, and was found to have markedly lower ratings on regulation and social distance. An equivalent reduction was found whether the houses had a low or a high staff:patient ratio. This is very similar to the TAPS data from the Environmental Index. The patients' appreciation of their increased freedom was even more marked in the Cane Hill sample. However, a smaller proportion of the Cane Hill patients (64 per cent) wished to remain in their community homes than of the TAPS sample (74 per cent), and a higher proportion (18 per cent) wanted to return to hospital compared with a handful of the TAPS patients.

On those measures that could reasonably be compared between the two studies, there were no outstanding differences either in the characteristics of the patients or their outcome following discharge. We are reasonably confident, therefore, that the beneficial outcome for long-stay patients from Friern and Claybury hospitals is likely to be repeated in reprovision programmes for other large psychiatric hospitals in the UK, provided that the funding arrangements are similar. One of the crucial measures in the reprovision for Friern, Claybury and Cane Hill hospitals was the regulation of finance, which ensured that revenue was transferred from the hospital budget into the budget for the replacement psychiatric services in the community. Without this "ringfencing", there is a great danger of inadequately resourced services being provided, making managing authorities reluctant to embark on a hospital closure programme. This has been the position in the USA until recently, as we shall explain below. But first we will review the situation in Europe, since there has been a wide variety of approaches to reforming psychiatric services.

A VIEW ACROSS EUROPE

Italy

Most attention has been focused on Italy because of the dramatic way in which psychiatric reform was brought about in the political arena. Following a vigorous public campaign by left wing parties, Law 180 was passed in 1978. It contained four main provisions:

1. No new patients to be admitted to psychiatric hospitals.
2. 15 bedded psychiatric units to be set up in general hospitals, with a ratio of 1 per 150 000 population.
3. Patient stay to be limited to 48 hours, renewable for a further 7 days by the mayor and a judge.
4. "Alternative structures" to be set up in the community.

Law 180 sanctioned two of the measures posited by Leona Bachrach (Chapter 2) as constituting deinstitutionalisation, but neglected the third, reprovision for the long-stay patients in the psychiatric hospitals. The barring of admissions to these hospitals has become known as a "front door" policy. By contrast, a programme that focuses on moving long-stay patients out is termed a "back door" policy. The consequence of Italy's front door policy has been the patchy development of psychiatric services nationally. Some places, such as Trieste, where the Democratic Psychiatry movement began, and Arezzo in Tuscany, have comprehensive, well-functioning community services. Others, particularly in the South, leave much to be desired. However, few of the long-stay in-patients have benefited from the reform. On the contrary, since many nurses have moved out of the hospitals to staff the community facilities, their standard of care has often deteriorated.

Belgium

The Belgian policy has been largely a back door one (Coucheir, personal communication), although in 1953 "dispensaria" were created, which were the equivalent of community mental health centres. They were usually situated in large houses, some distance from the psychiatric hospital. Long-stay patients are being discharged to what are termed psychiatric nursing homes. These are established in ordinary streets, and range in size from 10 to 60 places, offering single or double bedrooms. In Flanders 2500 beds have been closed and 2800 places created in nursing homes. Of these, 1300 are considered to be permanent, while 1500 are expected to be closed down as patients are discharged to more independent accommodation. Our experience with the TAPS project suggests that this may be overly optimistic (Trieman and Kendal, 1995). However, only patients who are stable are considered for discharge. We can also infer this from the staff:patient ratios in the nursing homes, which range from 1 : 8 to 1 : 6. A large number of chronic patients must remain in the psychiatric hospitals, since the number of long-stay psychiatric beds in Belgium in 1994 was 1.7 per 1000 population, several times the rates for the UK and USA.

Finland

Since 1980 the Finnish government has been supporting a policy of balanced deinstitutionalisation (Pylkkanen, personal communication). The National Schizophrenia Project has dual aims; to reduce by 50 per cent the number of both old long-stay and new long-stay in hospitals. Hence it is a combination of a back door and a front door policy. The front door strategy has been to establish multi-disciplinary crisis teams, consisting of three members who supervise family- and milieu-oriented activities. Each team deals with a population of 80 000 and handles about 80 crises per year. Sixty teams are now established, and have succeeded in reducing the need for psychiatric admission. The back door strategy is to establish rehabilitation wards in hospitals, and to set up domestic style rehabilitation homes in the community.

The success of the programme can be judged from the fact that between 1982 and 1992, staff working in community care increased by 104 per cent, the number of new long-stay patients decreased by 60 per cent and of old long-stay patients by 68 per cent. Hence this balanced policy appears to have worked extremely well for a small population of 5 million, which is, however, geographically dispersed, producing difficulties for outreach services. Unfortunately, no figures are available for the cost of this programme.

When we compare the British situation with the other European examples, it becomes apparent that the UK has successfully pursued a back door policy, and has advanced further than other countries, closing one third of its psychiatric hospitals to date. However, Britain has been less successful in creating an adequate network of alternative structures to replace the functions of the psychiatric hospitals. As a result, there is a continuing crisis affecting the acute admission wards, which can only be resolved by the investment of more money in community services. Where does the USA fit into these patterns?

The USA

The state of psychiatric services in the USA has been extensively analysed by Leona Bachrach (Chapter 2) so will not be reviewed here. However, some aspects of their history need emphasis in the context of the comparisons we are making across countries. The USA has operated both a front door and a back door policy, although the balance has not been as even as in Finland, and not consistent from state to state.

The front door policy was initiated by the Joint Commission on Mental Health in 1961 under the title of Action for Mental Health. It proposed the establishment of Community Mental Health Clinics to reduce the need for prolonged or repeated hospitalisation, and admission units in general hospitals for short-term treatment. President Kennedy took office a few days after the Commission's report was published and backed its recommendations. In 1963 he made a speech about combating mental illness and mental retardation, which was followed two years later by the establishment of Community Mental Health Centres. These were expected to provide inpatient and outpatient services, partial hospitalisation, emergency services, including 24 hour walk-in availability, and consultation and education services including public education. The plan was an excellent one and the centres attracted many enthusiastic and idealistic workers. However, they were met by considerable opposition from sections of the public, and were undermined by financial cuts by subsequent administrations (Brown, 1985). By 1975 there were 603 centres. Fifteen years later they had grown to over 800, but their budgets had been cut drastically.

Over the same period, a vigorous back door policy was being pursued. In fact the USA emptied its psychiatric hospitals faster than any other country. Surprisingly, though, relatively few psychiatric hospitals have been closed; 26

state mental hospitals in 17 states since 1970 (Rothbard, personal communication). Relative to the size of the population, this represents less than one quarter of the UK closures. A major reason appears to be the lack of surety that revenue and capital resources saved by the closures will be reinvested in community psychiatric services. This issue has recently been highlighted by legislation enacted by New York State. The Community Mental Health Reinvestment Act of 1993 linked reinvestment of funds in community mental health resources with the closure of state psychiatric hospitals (*OMH News*, 1993). Five psychiatric centres housing over 1500 patients were expected to close over the subsequent five years, releasing $180 million. The funding formula was based on a calculated annual cost of $57 500 per hospital bed, which is approximately £700 per week, somewhat higher than the equivalent figures for Friern and Claybury hospitals (see Chapter 6). A key requirement of the Act is that local government units establish a local planning process for the expenditure of reinvestment allocations. Users and family members were expected to become members of the planning subcommittees.

If this initiative by New York State goes according to plan, and state hospital funds are used sensibly to create a network of community services, it is likely that other states will follow this lead. This will result in the large-scale closure of state psychiatric hospitals across the USA. Given the force of these sweeping changes, in the light of the experience of the TAPS Project, does the psychiatric hospital have a future in the western world?

PSYCHIATRIC HOSPITALS: THE FUTURE

As we have argued, the problem in the UK affecting the admission services is not an inevitable consequence of closing the psychiatric hospitals. It could be remedied by further development of community services, particularly rehabilitation facilities to replace those available in the psychiatric hospital. While acutely ill patients preferred the admission wards in the old hospitals to the units in general hospitals, their attitudes could be changed by better design of DGH units, including the provision of secluded grounds in which they could walk around.

One group of patients whose existence might argue for the retention of the psychiatric hospital is the difficult-to-place (DTP). Some believe that the asylum function of the hospital is required for these patients, both to protect the public from them and to protect them from the public (Wing and Furlong, 1986). Others (Levene et al, 1985) regard the physical problems of long-stay patients, such as incontinence, as presenting a major obstacle to hospital closure. This view stems from the traditional role of the psychiatric hospital in providing nursing care for highly dependent patients. In a subtle way, it also reflects the anxiety of some professionals concerning the trend toward demedicalisation in the new system of care, and the narrowing role of professionals such as psychiatric nurses and psychiatrists.

In practice, we found that the existing range of supported accommodation, such as residential and nursing homes, was capable of caring for the most dependent patients (see Chapter 4). The DTP patients could have constituted an insurmountable obstacle if alternative facilities proved to be ineffective. However, the TAPS study (Trieman and Leff, 1996) showed that DTP patients could be maintained successfully in a variety of specialised units, as part of comprehensive community services. Moreover, we found that most improvement in aggressive behaviour occurred in a setting that was as open and free as the standard community homes, and was situated in a busy residential area. High staffing levels ensure that the risk to the public of being disturbed or assaulted is minimised. We consider the highest risk to the public to stem from patients who are living in unsupervised settings or with family, and in the latter case it is the family members themselves who face the greatest likelihood of assault. Most of the serious assaults that have occurred over the past decade were committed by patients who were acutely psychotic and who were often disconnected from psychiatric and social services. It is the pressing problem of how to sustain service support for these patients which poses the greatest challenge to the professionals and to the politicians. If we are not willing to turn the clock back and massively reinstitutionalise psychiatric patients, then we must face this challenge to the new system of care. Solutions must ensure better accessibility to acute admission units, and a much more active and systematic outreach policy.

In our view, the relatively small number of DTP patients does not justify the retention of the massive buildings that are inseparable from the image of psychiatric institutions. In this sense, psychiatric hospitals have no future and in 50 years time will probably not exist as institutions anywhere in the western world. The buildings in which 19th century governments invested so much money and careful planning, and in which they took such pride, will not entirely vanish, but will radically change their function. How many visitors to the Imperial War Museum in London are aware that it once housed the Bethlem Hospital? It will take some effort to discover that these buildings are the vestige of a past era in which the mentally ill were, with the best of intentions, banished from society.

REFERENCES

Brown, P. (1985) *The Transfer of Care: Psychiatric Deinstitutionalisation and its Aftermath*, Routledge and Kegan Paul, Henley-on-Thames.

Gooch, C. and Leff, J. (1996) Factors affecting the success of community placement. The TAPS Project. 26 *Psychological Medicine*, **26**, 511–520.

Jones, D. (1993) The TAPS Project. 11: The selection of patients for reprovision. *British Journal of Psychiatry*, **162** (suppl. 19), 36–39.

Levene, L.S., Donaldson, L.J., Brandon, S. (1985) How likely is it that a District Health Authority can close its large mental hospitals? *British Journal of Psychiatry*, **147**, 150–155.

OMH News (December, 1993) **V**(10). New York State Office of Mental Health, New York.

Pickard, L., Proudfoot, R., Wolfson, P., Clifford, P., Holloway, F. and Lindesay, J. (1992) *Evaluating the Closure of Cane Hill Hospital*, Research & Development for Psychiatry, London.

Trieman, N. and Kendal, R. (1995) The TAPS Project. 27: After hospital: pathways patients follow in the community, *Journal of Mental Health*, **4**, 423–429.

Trieman, N. and Leff, J. (1996) The TAPS Project 36: The difficult to place long-stay psychiatric inpatients: outcome one year after relocation, *British Journal of Psychiatry*, **169**, 289–292.

Wing, J.K. and Furlong, R. (1986) A haven for the severely disabled within the context of a comprehensive psychiatric community service, *British Journal of Psychiatry*, **149**, 449–457.

INDEX

Related titles of interest from Wiley...

Out of the Shadows
Confronting America's Mental Illness Crisis
E. Fuller Torrey

Drawing on stories of real people, this book explores the causes of the crisis and the tragic toll it is having on individuals, families and communities across the US.

0-471-16161-6 256pp 1996 Hardback

Families Coping with Schizophrenia
A Practitioner's Guide to Family Groups
Jacqueline Atkinson and Denise Coia

Provides a comprehensive guide to setting up relatives' education groups, looking at practical problems and issues, as well as considering some of the ethical and political issues which are raised by the provision of service for, and involving relatives.

0-471-94181-6 294pp 1995 Paperback

Community Psychology
Theory and Practice
Jim Orford

0-471-93810-6 302pp 1992 Paperback

Journal of Community and Applied Social Psychology

Reviews and reports concepts, methods and experience relating to individual and social behaviour in the context of community problems.

ISSN: 1052-9284

Journal of Community Psychology

Devoted to research, evaluation, assessment, intervention, and review articles that deal with human behavior in community settings.

ISSN: 0090-4392

Visit the Wiley Home Page at http://www.wiley.co.uk